NATO AND WARSAW PACT TANKS OF THE COLD WAR

NATO AND WARSAW PACT TANKS OF THE COLD WAR

MICHAEL GREEN

Pen & Sword
MILITARY

First published in Great Britain in 2022 by
PEN & SWORD MILITARY
an imprint of
Pen & Sword Books Ltd
47 Church Street
Barnsley
South Yorkshire
S70 2AS

Copyright © Michael Green, 2022

ISBN 978-1-39900-431-2

The right of Michael Green to be identified as author of this work has been asserted by him in accordance with the Copyright, Designs and Patents Act 1988.

A CIP catalogue record for this book is available from the British Library.

All rights reserved. No part of this book may be reproduced or transmitted in any form or by any means, electronic or mechanical including photocopying, recording or by any information storage and retrieval system, without permission from the Publisher in writing.

Typeset by Concept, Huddersfield, West Yorkshire HD4 5JL.
Printed and bound in India by Replika Press Pvt. Ltd.

Pen & Sword Books Limited incorporates the imprints of Atlas, Archaeology, Aviation, Discovery, Family History, Fiction, History, Maritime, Military, Military Classics, Politics, Select, Transport, True Crime, Air World, Frontline Publishing, Leo Cooper, Remember When, Seaforth Publishing, The Praetorian Press, Wharncliffe Local History, Wharncliffe Transport, Wharncliffe True Crime and White Owl.

For a complete list of Pen & Sword titles please contact
PEN & SWORD BOOKS LIMITED
47 Church Street, Barnsley, South Yorkshire S70 2AS, England
E-mail: enquiries@pen-and-sword.co.uk
Website: www.pen-and-sword.co.uk

Contents

Foreword vii
Acknowledgements viii
Notes to the Reader ix
1. Immediate Post-War Tanks 1
2. Building Up the Numbers 45
3. Keeping Pace 75
4. The Odds Get Worse 115
5. Keeping Up 145
6. Height of the Cold War 183
7. NATO Catches Up 221

Dedication

The author dedicates this book to the late US Army General William E. DePuy. Taken from the introduction of a US Army publication is this passage on General DePuy's contributions:

> General William E. DePuy changed the US Army. As the first commander of the US Army Training and Doctrine Command (TRADOC), he created the mechanisms to restore the Army's self-image as a conventional combat force trained and configured for continental warfare. He made it a doctrinal Army for the first time in its 200-year history. He laid the foundation for the training revolution that followed in the 1980s and for the development and fielding of the extraordinary combat systems that proved themselves in Operation DESERT STORM. Personally, and as the leader of a major Army command, he took hold of a defeated and discouraged Army and put it on the road to victory.

Foreword

Michael Green in this book once again shows the depth and breadth of his writing and researching about all aspects of tanks. For well over thirty years, the author has written deftly about tanks and tank progress throughout the twentieth century, and that depth of knowledge and expertise culminates in this work on Cold War tanks.

Randy R. Talbot
Command Historian (Retired)
US Army Tank-automotive and Armaments
   Command (TACOM)

Acknowledgements

This book's images come from various sources, including the author's collection, Department of Defense (DOD) websites, the former Patton Museum of Cavalry and Armor, the US Army Tank-automotive and Armaments Command (TACOM) historical office and several stock photo agencies, as well as friends named in the caption credits.

As with all published works, authors depend on many friends for assistance in reviewing their work. Those that contributed their thoughts include Joe DeMarco, Pierre-Olivier Buan, Peter Shyvers, Ed Webster and many others.

Notes to the Reader

1. Due to the publisher's space and format restrictions, the book is a broad canvas of those tanks that served in their respective period. It is not a comprehensive guide to Cold War tanks.
2. The chapter headings are arbitrary, and overlap in some cases due to the long service careers of many of the tanks described. The chapter headings also allow for the book's division into manageable sections.
3. The number of tanks built and the time frames can vary depending on reference sources. The same applies to various tanks' armour protection levels, as some remain classified and others are conjecture by uninformed sources.
4. The main focus of this book is on Cold War tanks that entered service and not the numerous prototypes and experimental models that never entered service.
5. All weights shown are approximated and listed in short tons (2,000lb per ton), in contrast to long tons/imperial tons (2,240lb per ton).

Chapter One

Immediate Post-War Tanks

In the immediate aftermath of the Second World War, the long-simmering tensions between the two vastly different political systems, the capitalism of the Western Allies and the communism of the Soviet Union, quickly reached a boiling point. Their mutual enemy, the Axis alliance, no longer existed. As neither side trusted the other, it led to a political and military stalemate that historians label as the 'Cold War', which began in 1947 and ended in 1991 with the political collapse of the Soviet Union.

Both the former Western Allies and the Soviet Union had post-war agendas. To prevent another invasion of their country, the Soviet Union had decided that most of the Central and Eastern European countries it occupied following the surrender of Nazi Germany were to remain under Soviet control, both politically and militarily. They were to act as buffer states. To disguise that fact, puppet governments soon appeared among them staffed by local Communist Party members, with all major policy decisions dictated from Moscow.

NATO's Appearance

To bring various non-communist countries (especially in Western Europe) together in a mutual defensive arrangement, in 1948 the US government secretly laid the groundwork to form the North Atlantic Treaty Organization (NATO) on 4 April 1949. The precursor to NATO, the Brussels Treaty Organization (BTO), was formed in March 1947. Each was to offset the large post-war Soviet military presence in Central and Eastern Europe and any armed aggression on their part.

The founding members of the NATO transatlantic alliance included Belgium, Canada, Denmark, France, Iceland, Italy, Luxembourg, the Netherlands, Norway, Portugal, the UK and the US. As the United States was NATO's sole superpower, NATO's military leadership (during the Cold War) always fell to American senior officers.

France officially withdrew from the military aspect of NATO in 1966. However, unofficially it remained committed militarily to NATO given the possibility of Soviet aggression and stationed armoured divisions in West Germany throughout the Cold War. France officially rejoined NATO in 2009.

In another expression of the American government's strong commitment to NATO's future, President Harry S. Truman signed the Mutual Defense Assistance Act of 1949. It allocated $1 billion (then) to NATO members to acquire a wide variety of military equipment and services to strengthen their individual and collective defense capabilities.

The United States' View

Western Allied senior military leadership, particularly that of the United States, saw artillery and air power as the key pillars of its ground victory against Nazi Germany, with tanks only supporting the role.

As the most powerful superpower and the only one with the atomic bomb (Great Britain did not explode its first atom bomb until 3 October 1952), America's senior political leadership saw little need for a large standing army. Instead, they believed they were secure behind a nuclear shield, which could be delivered anywhere globally by the United States Air Force (USAF). Despite this belief, the US Army strongly believed that ground forces would still play an essential role in a Third World War, with the US Army planning for a potential war with the Soviet Union as early as 1947.

With funding authorized by the American Congress primarily going to the USAF and the US Navy following the Second World War, the US Army soon became a hollowed-out shadow of its wartime strength. For example, the American military had had 28,000 tanks at the end of the Second World War. When the Korean War began in June 1950, it had only 6,000, many of which were unserviceable. The US Army then had a single understrength armoured division, down from the sixteen divisions fielded during the Second World War.

The author of the article titled 'Tanks and the Korean War: A Case Study in Unpreparedness' that appeared in the September–October 2000 issue of *Armor* magazine noted the US Army's awareness of the situation:

> Meanwhile, early in 1949, an advisory panel on armor reported that the US Army had no tanks in production or in development capable of defeating the types possessed by the country's potential enemies. The panel considered this situation critical. Unless the Army's tank development situation was improved, the panel reported, the United States would not have enough tanks to support a major ground war for at least two and a half years after the beginning of hostilities.

The M4A3 76mm Gun-Armed Sherman

The US Army classified all the various versions of the M4 series of medium tanks (unofficially nicknamed the Sherman) in its inventory as obsolete in January 1946. The only US Army exception was the M4A3(76)W riding on the horizontal volute spring suspension (HVSS) system. In March the US Marine Corps followed suit, listing all its wartime tanks as obsolete. The US Marine Corps never took into service any 76mm gun-armed Sherman tanks.

A total of 4,452 examples of the 37-ton M4A3(76)W had rolled off the assembly lines between March 1944 and June 1945. The first 1,925 examples rode on the earlier vertical volute spring suspension (VVSS) system, with the remainder on the HVSS system.

The US Army's preference for the M4A3(76)W HVSS over other 76mm gun-armed Sherman tanks centred on its gasoline-powered engine, labelled the GAA;

it was considered the best in its class. Not until 1955 would the US Army embrace diesel-engine-powered tank development.

The M4A3(76)W HVSS was a second-generation Sherman tank, as it had a reset 47-degree front to the upper front hull (referred to as a glacis) to resist penetration, the 'Wet' main gun ammunition stowage arrangement to reduce fire danger, and larger front hull hatches to facilitate crew entry and escape. First-generation M4 series tanks lacked these design features. All came with an elevation-only stabilizer system such as on naval guns, the only Second World War tanks to have such a feature.

Korean War Action

The M4A3(76)W HVSS was the most numerous US Army tank to see use during the Korean War. Its firepower and armour protection equalled that of the T-34-85s supplied to the North Korean Army. However, there were few tank-on-tank engagements during the last two years of the conflict.

From the files of the US Army Center for Military History comes the following passage describing an M4A3(76)W HVSS encountering an enemy tank during the Korean War:

> The first shell struck the ground next to the enemy [towed anti-tank] crew, and the burst blew away some foliage that was camouflaging an enemy tank dug in on the approach side of the pass on the right side of the road. As soon as the camouflage was disturbed, the enemy tank fired one round. The tracer passed between [tank commander] Nordstrom's head and the open hatch cover. In these circumstances, he did not take time to give fire orders; he just called for armor-piercing shells, and the gunner fired, hitting the front of the enemy tank from a distance of less than a hundred yards. The gunner continued firing armor-piercing shells, and the third round caused a great explosion.

Typically, US Army Sherman tanks in Korea had to deal with enemy infantry, as detailed in this extract from an article titled 'Armor Holds the Hill', which appeared in the January–February 1953 issue of *Armor* magazine:

> North Korean troops crawled up onto the tanks, blocking the vision devices, exploding shaped charges [unknown type] and attempting to jam the 76mm gun tube and plug the .30 caliber coaxial machine guns in an effort to silence the fire from the tanks. The tankers fired on one another, traversing their turrets to knock enemy troops from the decks. The fighting raged all night as the enemy reinforced the assault force to battalion size ... One Red soldier was observed firing the .50 caliber machine gun from the top of one of the tanks. He was shot off by friendly fire.

The M4A3(76)W HVSS remained in US Army service until the late 1950s. The Marine Corps Reserve had both second-generation M4A3 tanks armed with the

75mm main gun and a 105mm howitzer-armed model in service in the immediate post-war period. The latter saw service during the Korean War.

The M4A1 76mm Gun-Armed Sherman

The second most numerous second-generation 76mm gun-armed M4 series tank in the US Army's inventory in the immediate aftermath of the Second World War was the M4A1(76)W. It rode on either the VVSS or HVSS system.

A total of 3,426 M4A1(76)W tanks came off the factory floor between January 1944 and July 1945. An August 1948 inventory showed the US Army had 1,956 examples in storage within the US, 1,272 of which were equipped with the HVSS.

The post-war M4A1(76)W was classified as 'substitute standard' since the US Army disliked its gasoline-powered radial aircraft engine as it was not as reliable as the GAA gasoline engine in the M4A3(76)W HVSS tank.

As a substitute standard tank, the M4A1(76)W remained in service as there were insufficient M4A3(76)W HVSS tanks available. Hence, some US Army National Guard tank units had the M4A1(76)W HVSS tanks until the late 1950s.

The M4A2 76mm Gun-Armed Sherman

Besides the M4A1 and M4A3 armed with the 76mm main gun, American factories had built a second-generation diesel-engine-powered Sherman designated the M4A2(76)W, riding on both VVSS and HVSS systems. As the US Army wanted only gasoline-engine-powered vehicles, the M4A2 armed with the 76mm main gun was allocated to Lend-Lease.

Of the 2,915 examples of the M4A2(76)W tank constructed between January 1944 and July 1945, 5 went to the British Army and 2,073 to the Red Army; the rest remained in the United States for training purposes.

Upon the conclusion of the Second World War, there remained in the United States a total of 829 examples of the M4A2(76)W HVSS. The Canadian government purchased 300 of them in 1946 for training their army. The remaining 529 examples were eventually stripped by American industry for parts in the late 1940s and early 1950s. Many of those parts were used to convert the US Army's remaining inventory of M4A3(75)W tanks into the preferred M4A3(76)W HVSS tanks.

75mm Gun-Armed Sherman

Besides the various 76mm gun-armed second-generation Sherman tanks, the post-war US Army storage inventory contained, as of October 1948, a total of 1,413 first-generation 75mm gun-armed M4A3 Sherman tanks. Another 120 served with various US Army National Guard units. First-generation Sherman tanks had the original 56-degree sloped glacis, lacked the wet stowage feature, had small front hull hatches and rode on the VVSS.

The 1948 Army plans called for the first-generation M4A3 Sherman tanks to be stripped for useful parts, such as their GAA engines, and the remainder scrapped. That changed with the outbreak of the Korean War; the remaining

1,181 examples in 1950 remained in the inventory as an emergency measure. The US Army also scoured the Western Pacific for abandoned wartime M4A3 tanks, which were shipped to occupied Japan to be upgraded.

In January 1951, the US Army had industry rebuild all its remaining first-generation M4A3 tanks. A few would go as military aid, but five years later most were declared obsolete in 1956 and sold to scrap yards.

Military Aid Programme

With more M4A1(76)W tanks than required, the US Army had industry rebuild its remaining inventory beginning in late 1948, intending to transfer them to future NATO allies' armies. They would go out under a plan referred to as the Mutual Defense Assistance Program (MDAP). The recipients included the armies of Belgium, the Netherlands and Portugal.

In the early 1950s, under MDAP, the Danish and Portuguese armies also received a small number of M4A3(76) tanks out of 310 converted. These consisted of industry-modified M4A3(75)W tanks riding on the VVSS. They kept their original turrets and had their 75mm main guns replaced by 76mm main guns. American industry also modified 413 first-generation M4A1s to mount a 76mm main gun, designated the M4A1E6. Both tanks also went to non-NATO armies.

French Army Sherman Tanks

The French Army received the largest number of M4A1(76)W tanks under MDAP, a total of 1,254 examples: 833 riding on the HVSS and 421 on the VVSS. These joined the existing French inventory of Sherman tanks acquired during the Second World War via Lend-Lease.

The tanks originally delivered under Lend-Lease included both diesel-engine-powered M4A2 and gasoline-engine-powered M4A4 tanks. These tanks, supplemented by gasoline-engine-powered first-generation M4A1 and M4A3 tanks and second-generation versions of both tanks were armed with the 76mm main gun. The latter came from US Army stockpiles in wartime Western Europe to make up for Free French Army combat losses.

Post-war, the French Army replaced its inventory of M4A4 Sherman tanks, which were powered by Chrysler A-57 Multibank engines, with the same gasoline-powered radial engine that powered the M4 and M4A1 Sherman tanks. Those converted received the designation M4A4T.

The French Army employed Sherman tanks in the First Indochina War (1946–54) and the Algerian War (1954–62). Some eventually went off to the Middle East to help equip the Israeli Army formed in 1948.

The last French military force to employ the Sherman proved to be an internal security organization that retained some of them until 1965.

Other Sherman Tank Sources

Before the MDAP, some of the cash-strapped NATO armies depended on other means to acquire Sherman tanks. Between 1947 and 1952, the Italian Army took into service a wide variety of Sherman tank types left behind by the departing US Army, the British Army and its Commonwealth allies.

In 1948, the Belgian Army bought 200 ex-British Army 17-pounder-armed Sherman tanks from in-country scrap yards. The newly-formed Dutch Army also started with scrap-yard-acquired Fireflies. Both armies later acquired a collection of other models of Sherman tanks. Both armies would receive rebuilt M4A1(76)W tanks through MDAP beginning in 1950. These would eventually be placed into storage and brought out for part-time reserve training exercises until 1959. Some of the M4A1 tanks came from MDAP with dozer blades. These would last in service until 1961 with the Dutch Army.

The M26

The US Army's late-war replacement for the second-generation Sherman M4A3(76)W proved to be the 46-ton T26E3 Heavy Tank, with a 90mm main gun. Power came from the same liquid-cooled 500hp gasoline-powered engine used in the M4A3(76)W, riding on the VVSS and the HVSS systems, although the T26E3 weighed about 10 tons more. The five-man T-26E3 rode on a torsion bar suspension system.

The first T26E3 production examples came off the factory floor in November 1944. A total of twenty reached Western Europe in January 1945, seeing combat in the final few months of the war. In March 1945, the T26E3 received the designation of the M26 Heavy Tank and was officially nicknamed the 'Pershing' by the US Army in honour of General John J. Pershing who led US forces in France during the First World War.

By May 1945 310 M26 tanks had found their way to Western Europe. With Germany's surrender that same month, the US Army had envisioned the tank playing a role in the planned invasion of Japan. The first batch of twelve M26 tanks reached Okinawa on 21 July 1945, too late for combat as the island had fallen one month earlier.

US Army plans for the number of M26 tanks ordered varied: initial estimates in 1944 called for approximately 2,000 examples. The following year this grew to almost 5,000 examples. When the Japanese announced their surrender on 15 August 1945, M26 production ended with a total of 2,002 examples completed.

Post-War Pershing Employment

In May 1946, the US Army reclassified the M26 as a medium tank. With the beginning of the Korean War, the M26 was the US Army's answer to the North Korean T-34-85 tanks. Neither the M26 nor T-34-85 had a stabilizer system.

The first three M26 tanks arrived in July 1950 from army storage in Japan, but promptly broke down and found themselves abandoned during combat operations. A second larger batch of M26 tanks arrived in August 1950 and quickly established their dominance over Soviet tanks.

Both the M26 and the T-34-85 depended on a stadiametric rangefinder incorporated into the gunner's optical sight reticle to determine range to targets. The

M26 had hydraulically-operated turret traverse and elevation systems. Late-production T-34-85s came with an electro-hydraulic traverse system; however, elevation and depression of the main gun had to be done manually.

An upgraded version of the M26 tank, the M26A1, also appeared during the Korean War. The external differences between the M26A1 and the M26 included an improved 90mm main gun with a new single baffle muzzle brake and a 'bore evacuator', referred to by the British Army as a 'fume extractor'.

> **Bore Evacuator**
> Former US Army armour officer James E. Brown explains how a bore evacuator works:
>
> A bore evacuator is a chamber set over the tube, which covers several holes through the wall of the tube. The holes are inclined, so their inner bore ends are closer to the muzzle than are their outer ends. When the projectile passes the holes, some propellant gas is vented through the holes and pressurizes the bore evacuator chamber. Once the projectile leaves the tube, the bore returns to near atmospheric pressure. The gas in the bore evacuator escapes through the holes, whose inclination causes them to have a net velocity towards the muzzle.

By the winter of 1950, United Nations ground and aerial forces had destroyed the bulk of the North Korean fleet of T-34-85 tanks. With the threat gone, and as the US Army advanced northward up the rugged Korean Peninsula, the M26 quickly fell out of favour. It proved severely underpowered and unable to negotiate the country's mountainous terrain. At that point, US Army armour units in Korea began to prefer the 10-ton lighter M4A3(76)W HVSS for its superior off-road performance.

A problem for both M26 and the M4 series during the Korean War's first year was their unreliability. This was due to the critical shortage of logistical and maintenance support assets deployed to Korea.

More American Tanks Go To NATO

Because of concerns regarding a possible Soviet military invasion of Western Europe during the Korean War, the US government approved the transfer under MDAP of both M26 Pershing tanks and an upgraded model to various NATO countries.

The fear of a Soviet tank-led invasion of Western Europe and what could be done appears in a passage from an article in July–August 1951 *Armor* magazine titled 'A Concept – Armor' by Colonel Rothwell H. Brown:

> There is only one weapon which can possibly hope to cope with the mobility and momentum which could be generated in a mass Soviet armored attack which could be launched at any moment across Europe. This weapon is a superior armored force. Superiority in quantity may not be necessary but we

> **The US Army Reacts**
>
> Senior American political and military leadership perceived the Korean War (1950–53) as a possible opening move by the Soviet Union, to be followed by their invasion of Western Europe and the start of the Third World War. Without any modern tanks, the US Army declared a 'Tank Crisis' in 1950.
>
> The US Army's response was a sudden rush to field a new generation of post-war tanks, including light, medium and heavy models. Since the end of the Second World War, the Army had been developing these tank classes. However, due to funding shortages, design concerns and uncertainty regarding tanks' future, they were not ready for production when the Korean War began.
>
> With the Cold War threat growing hot, the US Army addressed its Tank Crisis by beginning a 'Crash Programme' to speed up fielding all its post-war-designed tanks. As events unfolded, however, none would see combat during the Korean War, and all suffered serious design issues from the lack of pre-production testing.

must have superiority in quality and near quantity. Otherwise, Soviet armor will cast aside everything that opposes it.

M24 Chaffee

Another American wartime tank seeing service in various NATO armies in the immediate post-war period was the 20-ton M24 Light Tank, best known by its British Army-applied official nickname of the 'Chaffee', honouring American general Adna R. Chaffee, a pioneer in overseeing the adoption of tanks by the US Army.

Between April 1944 and August 1945, two commercial firms built a total of 4,731 examples of the M24. Armed with a low-velocity 75mm main gun almost identical to those in the M4, the five-man tank rode on a torsion bar suspension system derived from that of the M-18 Hellcat tank destroyer. Its thickest armour was the gun shield (known as a mantlet by the British Army) at 38mm (1.5in).

As with the M4 series of medium tanks and the M26 series, the M24 depended on a stadiametric rangefinder incorporated into the gunner's optical sight reticle.

Power for the M24 came from two liquid-cooled 346 cubic inch Cadillac automobile engines. The tank lasted in service with the US Army throughout the Korean War, and was replaced by a new post-war-designed light tank, the M41.

The British Army acquired 289 examples of the M24 by way of Lend-Lease before the Second World War ended. They would continue to serve with the British Army in the immediate post-war era until replaced by new post-war-designed vehicles.

Other NATO armies that would take the M24 into service in varying numbers through MDAP and other means included Belgium (224), Canada (32), Denmark (63), France (1,245), Greece (170), Italy (518), the Netherlands (50), Norway (123),

Stadiametric Sights, by Ted Dannemiller

Choke that target, Gunner! Or what is a stadiametric sight and how does it work? And what is this WORM formula everyone talks about?

Stadiametric rangefinders (RF) use geometry as described in rules about triangles. That's all the math you need to know. The so-called worm formula is written as R=W/M (range, width, mils). Said longhand, it sounds like 'Range (km) equals Width (of target) in meters divided by Mils in width (seen on a binocular for example), or WORM for short'. Scouts and artillery observers are adept at using WORM.

On a stadiametric RF of an American tank, we use a standard tank length of about 7.6 yards, and a standard width of about 3.8 yards to create a known width (or length if presented sideways). Engineers work out how that appears using two curved lines, wide at the top and narrow at the bottom as seen in the illustration. Choking is the act of squeezing the target between the curved stadia lines or between the vertical centerline and one of the curved lines if the target presents end-on.

Squeezing the target near the bottom means a greater distance. The guns (main gun and co-ax) are slaved to the telescope (containing the reticle). For a target presented end-on, the gunner also chokes. Bracketing the target between the centerline and the right edge gives a choked range based on the center of mass of a tank. Skilled gunners can do this rapidly and are trained to apply leads for moving targets based on the estimated speed of the target.

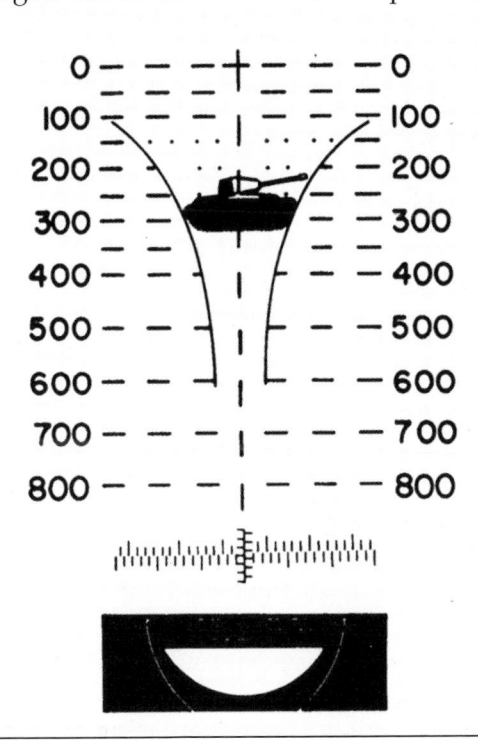

Portugal (16) and Turkey (238). They remained in service ranging from the late 1950s to as late as 1993 in the Norwegian Army.

The best-known use of the French Army's M24 fleet took place during the First Indochina War. Ten disassembled examples were air-dropped to the besieged (March to May 1954) French garrison at Dien Bien Phu and reassembled on site. Despite the tanks' presence, the enemy still prevailed due to French Army command and supply failures.

British Wartime Tanks in NATO

In the aftermath of the Second World War, the British Army retained many wartime-designed and built tanks. These included various M4-series Sherman tanks and some M3- and M5-series light tanks. Some were converted for a specialized purpose. The majority were placed into storage before disposal by various means, including scrapping.

The only wartime gun tanks that the British Army retained in front-line service in the immediate post-war period was the five-man Cruiser Tank officially named the 'Cromwell', and the five-man Cruiser Tank named the 'Comet'.

The 31-ton Cromwell, armed with a 75mm main gun, first appeared in British Army service in 1943. Some 3,000 were completed between 1944 and 1945. Riding on a Christie-type suspension system, the Cromwell received power from a liquid-cooled gasoline engine. Some would see service during the Korean War, with the last examples retired from British Army service in 1955.

The 37-ton Comet was an upgraded Cromwell with a new turret, armed with a shortened version of the 17-pounder (76.2mm gun) labelled the 77mm. Production began in September 1944, with the first examples reaching Western Europe in December 1944.

By the time the Comet's production concluded, a total of 1,186 examples had rolled off the assembly lines. The tank would eventually go to British Army part-time reserve formations in the aftermath of the Second World War. In that secondary rode, it would last in use until 1958.

Centurion

Constant reminders of how inferior its tanks were to those in the German Army between 1940 and 1942 led to the British Army's decision in October 1943 to begin development on a new better-armed and armoured tank with a 17-pounder gun.

The tank itself took inspiration from the German Panther tank, introduced on the Eastern Front in June 1943. What eventually evolved out of that 1943 decision was the 'Centurion Mk 1', with the first examples coming off the factory floor in November 1945. The British Army accepted delivery in February 1946, with the last example of the Mk 1 leaving the factory in 1948. The tank's thickest armour was the gun shield at 152mm (6in) and the glacis plate at 76mm (3in).

The 100 examples of the 54-ton Centurion Mk 1 were closely followed off the assembly lines by 250 examples of the Centurion Tank Mk 2 between 1946 and 1948. It featured a new cast-armour turret, replacing the welded armour turret of

> **Suspension Systems: Pros and Cons**
> US Army General Donn A. Starry wrote a message to the M60 Program Manager on 17 March 1977 regarding his thoughts on torsion bars compared to externally-mounted suspension system assemblies:
>
>> Any externally mounted suspension system is bound to be more vulnerable to fragments and direct fire than are torsion bars. However, here we're using the wrong measures of effectiveness. To begin with, suspension components are pretty well below that center of mass hit distribution pattern derived from the October War [1973 Yom Kippur War]. The probability of a direct fire hit is very low, of a frag hit equally low. Secondly, externally applied suspension components should add protection for the crew along the hull sides. Crew protection is a more important MOE [Measure of Effectiveness] than suspension protection. Third, if properly designed, ease of replacement of externally affixed suspension components is a big plus in their favor. Ease of replacement should be an MOE [Measure of Effectiveness].

the Mk 1, a commander's cupola and thicker hull armour, while retaining a now fully-stabilized 17-pounder gun.

All Centurion versions rode on modified Horstmann double-bogie wheel assemblies, with three externally mounted on either side of the hull. The design's advantage is that the bogies did not encroach on the tank's hull's internal space as did torsion bars, and were easier to replace than torsion bars when damaged by anti-tank mines.

Power for the entire Centurion tank series came from a modified liquid-cooled gasoline engine that had powered Cromwell and Comet tanks. The gasoline Rolls-Royce Meteor engine limited the Centurion's operational range to around 50 miles, reportedly as low as 30 miles off-road. One answer to the problem proved to be wheeled fuel trailers towed behind the tanks, which when entering combat could be disengaged from inside the vehicle.

The Centurion Mk 3

Production of the 56-ton Mk 3 version of the Centurion began in 1947, with an initial 600 vehicles ordered. By 1956, a total of 2,883 examples of the Mk 3 came down the assembly line, including 100 examples of the Centurion Mk 2 brought up to the Mk 3 standard.

The Centurion Mark 3 proved to be the most numerous of the Centurion series. It had as its main armament a 20-pounder (83.4mm) gun. The up-gunning came about in response to the Soviet Army IS-3 heavy tank's thick frontal armour.

The 20-pounder could fire a wide range of tank-defeating rounds, and specialized rounds such as the High-Explosive Squash Head (HESH). The American military refers to HESH rounds as High-Explosive Plastic (HEP) rounds.

> **HESH/HEP Rounds**
> HESH/HEP rounds were considered to be relatively effective tank-killing rounds until the 1960s. A US Army gunnery manual describes how they work: 'When plastic explosive detonates against a hard surface, the other side of that surface shatters into small pieces. This effect is called "spalling" in the case of armor and "scabbing" in the case of concrete.' Another US Army gunnery manual mentions a couple of problems inherent in HESH/HEP rounds:
>
>> Because the ballistic characteristics of the HEP-T projectile allow it to be affected more readily than most other projectiles by wind, drift and cant [slope], a first-round hit is more difficult when engaging distant stationary or moving targets. When engaging close-in targets, obscuration produced by firing presents a problem in adjustment of fire.
>
> A projectile is that part of a round expelled at high velocity from a gun bore by the fast burning of the round's propelling charge (contained within a metal cartridge case). The latent chemical energy of the propelling charge is converted to kinetic energy by combustion.
>
> Armour-piercing (AP) projectiles are metal cylinders with pointed cores to obtain the desired flight characteristics of stability, minimum air resistance and penetration. By virtue of their shape, they focus the kinetic energy on the smallest possible area of the impacted surface, to either penetrate, cause spalling on the interior, or transmit sufficient heat and/or shock to detonate stowed charges or start a fire among flammable liquids (e.g. fuel or hydraulic fluids) or ammunition.

The Centurion Mk 3 had an electrically-powered turret traverse and gun elevation system, as did follow-on models. An electro-mechanical two-axis gun stabilization system (horizontal and vertical planes) contributed to the effectiveness of the main gun and coaxial machine gun. This feature allowed Centurion gunners to acquire and fire on the move or from a short halt, a design feature not present in any previous tanks.

Into Action

The Mk 3 had its combat debut during the Korean War. A New Zealand officer shared his thoughts on the tank's main gun in a March 1952 report titled 'Centurion Tanks in Korea' which he authored:

> Let me state that the 20 pdr is the best tank gun we have had so far. Once my tp [troop] spent a week sniping individual Chinamen at a range of 3,600 yds with a most satisfactory degree of success. (One morning, we got two before breakfast.) It will put a shot into a bunker mouth at 4,000 yds once ranging has been completed, although it may take up to three shells to put one right in. Therefore 4,000 yds is considered the economic max for pin-point shooting with HE.

A few US Army comparisons of the British tank to the American M46 tank appear in a report titled 'Employment of Armor in Korea – The Second Year':

> The Centurion III engines are considered good but not powerful enough for the weight of the tank; however, it has been noted that this tank does have a good cruising speed on hard surface roads and has been able to climb steep hills ... The tank has forded water approximately 4 feet deep. Rice paddies, with mud 10 inches deep, were easily traversed ... The Centurion III tank is reported to handle very well; turns are relatively long and gradual.

Former British Army tanker Rob Griffin explains how the Centurion made its turns: 'The radius of turn depends on gear selected; also the gearbox allowed "neutral" turns on the spot to be made. This was achieved by having the gear in neutral and then pulling either the left or the right steering tiller; the tank then would pivot on the spot.'

French Army Solutions

It was not uncommon for some of the armies that fought Nazi Germany to employ captured tanks against their former owners. The Red Army pulled into service a wide variety of captured German tanks during the conflict.

The Free French Army did the same, including fifty-nine examples of the Panther medium tank in 1944 and 1945. Following the Second World War, the French Army retained forty-nine examples of the Panther to supplement its Sherman tank wartime inventory. At that point, it was the best-armed and armoured tank in the French Army. However, for a couple of reasons, the Panthers were retired from service in 1950. The supply of spare parts dwindled, and the French Army anticipated taking into service a new French heavy tank, the ARL 44, the development of which had begun in secret in 1943.

The 50-ton ARL 44, armed with a 90mm main gun, proved a design dead-end. Powered by a wartime German liquid-cooled gasoline tank engine, the tank rode on a suspension system based on the pre-war French heavy tank, the Char B1 Bis. Sixty examples of the ARL 44 came out of the factory between 1949 and 1951. Unfortunately for the French Army, they proved unreliable in service and France withdrew them from use in 1953.

Warsaw Pact Appears

Following the surrender of Nazi Germany in May 1945, those Western European countries freed by the Western Allies from Axis occupation quickly formed new governments, an option not available to those Central and Eastern European countries the Red Army occupied when the German capitulation took place.

In response to the United States' early 1950s push to establish a West German Army, later formed in November 1955, the Soviet Union went forward with a plan it already had under consideration. It called for bringing together most of the various indigenous military formations it had established in Central and Eastern Europe in a mutual defensive arrangement, overseen by Moscow.

The Soviet-arranged mutual defensive agreement involved Albania, Bulgaria, Czechoslovakia, East Germany, Hungary, Poland and Romania. Becoming official in May 1955, it bore the official title of the Treaty of Friendship, Cooperation and Mutual Assistance, but soon became better known as the 'Warsaw Pact', as the meeting location for it had been in the Polish capital of Warsaw. Another name for the countries of the Warsaw Pact was the 'Eastern Bloc'.

The relationship between the political leadership of the Soviet Union and some of its Warsaw Pact buffer states appears in a late 1968 statement by Leonid Brezhnev addressed to the political leadership of Czechoslovakia when the Czechs began considering leaving the Warsaw Pact: 'Your country is in the region occupied by Soviet soldiers in World War II. We paid for this with great sacrifices, and we will never leave. Your borders are our borders.'

Two Eastern European countries that left the Warsaw Pact without a military response from the Soviet Union were Albania in 1968 and Romania in 1969. They contributed little to the Warsaw Pact, militarily or by their location.

By 1990, as non-Communist governments came to power in Central and Eastern Europe, they began to withdraw from the Warsaw Pact, leading to its break-up in March 1991.

The Soviet View

The Soviet Union's senior political leadership depended on a large standing army as their protection from the threat posed by NATO's perceived aggressive stance, such as the American-organized 1947 Marshall Plan. The Soviet Union's senior military leadership believed that the most critical components in that force structure were its ground forces, artillery and tanks.

T-34-85 Medium Tank

In the Red Army, officially renamed the Soviet Army in 1946, its first line medium tank at the end of the Second World War was the diesel-engine-powered T-34-85. Approval for the tank occurred in December 1943, with the first examples coming off the factory floors in February 1944. Soviet industry completed around 12,000 examples of the T-34-85 tank by the end of 1944, with another 7,000 the following year.

The impetus for the development of the 35-ton T-34-85 came about due to the Red Army's experiences at the Battle of Kursk in July 1943. The German Tiger E (Tiger 1) heavy tank had been expected, as the Red Army had first encountered them in platoon strength in September 1942; however, there were so many Tiger Es at Kursk, and the Soviets were also surprised by the introduction of the new German Panther medium tank, armed with a potent higher-velocity long-barrelled 75mm main gun. Thus the Red Army's original T-34s, armed with a 76.2mm main gun, suffered heavy losses.

In response to the Germans fielding more potent tanks, the Red Army eventually decided to up-gun a modified version of the original T-34 chassis. It featured a new turret, based on one originally designed for the experimental T-43 medium tank, mounting an adaptation of the Red Army's 85mm anti-aircraft gun.

The first production examples of the T-34-85 began reaching field units in small numbers in March 1944. These went to elite (Guards) armoured units and proved a great morale-booster to Red Army tankers, as it provided a level of parity between the warring sides' armoured formations. Another bonus was that most had radios, not a feature of most first-generation T-34-76 tanks.

Besides the bigger gun, the new larger and better-armoured turret of the T-34-85 housed three men rather than the two of the original T-34, leading to an increased degree of combat effectiveness by the turret crew as the vehicle commander no longer had to double up as the tank's gunner.

Early Post-War T-34-85s

Following the Second World War, Soviet industry continued to churn out more T-34-85s until 1950, with estimates put at almost 23,000 additional examples, adding to the 19,000 built between 1944 and 1945. The need for more T-34-85 tanks in the immediate post-war period was no doubt in response to the steep losses incurred by the Red Army between 1944 and 1945, which totalled almost 36,000 tanks. More than half of these were T-34-85s.

In addition to the T-34-85 tanks built in Soviet factories, in the immediate post-war period, Polish and Czech factories produced another 4,000 or so combined licence examples of the T-34-85 tank in the 1950s.

The Czechs sold many of their post-war-built T-34-85 tanks to other Warsaw Pact countries' armies. The T-34-85 would survive in service as training tanks with the East German and Polish armies until the 1970s.

Many of the T-34-85s went off to Third World militaries that had come within the Soviet Union's political sphere of influence in the early post-war period. The best-known examples went off to the North Korean Army in 1948.

A now-declassified September 1951 CIA report titled 'Engineering Analysis of the Russian T-34/85 Tank' lists some of the desirable design features of the late 1945 Soviet-built T-34-85 from analysis of one captured in Korea:

1. Manufacturing methods had been adequate for the job, with crude exterior finish being countered by precision machining on functioning parts, according to need.
2. Materials were found ample for the job; better than those to be used in American tanks, in some instances.
3. Design was simple to the degree that the average mechanically trained crewman could attempt repairs with some assurance of success.
4. Fire hazard was minimized through the use of a diesel engine rather than one requiring gasoline, and a major source of radio interference was eliminated [spark plugs].
5. Armor thicknesses were approximately the same as those on US tanks.

T-34-85 Road Report

Marc Sehring, the curator of the Virginia Museum of Military Vehicles, shares his impressions of the T-34-85 tank in their collection:

> The T-34 is crude, raw, noisy, smoky, smelly – a very charming, very Russian tank! I like the T-34; it is simple without frills, designed to fight and survive without considering crew comfort. Visibility isn't the greatest, particularly for the bow gunner, who can't see anything unless it's directly in front of his little scope. But it will take off and runs well – it is a fast, reliable tank.
>
> The driver has to be built like a horse to drive it, but once you're out in open country, it rides very well; the tracks are wide enough to give it good flotation. You are surrounded by fuel and ammunition, but the armor is thick and beautifully shaped – the shape of the vehicle was well ahead of its time.
>
> The V-12 engine is a great power plant, very well designed, and highly dependable. I've never had a problem with Soviet engines anyway. They do burn oil, but the Russians planned for that, and you've got a big tank to keep the crankcase filled – if you aren't burning oil in a T-34, it means there [is] no oil in the engine. And the air start system works well – the engine fires up every time.
>
> The gunner's sight is pretty good for its time – good field of view and a pretty bright sight system. The turret traverse system is simple but effective. The real problem is communication between the commander and the gunner, which has to be good because the gunner doesn't have a wide field of view.
>
> You can't sneak up on somebody with them, but they weren't designed for that – they were designed for the attack. And if they'd gone up against our American tanks of the time [Second World War], we'd have lost. The Russian tank is a much better design than the M4 Sherman, with a lower silhouette, much better gun, better armor, better slope, a great suspension system, simpler, easier to maintain – a superior machine.

As time went on, most of the Soviet, Polish and Czechoslovakian armies' inventory of the T-34-85 went through a rebuilding process in the 1960s using components of more modern medium tanks. These upgrades could include a new diesel engine and radio, as well as infrared driving lights.

The post-war rebuilding of older-generation tanks at regular intervals was a long-standing practice of the Soviet Army in order to keep them as viable as possible. As seen in a 1 December 1984 declassified CIA report titled 'Soviet Tank Programs':

> As a general rule, during a tank's 25 to 30 years in active service, it spends the first 10 to 15 years in the inventory of ready divisions in the western

USSR or the forward area and the last 10 to 15 years in other parts of the country in non-ready divisions. Tanks that emerge from their active service in relatively good condition may be placed in equipment reserves or refurbished for export. Other old tanks probably are cannibalized for parts, then scrapped.

T-44 Medium Tank

Despite the Red Army's concentration on fixing its T-34 series tank designs to maximize production numbers, the idea of replacing the T-34 became more agreeable to those bureaus otherwise extending the life of the T-34 series. Hence one design bureau began development in 1944 of a next-generation medium tank; that received the designation T-44.

The T-44's turret, armed with an 85mm main gun, remained similar to the T-34-85, but the chassis design was dramatically different from that of the T-34, with a broader and shorter hull achieved by doing away with the bow machine-gunner's position. The T-44 featured a torsion bar suspension instead of the T-34 series' Christie-style suspension, like the previous KV and IS heavy tank series.

The new 35-ton medium tank received power from a version of the same diesel engine in the T-34 series. However, instead of the inline engine arrangement of previous Red Army tanks, the T-44 had its engine mounted transversely in the rear hull coupled to a new transmission, allowing for the more compact hull design as well as increased interior space.

Despite its innovative features, the T-44 had unresolved design issues, especially with its power train. Another problem: the turret proved too small to mount a larger main gun, a critical requirement desired by the Soviet Army. Despite these and other design issues, Soviet industry built 1,823 examples of the T-44 between 1944 and 1947. None of the wartime-built examples saw combat. However, its hull design would play an essential part in subsequent post-war development of Soviet Army medium tanks from the T-54 to the T-62.

IS-2 Heavy Tank

Upon capturing a 60-ton Tiger I tank with its 88mm main gun in January 1943, it became clear to the Red Army that the existing 50-ton KV-1 heavy tank, armed with the same 76.2mm main gun as the original T-34, was badly under-gunned. Adding to the KV-1's design shortcomings was an unreliable transmission. To meet the Tiger I on equal terms, Soviet industry in response began constructing the 51-ton IS-2 heavy tank in February 1944. The prefix letters 'IS' translate to the abbreviation of Joseph Stalin.

Armed with a 122mm main gun in a new turret design, the Stalin chassis came from the earlier IS-85 heavy tank that had featured a new and more reliable transmission. Rather than the five-man crew of previous Red Army heavy tanks, with the advent of the IS-2, the bow machine-gunner position disappeared to allow for a better-designed glacis.

By the time production of the IS-2 concluded in 1945, a total of 3,854 examples had rolled off the assembly lines. Seventy-one examples went off to a Soviet-raised Polish Army formation in late 1944, entering combat for the first time in January 1945. No other future Warsaw Pact army would take the IS-2 into service.

Starting in 1954, the Soviet Army had its remaining IS-2 tanks upgraded, resulting in the designation IS-2M; the suffix 'M' stood for modernized. These would linger on in front-line service with the Soviet Army until the 1960s. They then went into long-term storage for use by lower-tier reserve divisions. As with its T-34-85s, some IS-2s would go off to friendly non-Warsaw Pact countries in the 1950s and 1960s.

IS-3 Heavy Tank

Even as the IS-2 entered Red Army service, Soviet tank designers were hard at work coming up with a redesigned IS-2 featuring a more ballistic turret and front hull glacis. That tank became the IS-3 and first appeared in December 1944. Red Army leadership liked what they saw and quickly approved the tank for production. Armament remained the D-25T 122mm main gun.

The four-man IS-3 featured a large, heavily-sloped, bowl-shaped hemispherical turret and a glacis consisting of two thick sharply-angled armour plates welded together, resulting in its unofficial nickname of the 'Pike'. The tank had a 250mm-thick (10in) gun shield, with the glacis plate coming in at 110mm (4in).

The use of sloped armour plates significantly increased the chances of an armour-piercing (AP) projectile glancing off when struck. AP projectiles also fall under the general heading of kinetic energy (KE) rounds.

Due to the extensive retooling necessary to build the diesel-engine-powered IS-3, the first examples did not come off the assembly lines until May 1945, arriving in Eastern Europe too late to see combat against the German Army.

Sloped Armour

Designers do their best to keep the surfaces of tanks, both turrets and hulls, sloped as much as possible so that projectiles will ricochet off. Another benefit of sloped armour is the increase in areal density. A vertical armour surface struck by a projectile with a horizontal line of fire defeats a threat based on its thickness alone. That same plate, when sloped, presents a thicker profile to an incoming projectile and possesses a higher areal density. If the slope's angle is sufficiently steep, projectiles will deflect off the surface rather than penetrate it.

The increase in protection provided by sloping tank armour is usually gradual below 30 degrees and increases as the angle goes up. Post-war British military studies indicated the optimum slope to resist penetration of a tank's glacis plate by an armour-piercing capped (APC) projectile lay between 50 and 70 degrees. Against attacks by an armour-piercing discarding sabot (APDS) projectile containing a sub-calibre tungsten core, a glacis slope of 60 degrees provided the optimum protection.

The Western Allies were unaware of the IS-3 tank's development. Upon observing fifty-two examples roll by during a victory parade held in Berlin, on 7 September 1945, the Allied generals were utterly taken aback. It appeared to be far superior to anything in their armies, thereby prompting heavy tank development in the immediate aftermath of the war by several NATO countries.

Looks Can Be Deceptive

Despite the IS-3's impressive appearance, in the rush to field it there had been some design constraints imposed. The most crucial was keeping the tank's weight down to 51 tons, the same as the IS-2. The designers took shortcuts to meet that benchmark, which weakened its hull's stiffness. That made the hull flex, which frequently broke hull welds and motor mounts and damaged the tanks' road wheel bearings.

Despite the IS-3 tank's unreliability, the Soviet Army had production continue until 1947, with 2,311 examples completed. It was not for lack of trying that the IS-3 never lived up to Soviet Army expectations. The tank went through three significant rebuilds and upgrade programmes between 1948 and 1959, resulting in the designation IS-3M. However, it still could not meet Soviet Army standards of reliability.

There was a fear among the French Army fighting in Indochina (1946–54) that the Soviet Union might provide their opponent with the IS-3, but that concern proved unfounded. During the Korean War (1950–53), the US Army also became concerned about encountering the IS-3. The US had no tank that could effectively defeat the IS-3's frontal armour array, but that problem also never occurred.

The only combat action Soviet Army-manned IS-3M tanks ever took part in occurred during the suppression of the Hungarian Revolution between October and November 1956. Hungarian insurgents destroyed a handful with Molotov cocktails. No Warsaw Pact army took the IS-3M into service. Many ended up as range targets or as dug-in pillboxes along the Sino-Soviet border during the 1970s and 1980s. Some eventually went to third-world countries as military aid.

> **Tank-Killing Rounds**
>
> A potent armour-piercing round for tanks came out of the Second World War and had a tungsten carbide core. It was employed by the US Army, the Red Army and the German Army. The American military referred to it as a High-Velocity Armor-Piercing (HVAP) round. Unofficially it was nicknamed 'Hyper-Shot' by American tankers.
>
> HVAP came to be known as an Armor-Piercing, Composite Rigid (APCR) round in other armies. Such an armour-piercing round falls under the general category of a kinetic energy (KE) round. The tungsten carbide core was centred within a lightweight jacket that matched the bore of tank guns.
>
> Because the diameter of the sub-calibre core was smaller than that of standard AP rounds, the APCR concentrated its penetrative energy on a

smaller area of the target, making it more effective than full-calibre AP rounds in penetrating armour at short and medium ranges.

A drawback of APCR was the fact that the core carried its lightweight jacket to the target. The jacket imposed aerodynamic drag and caused it to lose velocity during flight, reducing armour penetration at longer ranges compared to standard AP rounds.

The weight of an APCR round did not cause a loss of velocity, but required super-elevation to counteract gravitational forces. Another disadvantage with APCR rounds is that the cores require high-density materials to resist break-up on impact; tungsten, being highly dense, is relatively scarce given its preferred use in machine tools.

The British took the next obvious step and developed for its wartime 17-pounder gun a Super-Velocity Discarding Sabot (SVDS) round. In the US Army, the same type of round bore the label Armor-Piercing Discarding Sabot (APDS) but did not come into service until the late 1950s.

The significant advantage of APDS involved providing a given calibre cannon with a much higher muzzle velocity. It also resulted in shorter flight times with much flatter trajectories at short ranges than Second World War conventional projectiles, such as Armor-Piercing Capped (APC) or Armor-Piercing Cap/Ballistic Cap (APCBC). In American military verbiage an APCBC round is referred to as an Armor-Piercing Capped (APC) round.

A sabot projectile consists of three main parts: a soft jacket, a sub-calibre projectile core, and a metal base that has a rotating band. Upon firing an APDS round, the lightweight jacket supports the projectile as it passes through a gun's rifled bore giving it rotational velocity. Upon exiting a tank gun's muzzle, the lightweight jacket and metal base would separate due to centrifugal force, leaving the sub-calibre core to travel to the chosen target on its own.

The Egyptian Army had obtained about 100 examples of the IS-3M, which did see action during the 1967 Arab-Israeli War. They proved the most serious threat to Israeli tanks as their frontal armour was immune to the 90mm main guns on their American M48 tanks, and even caused problems for the Israeli M48 tanks armed with the 105mm main gun.

(**Opposite, above**) No longer the most modern tank in the US Army's inventory following the Second World War but still in service, this vehicle is listed as the Tank, Medium, M4A3, 76mm Gun, Wet, on its data plate; for the sake of brevity, labelled by the author as the M4A3(76)W. It's riding on the Horizontal Volute Spring Suspension (HVSS) system, with 23in-wide tracks. (*Richard and Barb Eshleman*)

(**Opposite, below**) In a photograph dated May 1950, some M4A3(76)W HVSS Tanks appear in storage. A total of 2,167 examples were built by April 1945. In the second generation of M4 series tanks, the preferred tank is due to its superior Ford GAA engine. Those in excess of the US Army's post-war manning requirements were retained for a wartime emergency. (*Sherman Minutia website*)

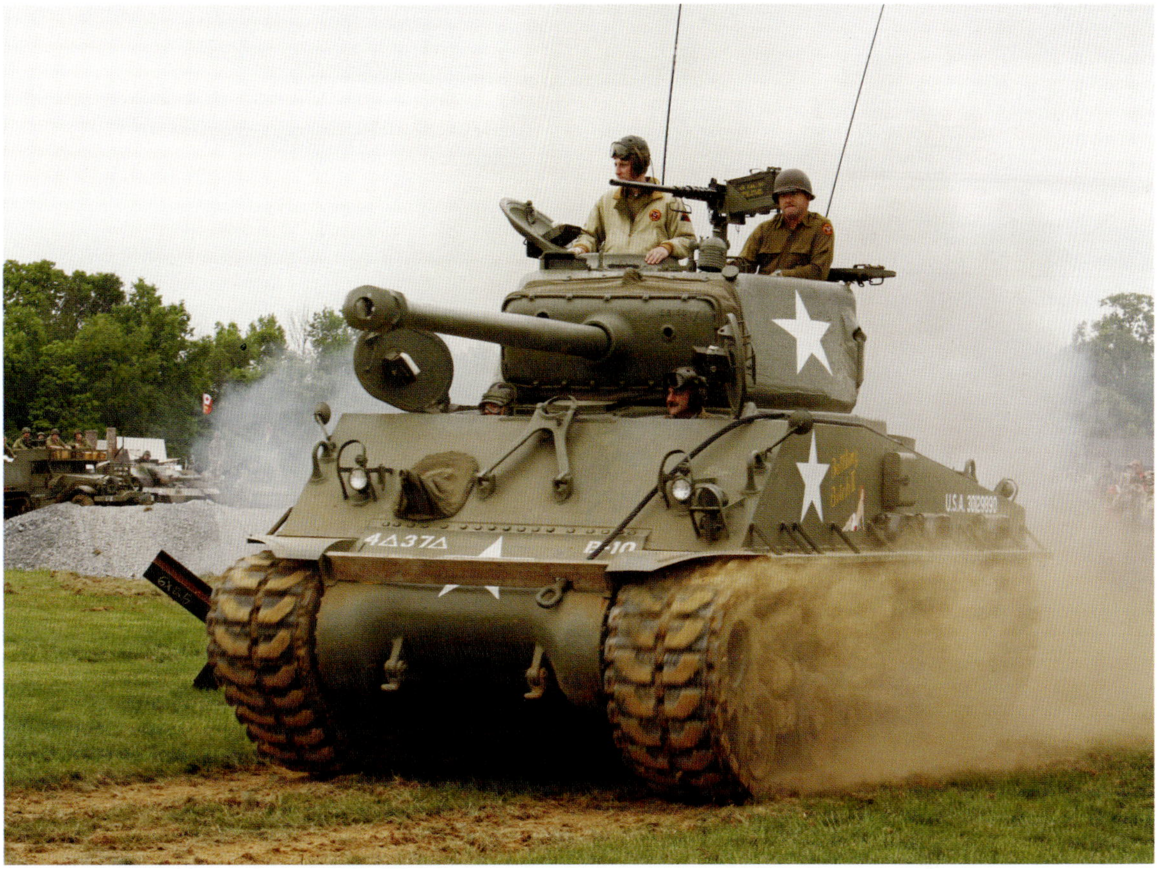

4Δ37Δ
B-10

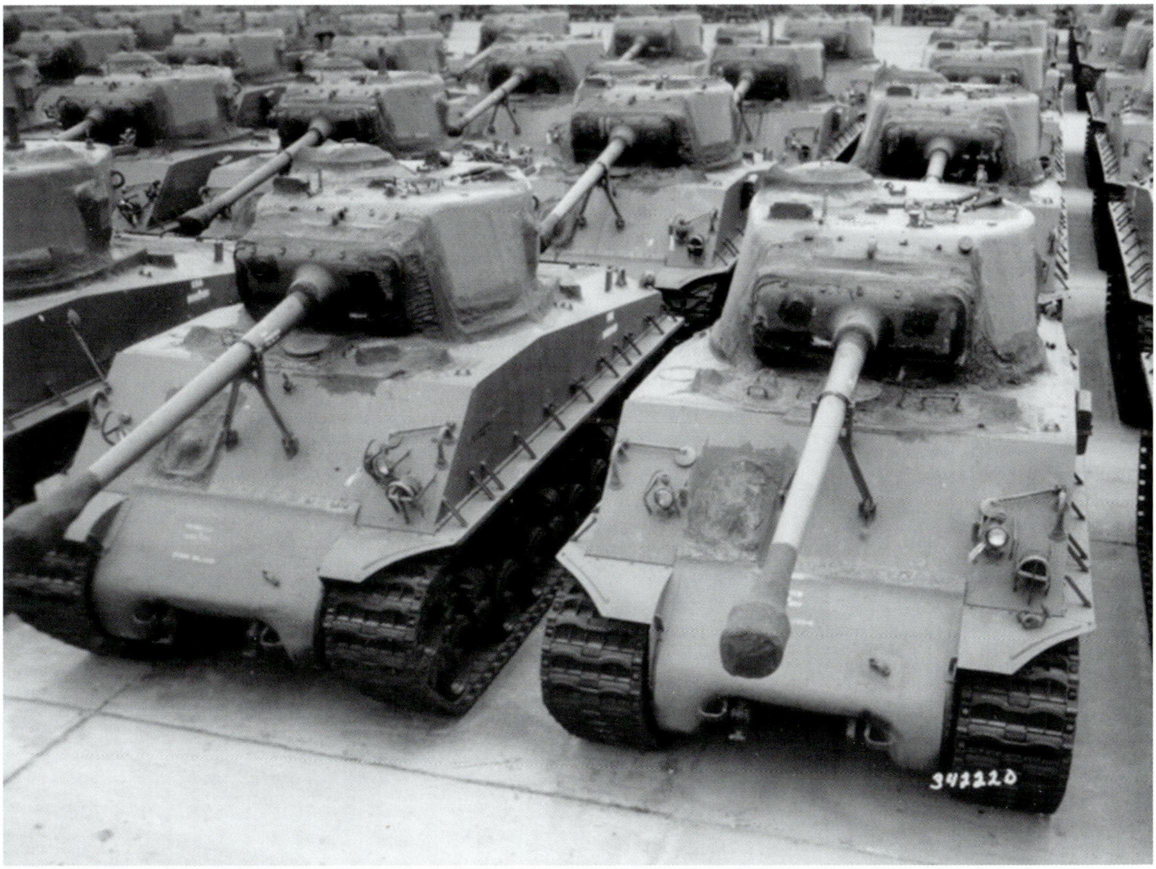

341220

(**Above**) In the immediate post-war period, the US Army kept some of the 3,071 examples of the second-generation M4A3 tanks with the wet ammunition stowage arrangement and 75mm main gun. Pictorial evidence shows them serving with US Army National Guard units and as training tanks. A total of 651 examples built with the HVSS system found themselves reworked into the M4A3(76)W configuration. (*Pierre-Olivier Buan*)

(**Opposite, above**) Of the 3,426 examples of the second-generation M4A1(76)W tank built between 1944 and 1945, a total of 1,255 rode on the HVSS system, as shown here. In the aftermath of the Second World War, the M4A1(76)Ws remaining in the US Army inventory were deemed obsolete due to their underpowered radial engines. They were therefore available for transfer under military aid programmes to countries friendly to the United States. (*Richard and Barb Eshleman*)

(**Opposite, below**) A principal recipient of US-built M4 series tanks during and following the Second World War was the French Army. A French Army officer is seen here standing on the turret of his second-generation M4A1(76)W tank before the beginning of a military parade. The German wartime occupation and the devastation wrought by the fighting to free France had decimated the French armament industry. (*Patton Museum*)

23

(**Above**) In the turret of a second-generation M4A1(76)W two French Army tankers are taking part in a training exercise. The vehicle commander is on the left, with the loader on the right. The commander's raised cupola has six laminated vision blocks around its circumference, with an overhead periscope in the roof of his overhead hatch. Note the circular ventilation exhaust between the loader and commander. (*Public domain*)

(**Opposite, above**) The French Army employed a wide array of American wartime and post-war-supplied military equipment during the First Indochina War (1946–54). Shown here is an M4A1 tank armed with a 75mm main gun and riding on the vertical volute spring suspension (VVSS) system. Due to French Indochina's terrain and the lack of suitable road infrastructure, tanks generally proved to be of limited usefulness. (*Patton Museum*)

(**Opposite, below**) During the last two years of the Second World War, the British Army had approximately 2,000 examples of American-supplied first-generation M4 series tanks up-gunned with the 17-pounder, as seen here. Upon the war's end, the British Army left most of them behind on the continent as scrap. Both the newly-formed Dutch and Belgian armies took advantage of this fact and took a number into service. (*Ian Wilcox*)

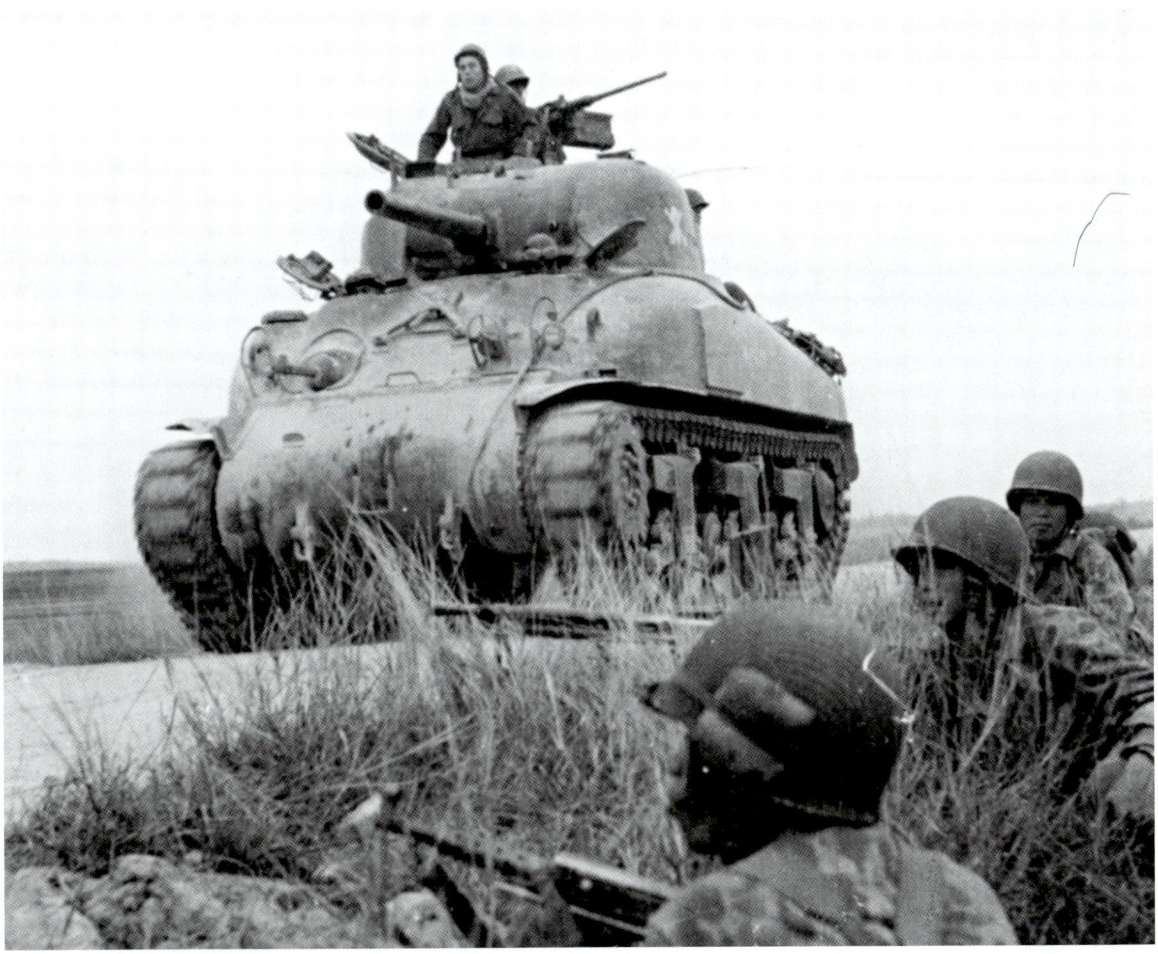

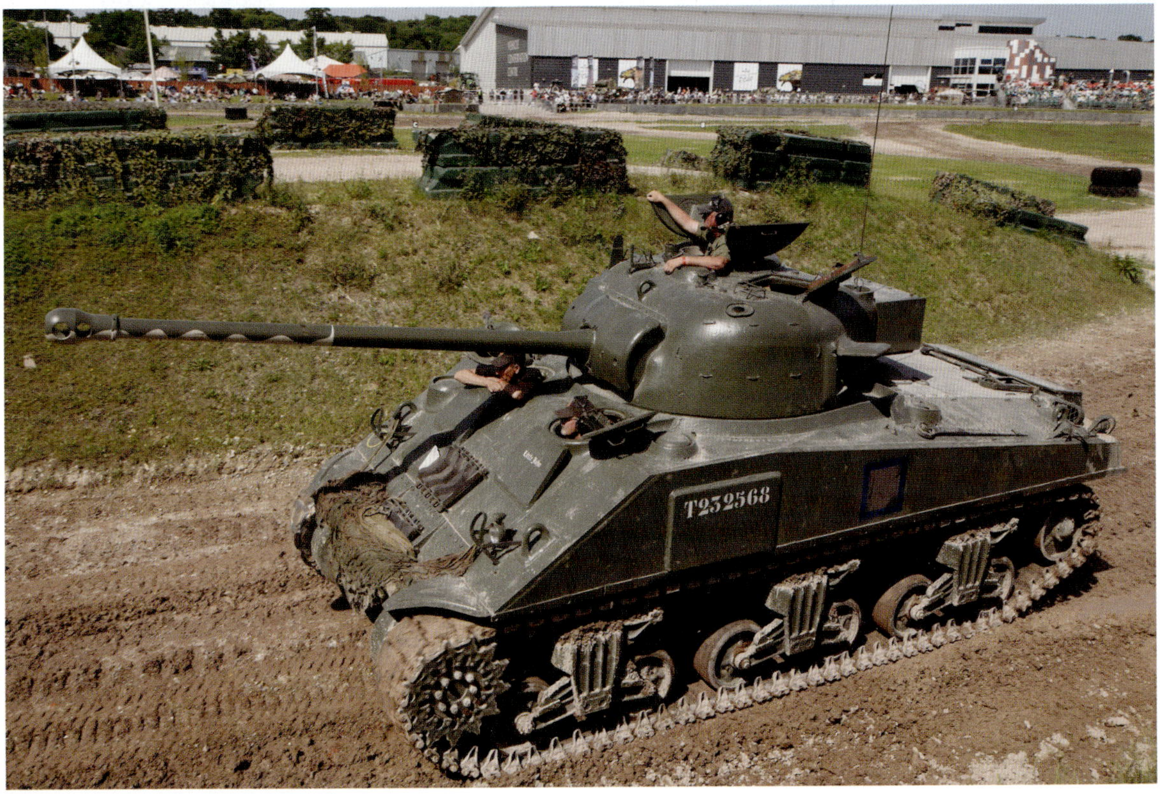
T232568

(**Above**) The most modern tank in the US Army upon the Japanese surrender in September 1945 was the M26 Heavy Tank. Following the war, the M26 was redesignated as a medium tank, as the US Army had much larger and heavier tanks in development. The M26's 90mm main gun fired an M82 Armor-Piercing Capped-Tracer (APC-T) round with a muzzle velocity of 2,800ft/sec that could penetrate 107mm of steel armour at 2,000 yards. (*WW2 Tank Museum*)

(**Opposite, above**) During the Korean War (1950–53), tank-versus-tank combat was fairly rare, apart from in the first few months. The biggest threat to American tanks, such as this M26 Medium Tank, proved to be land mines, as is evident in this picture. Another threat was American-made 3.5in rocket-launchers captured by the enemy and used against US Army and Marine Corps' tanks. (*Patton Museum*)

(**Opposite, below**) The M26 Medium Tank, powered by the liquid-cooled GAA gasoline engine, had a cruising range on level roads of around 100 miles. Unlike the M4 series of medium tanks with the transmission and controlled differential in the front hull and engine in the rear hull, the transmission, controlled differential and engine of the M26 all resided in the rear hull and, when required, were removed as a single unit for servicing. In this photo, the main gun is stowed over the rear deck. (*Patton Museum*)

REAR FENDER STOWAGE BOXES BRUSH GUARD

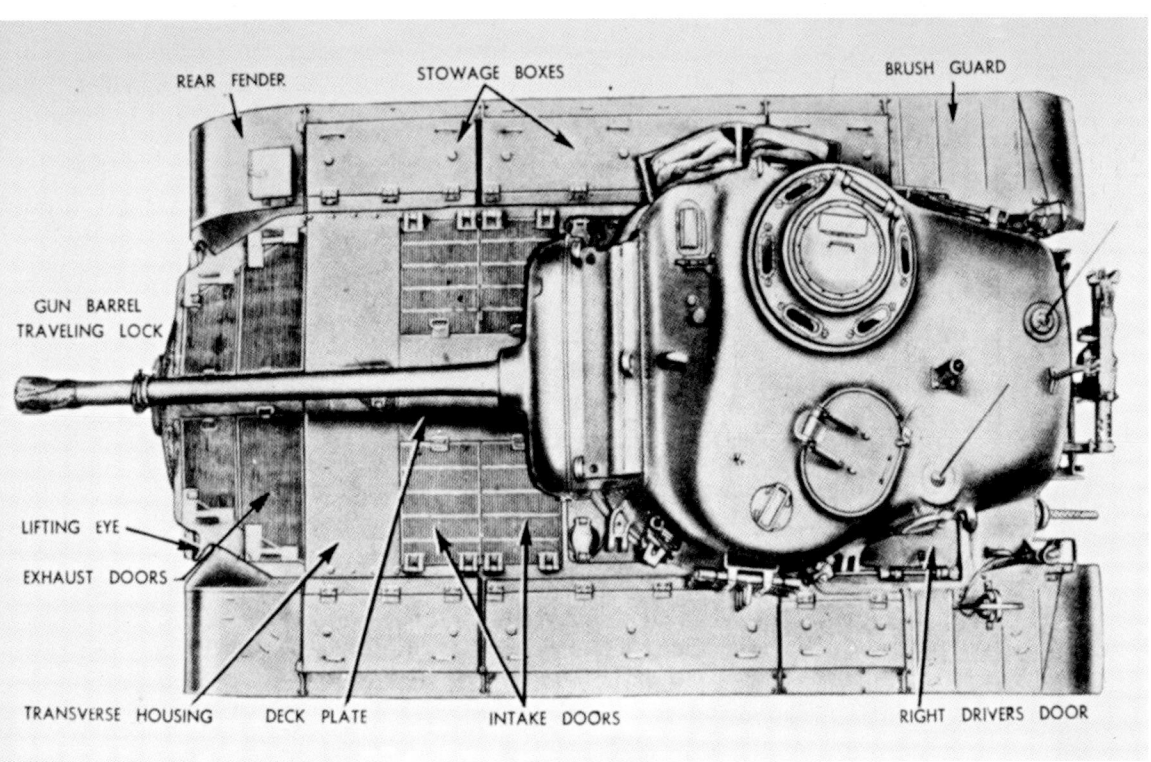

GUN BARREL
TRAVELING LOCK

LIFTING EYE
EXHAUST DOORS

TRANSVERSE HOUSING DECK PLATE INTAKE DOORS RIGHT DRIVERS DOOR

In an image taken during a post-war training exercise, the crew of an M26 Medium Tank is seen here loading main gun rounds. Besides the M82 APC, the tank carried the T30E16 Hypervelocity Armor-Piercing-Tracer (HVAP-T) shot round, nicknamed 'Hyper-Shot' by tank crews. It had a muzzle velocity of 3,350ft/sec and could penetrate 155mm (6.1in) of steel armour at 2,000 yards. The term 'shot' referred to a round with no high-explosive element. (*Patton Museum*)

The M24 Light Tank shown here during the Korean War proved to be a liability in service with the US Army during the first months of the conflict. It was both under-gunned and under-armoured compared to the Soviet-supplied T-34-85 tanks of the North Korean Army. Once enough American medium tanks arrived in Korea, the M24s filled secondary roles. *(Patton Museum)*

The M24 Light Tank received power from two gasoline-fuelled car engines connected to a new automatic transmission. Top speed on level roads was 35mph. Surplus to US Army requirements, many M24s went off to friendly countries, including various NATO nations, in the immediate post-war period. The best-known were those employed by the French Army during the First Indochina War (1946–54). *(Pierre-Olivier Buan)*

(**Above**) No immediate post-war army could afford to dispose of all its wartime-built tanks while awaiting newer generations of replacement tanks. One of those wartime tanks that lingered on in service for a time into the Cold War was the British Army Cromwell. Armed with a 75mm main gun, some remained in service long enough to see limited use during the Korean War (1950–53). (*Pierre-Olivier* Buan)

(**Opposite, above**) The Comet tank was another wartime-built British Army tank that remained in service into the Cold War's early years. A modified hull of the earlier-production Cromwell tank featured a new turret armed with a scaled-down 17-pounder (76.2mm) main gun labelled the 77mm gun. It fired the same rounds as the 17-pounder, but the cartridge case was shorter to fit within the tank's turret confines. (*Ian Wilcox*)

(**Opposite, below**) The British Army's answer to the German Panther tank proved to be the Centurion series. The initial version, the Mk 1, of which 100 examples came off the factory floor, had a 17-pounder (76.2mm) main gun, a welded armour turret and a fixed vehicle commander's cupola. The up-armoured Mk 2 version shown here appeared in service in 1947. It retained the 17-pounder of the Mk 1 but featured a new all-cast-armour turret, fitted with a rotatable vehicle commander's cupola. (*Tank Museum*)

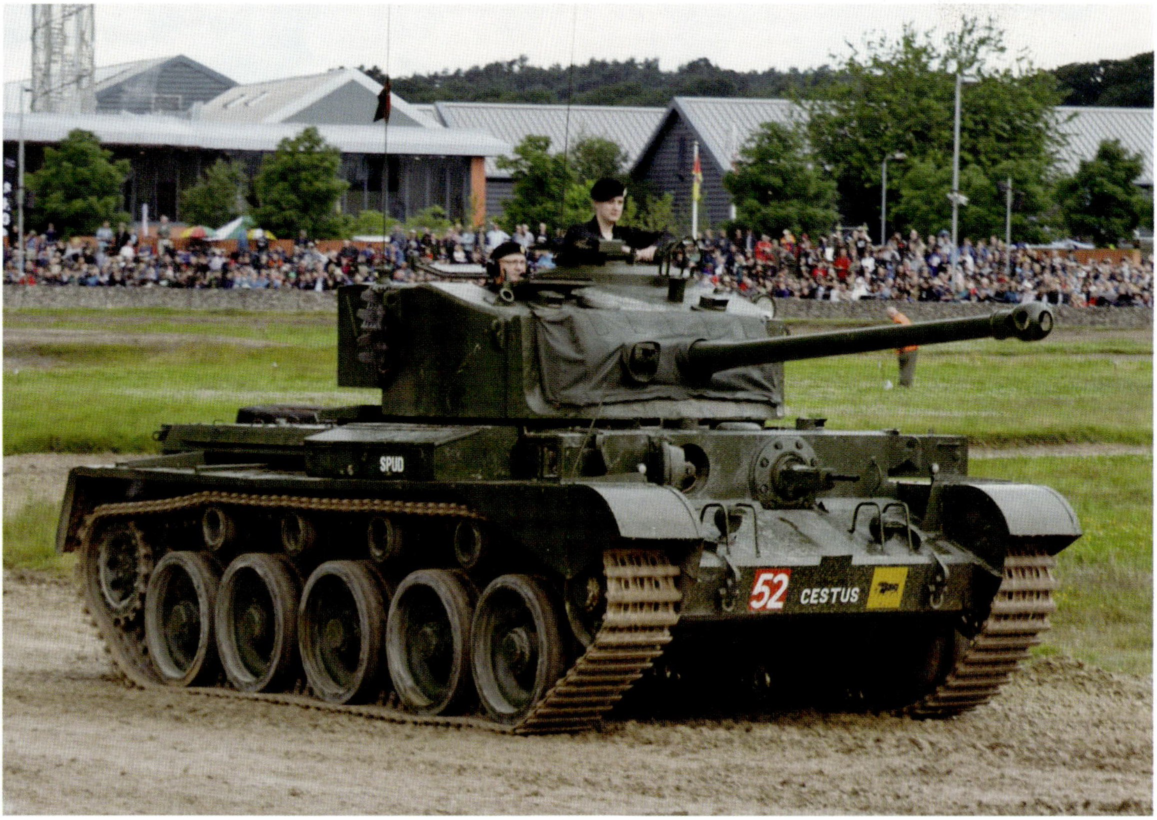
SPUD
52
CESTUS

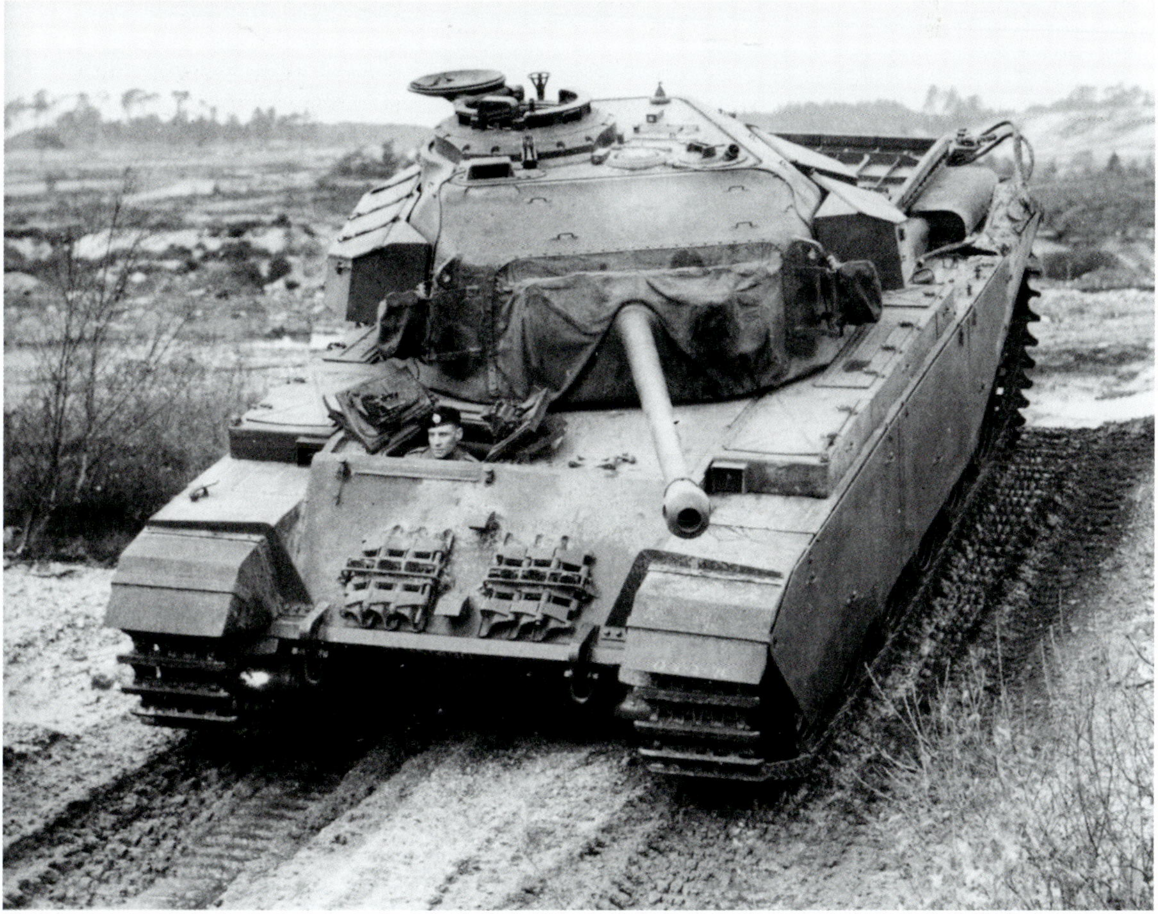

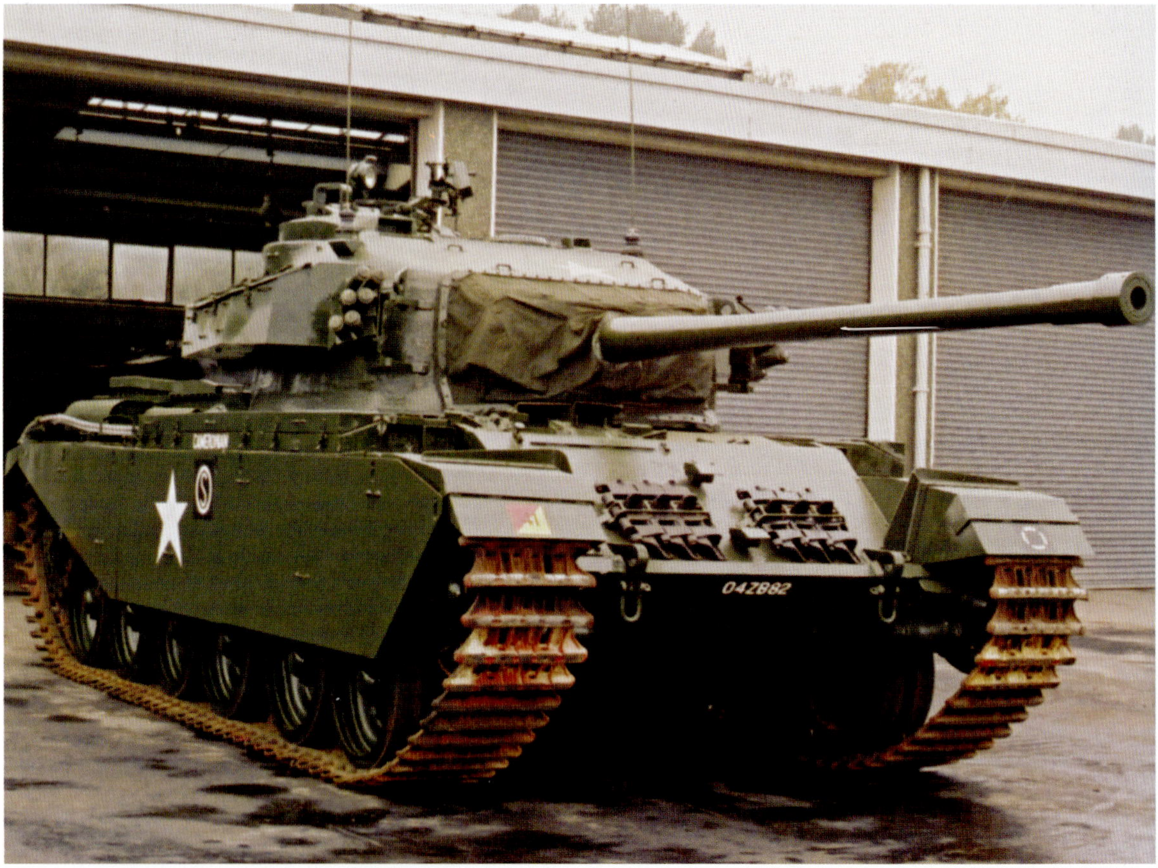
04ZB82

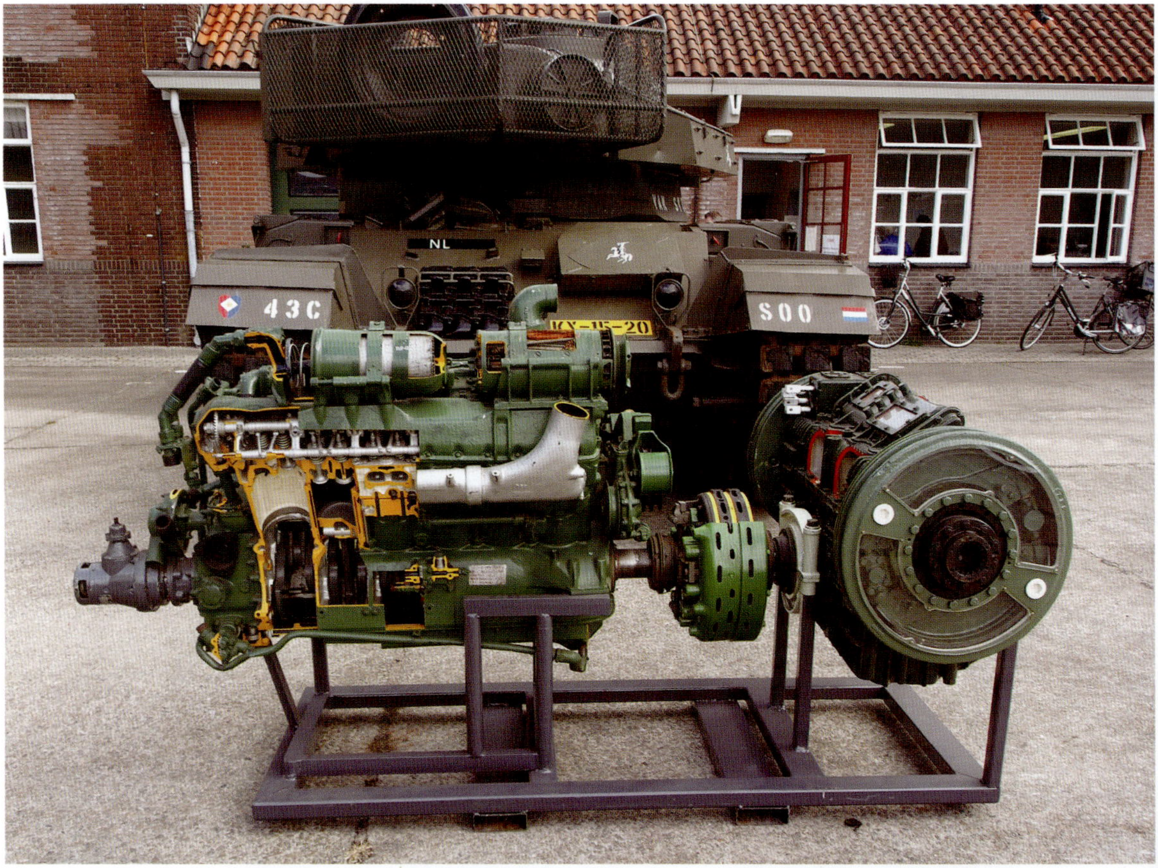
NL
43C
S00

(**Opposite, above**) The first combat action for the Centurion tank series was the Korean War (1950–53). The British Army units served as part of the United Nations (UN) and deployed the Mk 3 version. This example is armed with a 20-pounder (83.4mm) main gun. It is featured in Korean War markings, with the white star on the side of the tank's armoured skirting plates intended as an identifying feature for those who might be unfamiliar with the vehicle. (*Tank Museum*)

(**Above**) On display here at a Swiss Army museum is a Mk 3 Centurion tank armed with a 20-pounder (83.4mm) main gun. At the end of the muzzle is a counterweight to aid in balancing the gun in its mount. It was fitted with a two-axis stabilization system that first appeared on the Mk 2 versions. The Mk 3 could effectively fire on the move, the first Cold War-era tank with that capability. All the earlier-production Mk 1 and 2 Centurion tanks were brought up to the Mk 3 standard by 1951. (*Dreamstime*)

(**Opposite, below**) On display here is the gasoline-powered engine of the British Army Centurion tank series and its transmission and controlled differential. These powered both the Cromwell and Comet tanks. The engine, from the British firm of Meteor, was derived from a Rolls-Royce engine that had powered some British wartime aircraft and the famous American-designed and built P-51 Mustang fighter plane. (*Dreamstime*)

A Centurion Mk 3 armed with the 20-pounder 83.4mm main gun; without the typical hull side armour skirting, the suspension system of the tank is visible. Rather than the torsion bar suspension system favoured by the American and Soviet armies for their tanks, the Centurion tank series had the externally-mounted Horstmann double bogies wheel assembly system, three on either side of the hull. (*Dreamstime*)

In the immediate aftermath of the Second World War and desperate for a tank that could deal with Soviet Army heavy tanks, the French Army used a limited number of German Panther tanks. With unreliable vehicles and a limited supply of spare parts, they did not last long in French military service. The example pictured here is a Model A restored to running condition at a now-closed Military Vehicle Technology Foundation. (*Chris Hughes*)

Pictured here is a former French Army Char ARL-44 Heavy Tank armed with a 90mm main gun. Powered by a German wartime-built liquid-cooled gasoline engine, the vehicle's design began in secret during the German occupation. Production began in 1949, with around sixty vehicles eventually completed. Already obsolete when it entered service, it lasted in use until 1954, when most went off to the scrapyards. *(Pierre-Olivier Buan)*

The Red Army tank fleet's mainstay of the last two years of the Second World War was the T-34-85. It first entered service with the Red Army in early 1944. Its 85mm main gun helped to offset the firepower advantage possessed by late-war German tanks. Not the equal of the Panther or the Tiger tanks on a one-to-one basis, the T-34-85 made up for that disadvantage in wartime numbers built, almost 24,000. *(Dreamstime)*

This T-34-85 is taking part in an historical military vehicle event. Besides the 24,000 wartime-built examples, the US Army concluded that an additional 23,000 came off Soviet assembly lines by 1950. In the early years of the Cold War, both the Czech and Polish industries received licence rights to build the T-34-85 tank for their armies. During post-war production of the T-34-85, the various factories switched from rounded front fenders to the squared front fender. (*Dreamstime*)

On display here at a Canadian Army museum is a T-34-85. The rubber-rimmed concave roadwheels visible first appeared in 1941 on the T-34-76. Note the two external fuel drums affixed to either side of the upper rear hull. The rear hull armour plate on the T-34-85 had a thickness of 45mm. Not seen on this museum vehicle are the two electrically-detonated smoke canisters seen on wartime vehicles. *(Dreamstime)*

An external spotting feature of some post-war Soviet Army T-34-85s is the relocation of one of the two armoured turret exhaust domes to a position in front of the loader's hatch, as seen on the tank here. Before 1946, both exhaust domes resided side-by-side at the rear of the turret roof. The vehicle also has the spoked rubber-rimmed roadwheel design for the T-34-85 that first appeared on 1945-built vehicles. *(Dreamstime)*

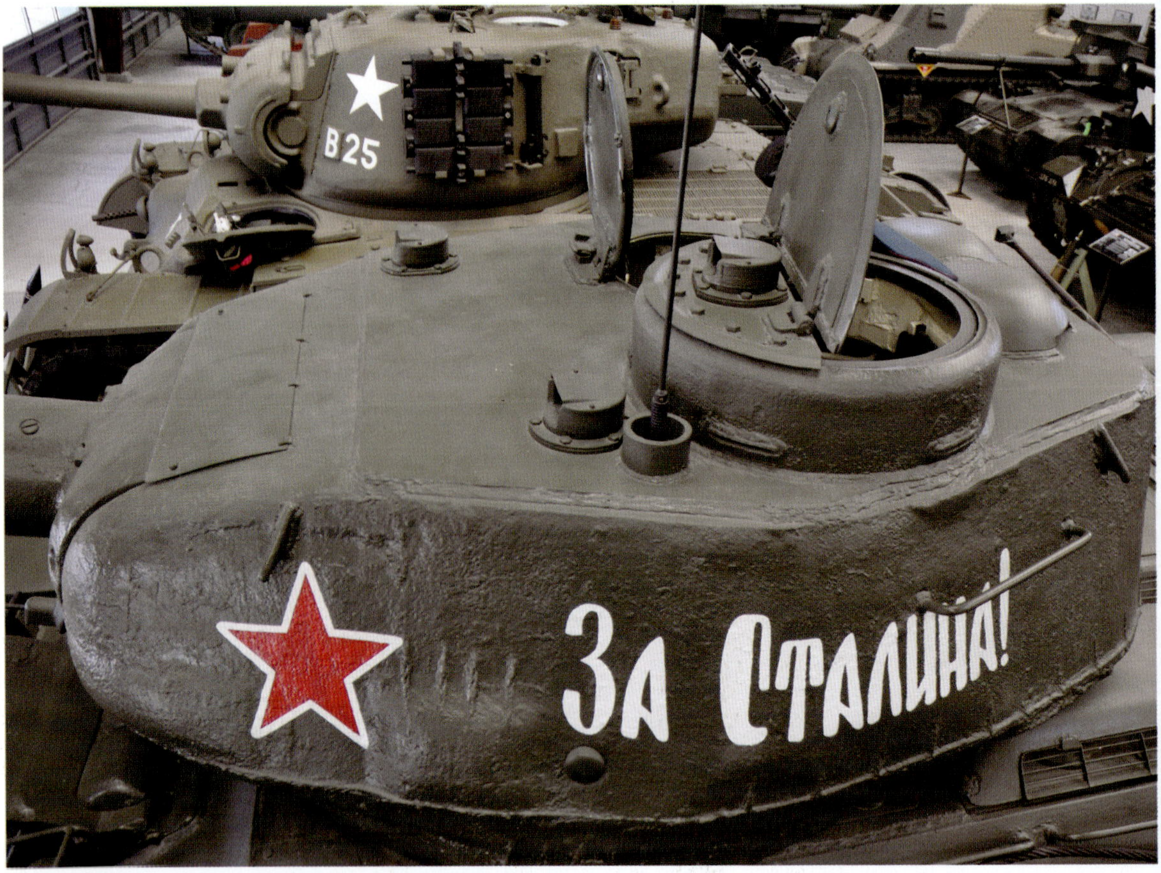
B25
За Сталина!

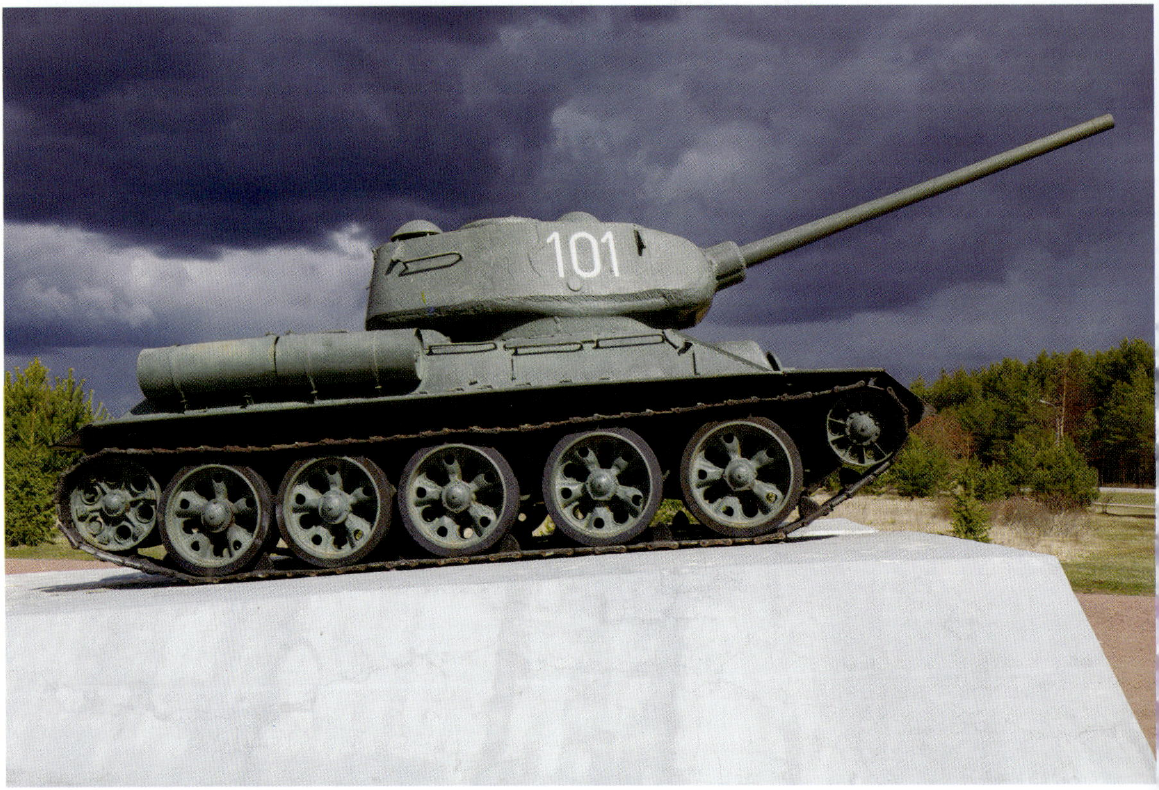
101

(**Opposite, above**) The rectangular bulge on the lower left-hand side of this T-34-85 turret, behind the red star, indicates that it is equipped with an electrically-powered turret traverse system. Elevation and depression of the main gun remained manually-operated. Note the two exhaust domes behind the vehicle commander's cupola. The T-34-85 had a height of 8ft 6in. (*Chris Hughes*)

(**Opposite, below**) Some reworked T-34-85s began to appear with a new spoked rubber-rimmed roadwheel design in the 1970s, as seen on this monument tank. The roadwheel design is based on a version of that developed for the post-war T-55 Medium Tank. Other design features added to Cold War-era rebuilt examples of the T-34-85 included automotive improvements, infrared driving lights, new radios and improved optics. (*Dreamstime*)

(**Above**) As the war on the Eastern Front in 1944 and 1945 swung in favour of the Red Army, Soviet industry continued to churn out untold thousands of T-34-85s. An opportunity arose for Soviet industry to begin developmental work on a replacement tank for the T-34-85. That tank proved to be the T-44 Medium Tank, which first appeared in 1944. It did not see combat during the Second World War. (*Dreamstime*)

The T-44 Medium Tank's turret remained similar in shape and size to that of the T-34-85; hence the retention of the 85mm main gun as nothing larger would fit. Although the T-44's turret design remained stuck in the past, Soviet tank designers outdid themselves with the new hull design, which proved to be both smaller and yet better armoured than its predecessor. It would prove to be the hallmark of follow-on Soviet Army medium tank hull designs through the 1960s. (*Dreamstime*)

The IS-2 heavy tanks did not go into action alongside the Red Army T-34 series tanks. Rather, they were organized into elite formations. These units were held in reserve until a large-scale offensive operation, in which case they would form the armoured spearhead of the initial assault wave. Their 122mm main gun firing high-explosive (HE) rounds proved highly effective against German defensive positions. (*Dreamstime*)

To field a heavy tank to effectively deal with late-war German tanks like the Panther and Tiger series, Soviet industry came up with the 122mm main gun-armed IS-2, officially nicknamed the 'Stalin'. The initial 150 production examples rolled off the factory floor in February 1944. Due to the size of the main gun rounds, it proved too heavy for a single loader, and therefore the projectile and the steel cartridge case were loaded separately. (*Dreamstime*)

(**Above**) Even as IS-2 heavy tank production continued, Soviet industry proved to be hard at work on a better-protected version of the tank. That modified tank became the IS-3 Stalin tank seen here. Its thickly-armoured and highly-sloped turret and front hull proved almost impenetrable against the 88mm AP rounds fired by the main gun on the Tiger B Heavy Tank. Maximum armour thickness on the front turret of the IS-3 was 230mm. (*Ian Wilcox*)

(**Opposite, above**) Production of the IS-3 continued until 1946, unlike the IS-2 Heavy Tank, whose production concluded with the end of the Second World War. None would see combat during the Second World War. Both the IS-2 and IS-3 would go through modernization programmes post-war. Upgraded tanks would have the suffix letter 'M' added to their designations. (*Dreamstime*)

(**Opposite, below**) The well-sloped contours of the armor arrangement on the IS-3 are very apparent with this derelict example. The sharply angled two-piece glacis of the tank made of thick interlocking steel armor plates led to its popular but unofficial nickname as the 'pike'. While the ballistic shape of the IS-3 was state-of-the-art, mechanical reliability proved a problem. So much so that many came straight off the production lines and were shipped directly to rebuild facilities for correcting their many design defects. (*Dreamstime*)

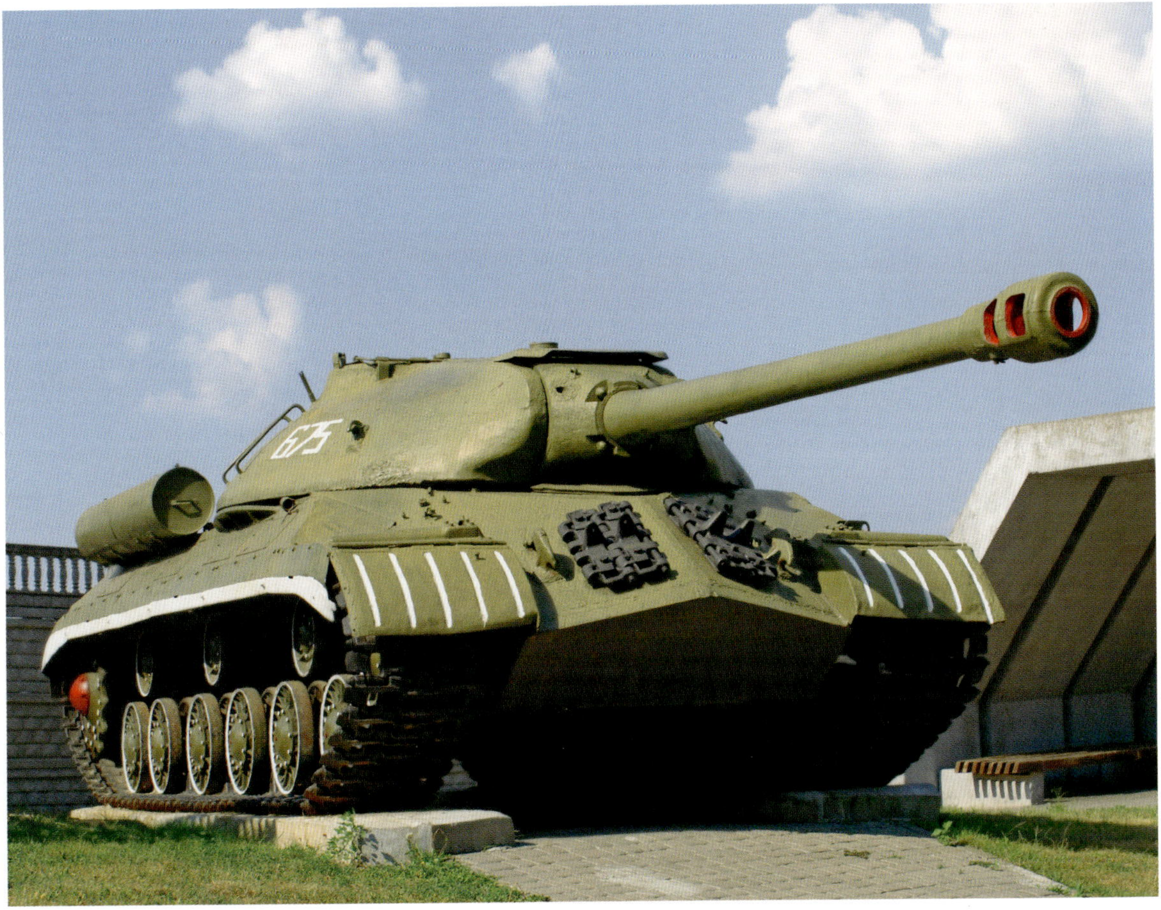
675

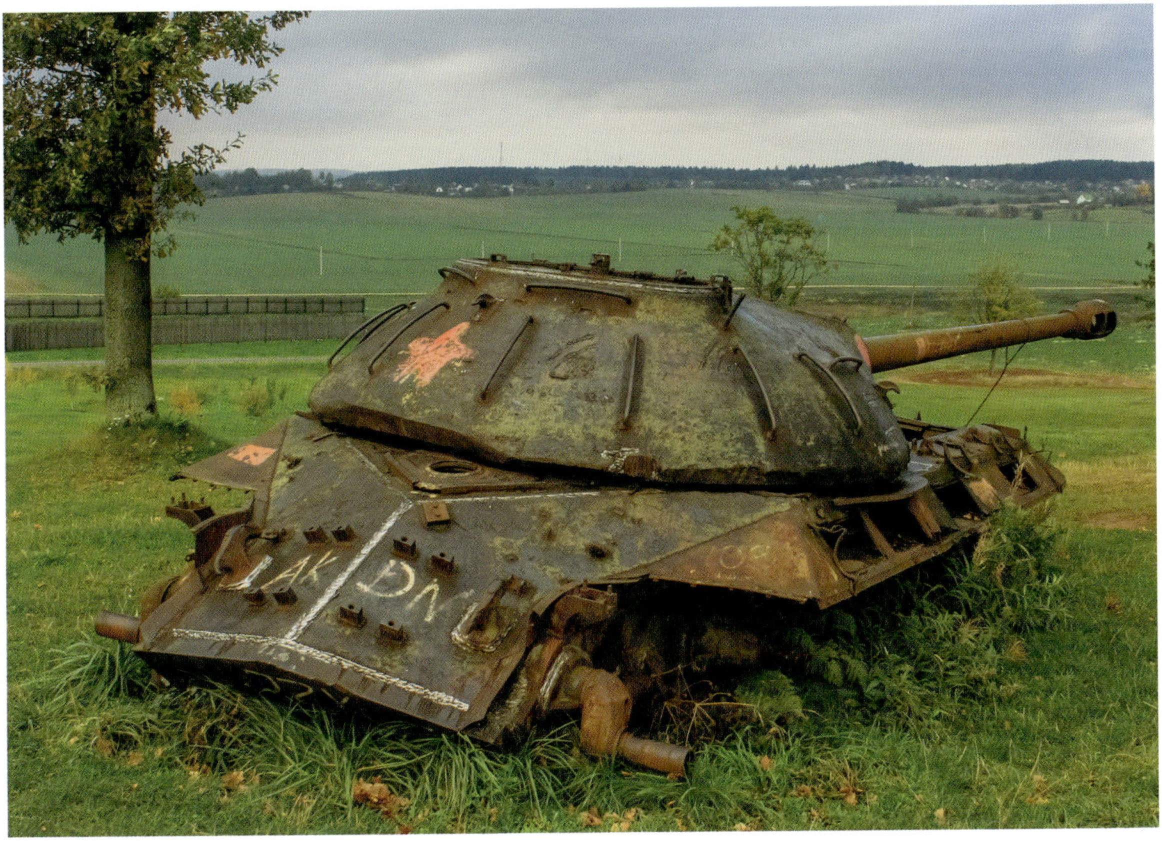

Chapter Two

Building Up the Numbers

The Soviet Army never stopped trying to field a suitable medium tank to build in large numbers at the lowest price. In 1946 it decided that a new medium tank design had most of the desired features. The first completed examples of the tank came off the assembly lines the following year as the T-54.

The T-54 consisted of a modified T-44 medium tank hull, with a new larger turret armed with a 100mm main gun. It was thereby overcoming the biggest shortcoming of the T-44, its 85mm main gun. The T-54 also featured a new, more powerful liquid-cooled diesel engine.

T-54 Series Tanks

To identify this first version of the T-54 from the subsequent models, the earliest versions of the series had an added suffix marking the year production was authorized. Hence the initial iteration of the T-54 became the Model 1947.

The Soviet Army had planned for thousands of the T-54 Model 1947 tanks to replace its wartime T-34-85s. However, many production problems were associated with the T-54 Model 1947, which translated into low reliability. Production quickly ground to a halt, with approximately 1,000 examples built.

The Soviet Army was also very concerned as the Model 1947's turret did not provide the desired protection. Thus production of the follow-on Model 1949 featured a redesigned turret. It was produced until 1951.

The Soviet Army remained unconvinced that industry could not develop an even better turret design for the T-54 series. Industry did, beginning production of the Model 1951 in 1952 and continuing until 1955. The T-54 Model 1951's half-egg-shaped turret presented no vertical surfaces or shot traps to incoming kinetic energy (KE) projectiles. It remained the standard on all subsequent T-54 versions.

T-54A Tank

Development of the T-54 series continued with a couple of its design features influenced by British and American tanks. These included a bore evacuator and a stabilization system. A bore evacuator first appeared on the T-54A, production of which began in 1954 and continued until 1957.

The T-54A had a single-axis (elevation only) stabilization system and a manually-operated turret traverse system. The Red Army had experimented with stabilization systems as far back as the 1930s. However, none appeared on its production tanks during the Second World War, possibly due to immature technology or as a possible trade-off of features versus production simplification.

Poland and Czechoslovakia were allowed to build the T-54A for their respective armies as well as for export. Other design features incorporated into the T-54A included an improved optical sight for the gunner, infrared driving lights and snorkelling equipment. As with the T-34-85, the T-54 gunner depended on a stadiametric rangefinder incorporated into his optical sight reticle.

The requirement for snorkelling equipment on the T-54A and all follow-on Soviet Army tanks was driven by the large number of rivers that had to be crossed during an invasion of Western Europe. The Soviet Army lacked engineer/bridging resources at the division level and below. Furthermore, providing more portable bridging equipment would further tax Soviet manufacturing capacity and material supplies.

The Red Army/Soviet Army had started experimenting with fording equipment for its tanks going back to the 1930s. However, the T-54A was to be the first Soviet Army tank fitted with it as standard equipment.

T-54B Tank

The follow-on to the T-54A was the T-54B, with production beginning in 1956. It featured an electro-hydraulic twin-axis stabilization system (both elevation and traverse). In practice, the stabilization system could only provide a fire-on-the-move capability at very low speed on level ground.

Soviet factories built around 16,000 examples of the T-54 series, with Warsaw Pact countries constructing another 5,500 vehicles.

In an article titled 'The Evolution of the Soviet Battle Tank: Part II' that appeared in the March–April 1968 issue of *Armor* magazine, a West German Army officer described what he considered to be the T-54 series tanks' key advantages over their NATO counterparts in the 1950s:

- Superior armament
- Superior strategic and tactical mobility
- Less breakdown-prone with greater logistical independence
- Simplified production possibilities
- Simplified training requirements

One of the T-54 series tanks' significant advantages was that they presented a lower profile to an opponent. A T-54's height was 7ft 7in without a machine gun fitted on the turret roof, and 8ft 8in with the gun fitted. In contrast, its 1950s NATO counterparts averaged about 11ft in height, with their roof-mounted machine guns.

Keeping a tank's height down and controlling its weight allows for thicker frontal armour as the designers have less vehicle volume to protect. The downside of lowering tank height is the reduced main gun depression angle in a hull-down defensive position; more of the tank is exposed. This was a limiting factor in Soviet Army tank designs, but accepted as a trade-off for fielding smaller, cheaper, lighter and more mobile vehicles, orientated for offence and not defence.

T-55 Tank

As early as 1955, Soviet industry proposed a new upgraded version of the T-54B, correcting all design flaws identified during its time in service. Various upgrades included making it easier and faster to build and improving its operational parameters such as range. With its internal fuel tanks, the T-55 series had a range of 311 miles. The external fuel tanks on the new version provided a further 124 miles of range.

The first iteration of this new version of the T-54 series became the T-55, with the first examples rolling off the assembly line in 1958. A second version of the T-55, first delivered in 1963, provided a higher level of protection from the effects of tactical nuclear weapons and received the designation T-55A.

The T-55A also featured a smoke generation system that involved spraying oil on hot engine surfaces, an arrangement eventually adopted by the US Army. Previous Red/Soviet Army tanks had depended on pyrotechnic smoke pots.

> **Nuclear Weapons and Tanks**
> A declassified CIA report titled 'Soviet Tank Programs' had this to say about the Soviet Army and its tanks regarding fighting in an environment that included tactical nuclear weapons:
>
>> After extensive study and debate, concluded that, although nuclear weapons would be decisive in any future general war, they had not rendered the tank obsolete. Indeed, the Soviets identified the tank as the weapon system most likely to survive on the nuclear battlefield and as the best system for rapidly exploiting nuclear strikes on the opposing forces. Soviet war plans, therefore, envisioned that tactical nuclear weapons would open gaps in enemy defenses through which tank troops could quickly pour to pursue surviving defenders, destroy reserves, and capture key installations in the rear area.
>
> In a March–April 1951 issue of *Armor* magazine is an article titled 'Tank Defense Against Atomic Attack' by a US Army armour officer, in which the author stated the following:
>
>> Since the best protection against blast is armor plate, in a large area under an atomic explosion, although buildings will be knocked down, wooded areas would be leveled, and debris would be thrown for miles, still a tank close to the ground center would have a chance of survival. Not only would the tank's armor plate protect against the initial blast, but more important, it would protect against flying debris ... It is well to remember that although an atomic explosion is a tremendous thing, it will not kill a person any deadlier than a .30 caliber bullet, and the hazards of atomic explosions are to be reduced by good training, proper use of equipment, and use of mobility, cover and concealment, just as other battlefield hazards have been reduced by similar procedures.

Like the T-54B, the T-55A had a two-axis electro-hydraulic stabilization system, as did subsequent Soviet Army tanks. Electro-hydraulic means that the hydraulic system is pressurized by an electrically-driven pump rather than being shaft-driven. The electrical drive can remain active even if the diesel engine is shut down, allowing it to not give away its position with smoke or noise.

The T-54/T-55 series had a 100mm (4in) glacis plate sloped at 60 degrees. The slope effectively doubled its thickness when struck by AP/KE rounds. The gun shields on both tank series presented a maximum thickness of 210mm (8in).

By the time production of the T-55A ended in 1977, Soviet factories had completed approximately 23,000 examples of the T-55/T-55A. Polish factories built around 7,000 T-55 series tanks, with Czech factories constructing another 8,000 vehicles. Many T-54s would eventually be retrofitted with components from the T-55, making it difficult to distinguish between them at a distance.

As with all tank-producing nations, the ever-rising cost of production has precluded wholesale replacement of older tanks. Consequently, it has been a long-time economic necessity to improve existing tanks. In the early 1980s, the Soviet Army began a modernization programme for T-55 and T-55A tanks. Those upgraded models respectively became the T-55M and T-55AM. The Polish- and Czech-built versions respectively became the T-55AM2 and T-55AM2B.

Shortcomings

In the September 1987 issue of *National Defense Magazine* there appeared an article titled 'Soviet Tanks – An Israeli View' by an Israeli Army officer, in which he quoted his army's ordnance experts regarding the basic T-55 tank:

> ... was a good tank with excellent automotive capabilities riding on one of the world's best suspension and track systems, its heavy armor but low weight added survivability. The tank had an extremely low silhouette and was fast even over rough terrain and sand. Its power-pack was fairly reliable and simple to maintain.

In the same article, design shortcomings of the T-55 are listed, one of which lambasts the Soviet designers' 'total disregard for human engineering for crew members ... bad ventilation in the cramped interior caused fatigue and exhaustion, reducing combat efficiency and endurance'.

The T-54/T-55's tight quarters also made it much harder on the tank's loader to manage more than four main gun rounds per minute. In contrast, well-trained NATO tank crews in larger and roomier tanks could fire four main gun rounds in fifteen seconds.

Main Gun Round Stowage

The T-55 series had a new main gun ammunition stowage arrangement that held forty-three rounds. In contrast, the T-54B and those in the series preceding it had room for thirty-four main gun rounds. The T-34-85 had stowage space for fifty-six 85mm main gun rounds, as did the T-44.

By way of comparison, the much larger and heavier 1950s-era American M47 medium tank had authorized stowage for seventy-one 90mm main gun rounds. Its British Army counterpart, the Centurion Mk 3, had stowage for sixty-four 83.4mm main gun rounds, all stored in the hull. Both the Soviet and American tanks had some of their main gun rounds stored within their turrets, significantly adding to their vulnerability.

Soviet military observers noted something troubling during the 1973 Yom Kippur War. Some T-55 series tanks exploded when tank-killing rounds struck the hull's right front even without penetrating, as the shock waves and resulting interior spalling detonated main gun rounds stored in that location.

Firepower

The T-54/T-55 tank series depended on a mixture of main gun rounds including an Armour-Piercing-Tracer (AP-T), Armour-Piercing Discarding Sabot (APDS) and High-Explosive Anti-Tank (HEAT). For non-armoured targets, there was a High-Explosive-Frag (HE-Frag) round.

There appeared for the T-54/T-55 series an Armour-Piercing, Fin-Stabilized, Discarding Sabot (APFSDS) round in 1967. Instead of the APDS round's blunt sub-calibre steel core, the sub-calibre core for the new APFSDS round consisted of a long dart-like tungsten carbide projectile stabilized in flight by aerodynamic fins that prevented it from tumbling.

By the 1980s, modernized Soviet Army T-55AM tanks and Czech- and Polish-built tanks were modified to allow their 100mm main guns to fire a laser-guided Anti-Tank Guided Missile (ATGM) with a shaped-charge warhead. The biggest downside of these specialized ATGMs was their cost.

> **HEAT Disadvantage**
> Tank expert Richard M. Ogorkiewicz brings up an interesting point regarding HEAT rounds and their shaped-charge warheads in an article titled 'Thoughts on Future Tank Designs' in the July–August 1968 issue of *Armor* magazine:
>
> Recent advances in armor penetration have been achieved almost entirely with APDS and HEAT ammunition. Of the two, HEAT ammunition offers superior penetration. But its relative performance needs to be qualified because shaped charges can penetrate armor without doing much harm. This became evident during World War II, when shaped-charge weapons were first introduced, and has been brought out again in Vietnam [the Vietnam War].
>
> Thus, shaped-charge projectiles or missiles must be capable of perforating a significantly greater thickness of armor than that which they are expected to defeat if they are to cause lethal damage behind the armor. In other words, the thickness of armor which HEAT projectiles or missiles perforate with lethal effect is less than the thickness which they can just penetrate.

> **T-55 Road Report**
> Marc Sehring, curator of the Virginia Museum of Military Vehicles, shares his impressions of the T-55 tank in their collection:
>
>> I am impressed with the way the Soviets put these vehicles together: they're crude, and they have lots of horsepower, lots of armor, lots of fuel, and a big gun, and the engine drinks oil – this is a man's tank!
>>
>> I love to drive the T-55; it is an awesome machine. That big V-12 diesel sounds just amazing, with a tremendous roar and a distinctive clinking from the track linkage. The T-55 steers very well, much better than US tanks of the same period. The night vision system, smoke capability, and deep fording capability made the tank a capable machine in its day.
>>
>> The T-55 has lots of little bells and whistles: compass, excellent compressed air or electric starters, lots of back-up systems – you can even clean the periscopes with air pressure from inside. The 100mm gun was excellent for its day, and you've got pretty good vision, even buttoned up.
>>
>> It is harder to maintain; the access to the engine is somewhat limited, although the filters can be cleaned in the field. It is designed to be maintained in the field, and it has enough back-up systems that you can overcome most failures. The components are beefy, particularly compared to US equipment. It is a very robust tank and hard to break; that means that in combat, you can worry about the enemy rather than your vehicle.

Like the T-54 series, the early-model T-55 series tank had a simple stadiametric rangefinder incorporated within the gunner's sight reticle, optimized for target engagements under 1,100 yards. It proved far less accurate than the stereoscopic and coincidence optical rangefinders on NATO tanks of the 1950s into the 1960s.

Soviet Army offensive tank tactics stressed platoon fire at individual enemy tanks, increasing the odds of hitting a chosen target to offset the lack of accuracy demonstrated by individual tank sights and crews. Western Europe's dense natural and man-made terrain led the Soviet Army to minimize concerns over the long-range inaccuracy of main guns on T-54/T-55 series tanks. In the Soviet Army's opinion, long-range tank-on-tank engagements would be rare during a Third World War in Western Europe. Instead, they saw short-range engagements as more typical in such a conflict.

NATO research suggested, however, that most potential targets in the mid-European zone fell within a range of 1.1 miles. Some 50 per cent would be under 1,094 yards (1,000m), 30 per cent between 1,094 yards and 1.1 miles (1,770m) and 20 per cent over 1.1 miles.

Amphibious Tank

In 1953, authorization was given to begin production of the PT-76 amphibious light tank; the prefix 'PT' stands for '*plavayushchiy* tank' ('floating tank'). Production of the 16-ton PT-76 continued until the late 1960s, with approximately

7,000 examples constructed. Many were allocated to Warsaw Pact and non-Warsaw Pact armies.

Like so many other Soviet Army tanks, the PT-76 went through many progressively-improved versions. Large and thinly-armoured for buoyancy, the PT-76 series had a maximum armour thickness of 17mm on the front of the turret, sloped at 35 degrees.

The three-man PT-76 series had several intended roles: reconnaissance, fire support in crossing water barriers and taking part in Soviet Navy amphibious operations. The tank came with a 76.2mm main gun. Power was derived from a six-cylinder diesel engine, based on the 12-cylinder diesel engine in the T-54/T-55 series.

Following several upgrades including a new muzzle brake and two-axis gun stabilization system, the PT-76 received the designation PT-76B. These appeared in 1962, and eventually all the early production examples were brought up to the same standard.

The PT-76 had a maximum speed of 27mph on land; in water its water-jet propulsion system provided a speed of 6.3mph. The tank required no preparation for entering the water other than raising a trim vane at the front of the vehicle's upper hull.

The PT-76 in Soviet Army service took part in invasions and occupations of Hungary in 1956 and Czechoslovakia in 1968, when each threatened to leave the Warsaw Pact. The US Army encountered the PT-76 in small numbers during the Vietnam War in 1969 and 1972.

Did Not Pan Out

The Soviet Army, concerned that a new tank design might not live up to its expectations, sometimes authorized manufacture of an alternative design as a back-up. One example of that proved to be the IS-4 Heavy Tank, initially conceived in 1944 and based on the IS-2 Heavy Tank. Production approval came in 1946, and the IS-4 began coming out of the factory doors the next year as the replacement for the troublesome IS-3.

Although armed with the same 122mm main gun as the IS-2 and the IS-3, the 58-ton IS-4 proved larger. Maximum armour thickness of 250mm (10in) was at the gun shield. The Soviet Army, however, quickly decided that the tank was even more problematic than the IS-3. Production of the IS-4 ended after only 179 examples had come off the factory floor.

The IS-4s were eventually modernized, as were the IS-3s, but were considered obsolete and quickly consigned to long-term storage in the 1950s. Some of their turrets were eventually mounted on concrete emplacements along the Soviet/Red Chinese border as pillboxes.

Last of its Kind

The Soviet Army, displeased with the IS-3 heavy tank series' design defects and believing there remained a requirement for heavy tanks to support its medium tanks, pushed along the development of a new heavy tank. That tank eventually became the T-10. Rather than simply an improved IS-3, the T-10 proved to be a brand-new tank, with a gun shield that was 250mm (10in) thick and a glacis plate coming in at 120mm (4.7in).

T-10 production began in 1953 and ended in 1965, with 1,539 vehicles delivered. NATO only became aware of the new four-man tank when it appeared in a Red Square parade in 1957. Like the IS-3, the T-10 made a powerful first impression on Western military observers as they knew nothing of its capabilities or how many of them existed.

The T-10 was considered a dangerous foe in the 1950s. By the time production ended, the T-10 was already obsolete and soon consigned to storage depots and target ranges, with none exported. Nikita Khrushchev, leader of the Soviet Union between 1953 and 1964, thought so little of heavy tanks that he had all development work ended in 1960. He also believed that tanks in general were then obsolete.

The only action the T-10 saw occurred during the Soviet Army's invasion and occupation of Czechoslovakia in 1968 when the country's leadership decided that it wanted to withdraw from the Warsaw Pact.

Description

The T-10 series included the original 55-ton version, followed by the T-10A and T-10B; the final and most numerous version was the T-10M entering production in 1958. Besides having a larger and more thickly-armoured turret than the IS-3, the T-10's hull was longer and had seven pairs of road wheels instead of the six on the IS-3. As with its predecessor, the T-10 series rode on torsion bar suspension.

The first three models of the T-10 series were delivered with the same 122mm main gun as the IS-3. The A model of the T-10 had a single-axis stabilization system, while the B model had a two-axis stabilization system. As with the two-axis stabilization system on the T-54/T-55 series tanks, that of the T-10B provided only a very limited fire-on-the-move capability at very low speeds when on level surfaces.

The 122mm main gun on the T-10 series initially fired an APC round and a HE-Frag round for non-armoured targets. In 1964 there appeared a HEAT round.

The parts of the main gun's rounds, due to their size and weight and the vehicle's cramped interior, were loaded into the breech separately with the assistance of an electromechanical rammer. This restricted the rate of fire to somewhere between three and four rounds per minute.

T-10M Upgrades

The T-10M model received a new, more powerful 122mm main gun, and with that and other features the vehicle weight rose to around 57 tons. Besides the two-axis turret stabilization system, it came with a two-axis stabilized optical gun sight that proved challenging to use and did not appear on any other Soviet Army tanks. The T-10M also was fitted with a Nuclear-Biological-Chemical (NBC) protective system and provisions for a fording kit.

Like the T-55 series, the T-10M eventually received a driver's infrared system, as well as an infrared night-fighting system. As with the T-54/T-55 Medium Tank series, the T-10 series had only a simple stadiametric rangefinder within the gunner's sight, optimized for target engagements at less than 1,100 yards (1,000 metres).

Based upon the new hull design of the T-44 Medium Tank, Soviet industry continued developing a medium tank with a turret large enough to mount a 100mm main gun. The first example appeared in 1946 as the T-54-Model 1946. The example pictured here has the correct turret, but the hull is not the original as it lacks the front fender-mounted machine guns and the tracks are too wide. (*Dreamstime*)

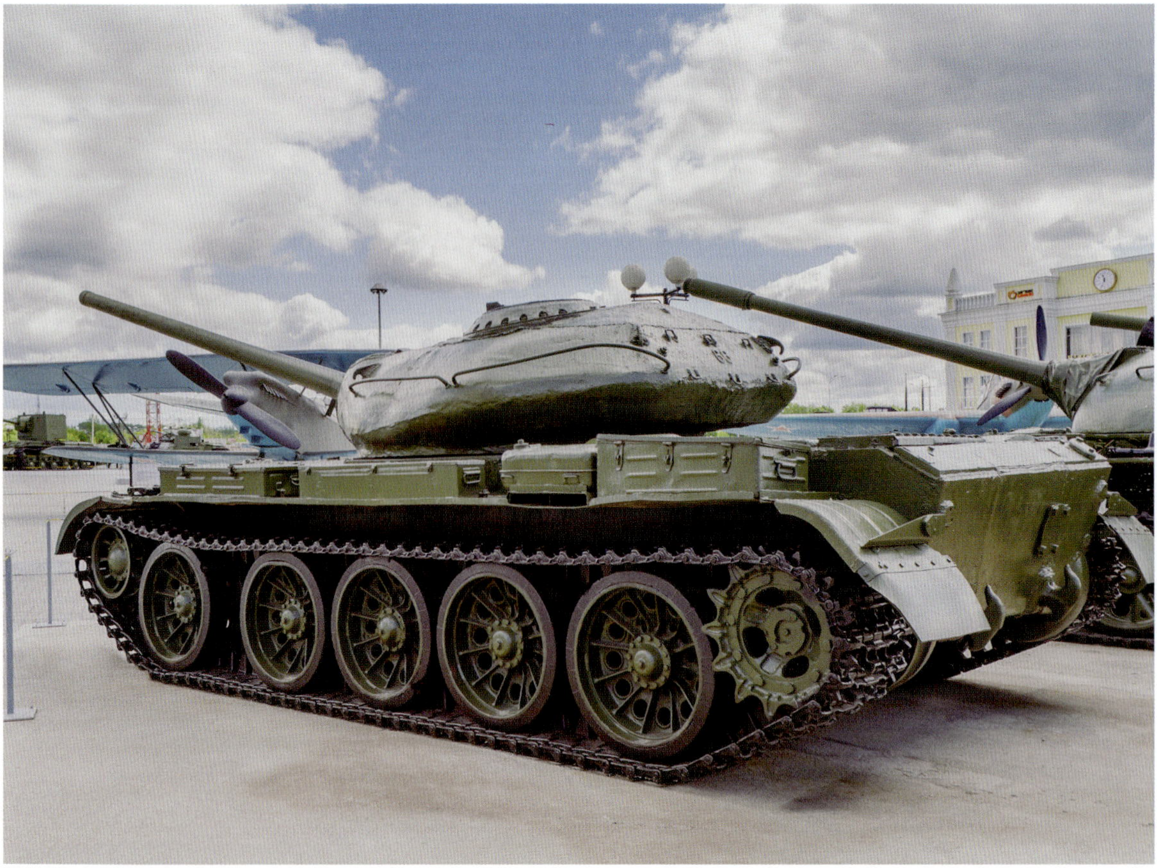

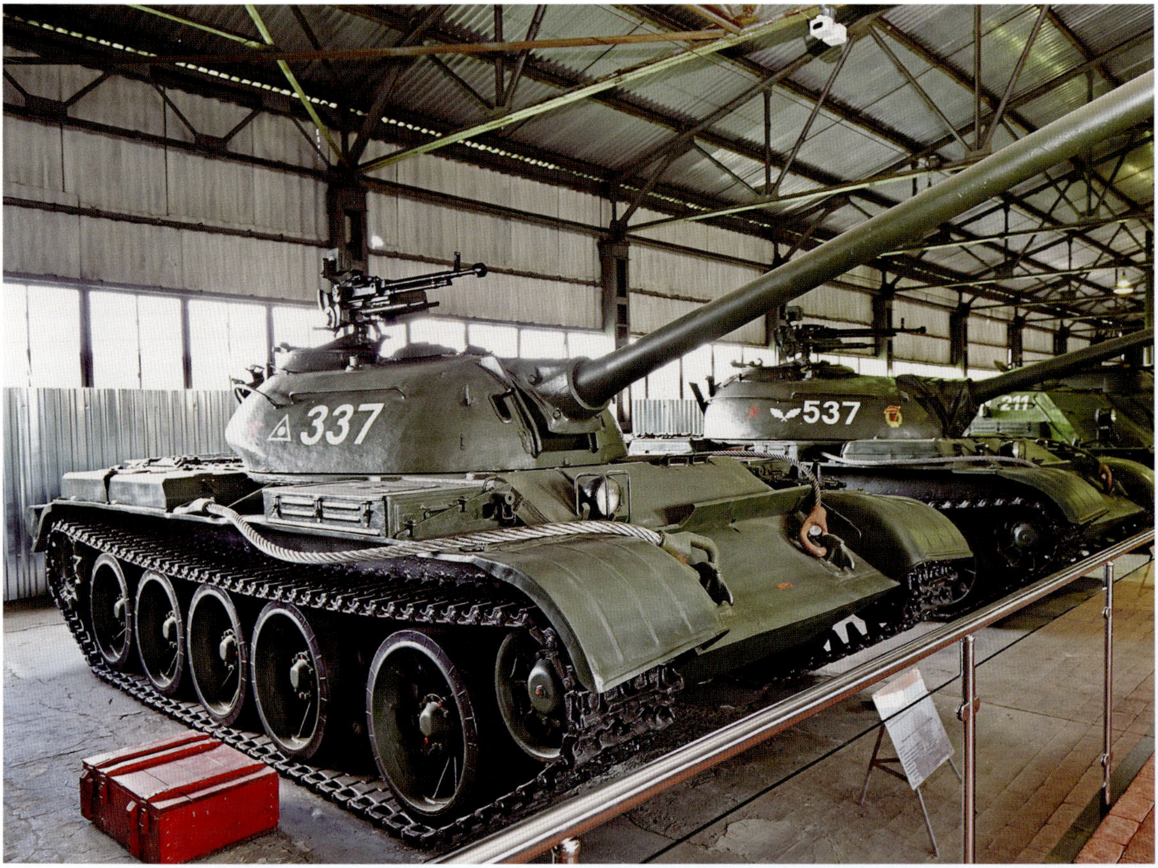
337
537
211

(**Opposite, above**) Another view of the turret from a T-54-Model 1946. The Soviet Army disliked the turret design due to its wide horizontal gun shield and the cleft shape of the lower portion of the turret, which created a shot trap around its circumference. Also, early troop trials of the T-54-Model 1946 demonstrated an insufficient level of reliability. The Soviet Army therefore cancelled production of the tank with approximately 1,000 examples completed. (*Dreamstime*)

(**Opposite, below**) In response to the Soviet Army's unhappiness with the T-54-Model 1946, Soviet industry came up with the T-54-Model 1949 pictured here. The tank's lower turret cleft shape now occupied only the rear half of the turret. A narrow vertical gun shield replaced the wide horizontal gun shield of the T-54-Model 1946. The Model 1949 also introduced wider tracks. Production soon ramped up as the Soviet Army expressed its satisfaction with the Model 1949. (*Dreamstime*)

(**Above**) Soviet industry continued to refine the design of the turret on the early versions of the T-54 series. Their work eventually eliminated the undercut on the lower rear portion of the turret with a new hemispherical turret design for the T-54 series seen here, with the introduction of the T-54 Model 1951. It entered production in 1952 and concluded in 1954. (*Dreamstime*)

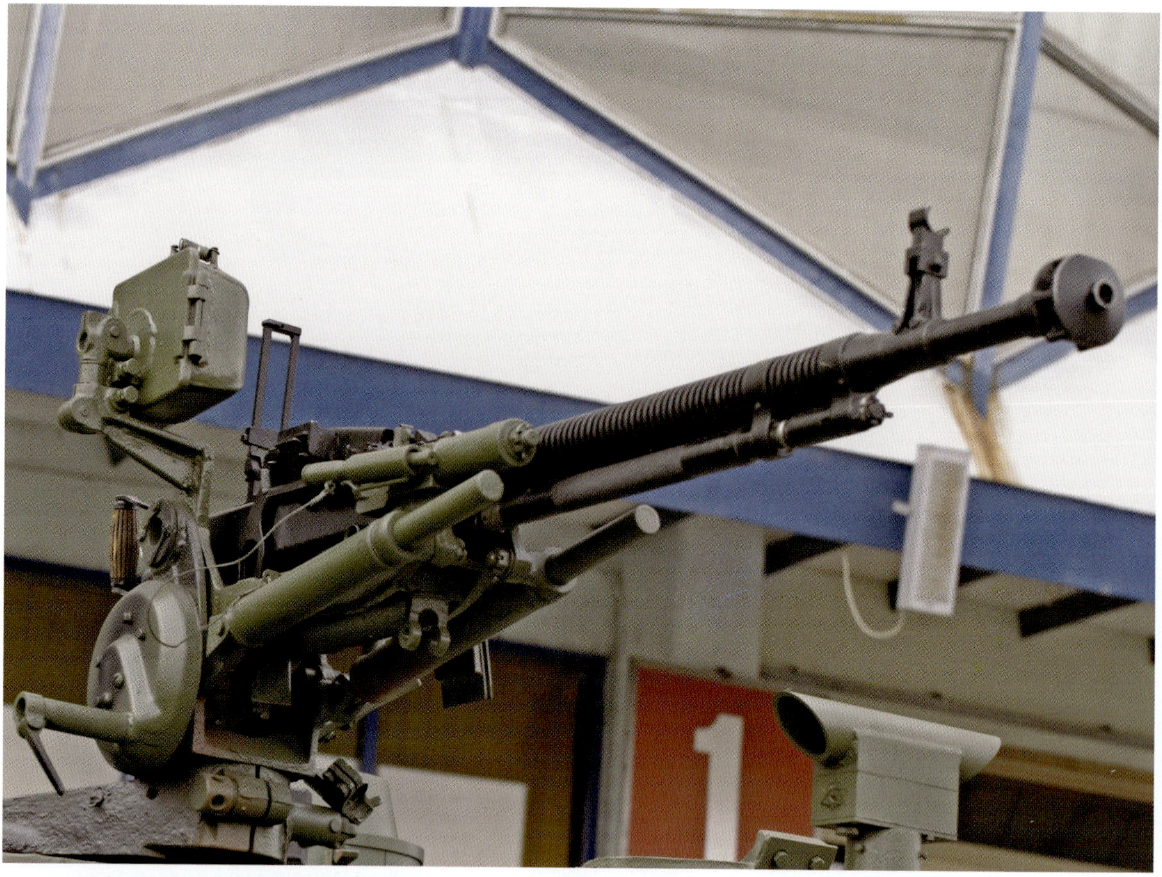
1

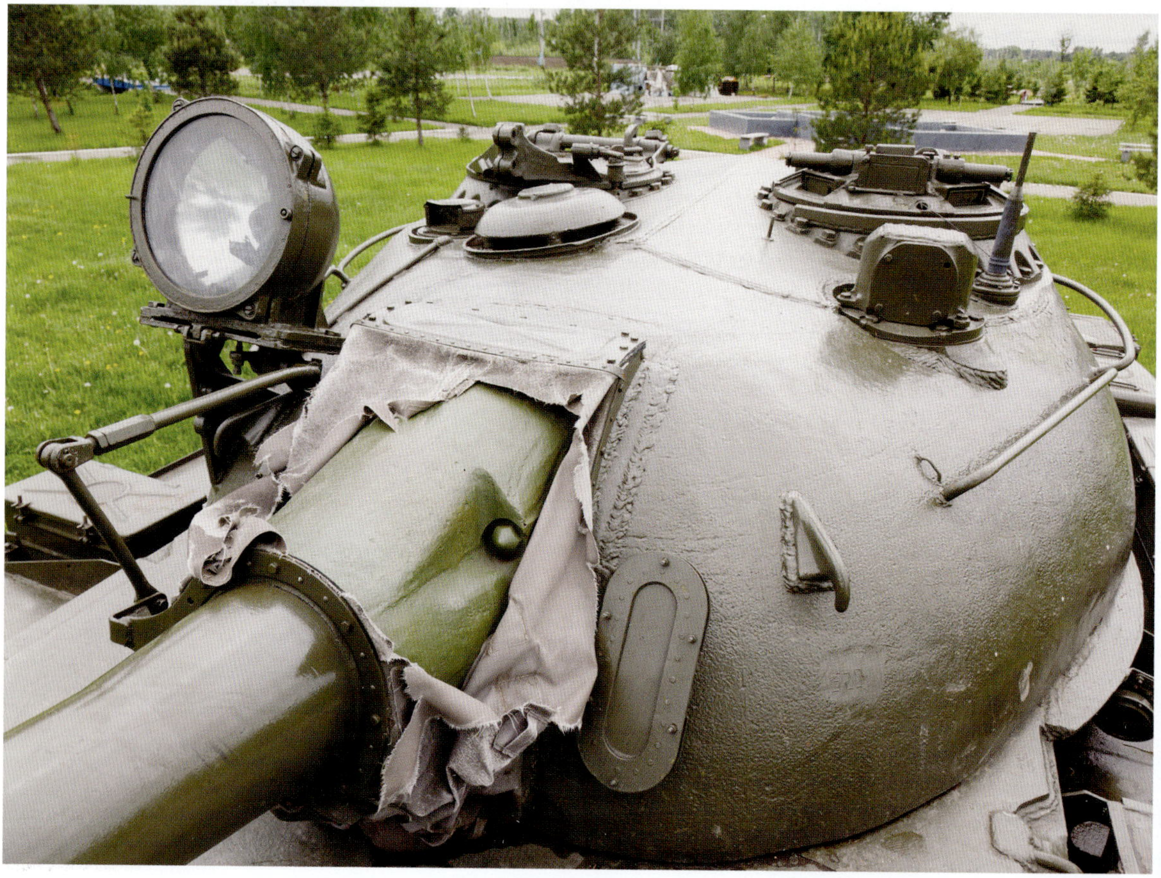

(**Opposite, above**) Shown here is a pintle mount mounting a gas-operated DShK(M) 1946 12.7mm machine gun fitted to the loader's overhead rotating turret hatch of the T-54 series. The original version of the belt-feed air-cooled weapon entered Red Army service in 1938 as an anti-aircraft weapon. It first appeared on the Red Army's IS-2 Stalin Heavy Tank during the Second World War. Firing 600 rounds per minute, it had an effective range of around 2,000 yards. (*Dreamstime*)

(**Opposite, below**) In this picture, the fixed vehicle commander's hatch is on the right side of the image and the traversable gunner hatch on the left. In front of the loader's hatch is the circular armoured dome that marks an electrically-powered turret exhaust fan design feature seen only on T-54 series tanks. In front of the vehicle commander's hatch is the upper armoured portion of his traversable periscope sight. A torn weather covering exposes the tank's gun shield. (*Dreamstime*)

(**Above**) The early-production T-54 series tanks lacked a turret basket and had no stabilization system for firing on the move. An identifying feature of those without a stabilization system is the muzzle counterweight seen here. Besides a coaxial 7.62mm machine gun, a second fixed forward-firing 7.62mm machine gun fired through a small hole in the tank's glacis plate. This feature eventually disappeared due to its limited usefulness. (*Dreamstime*)

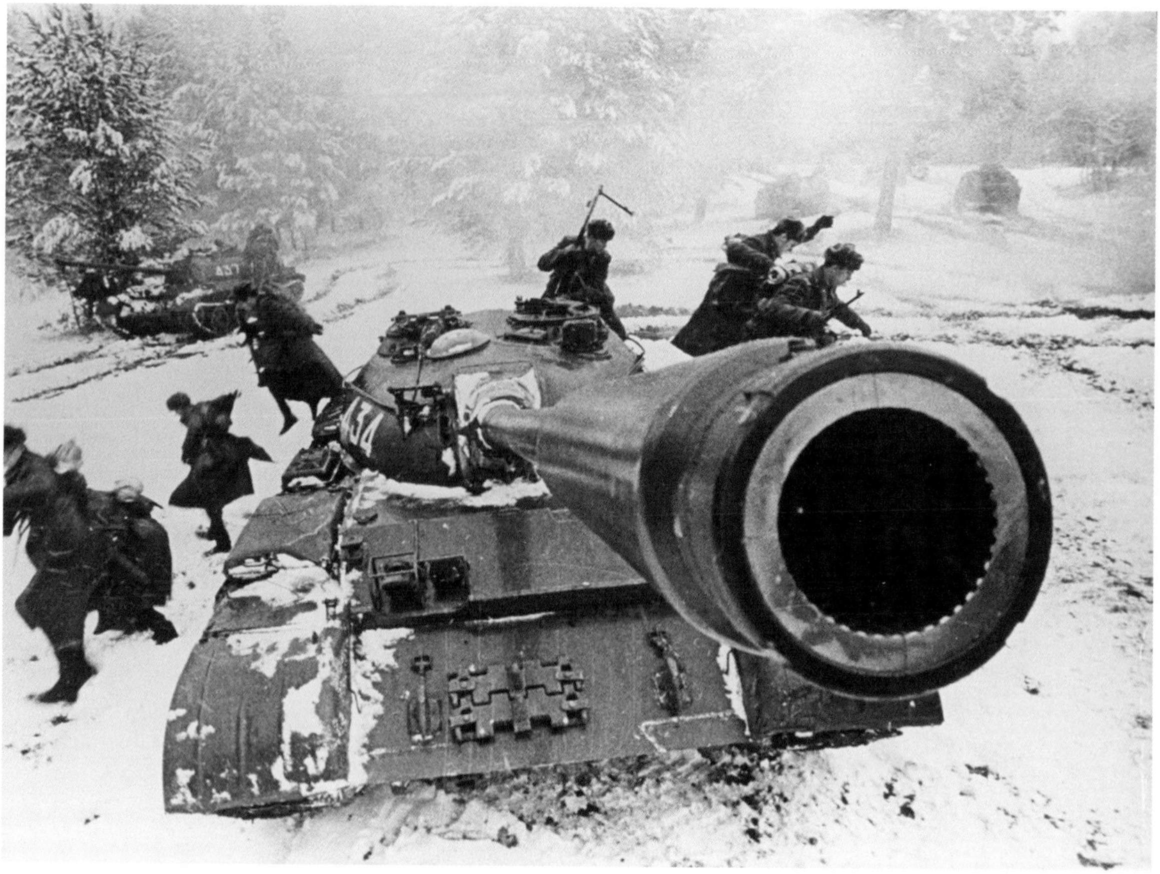
434

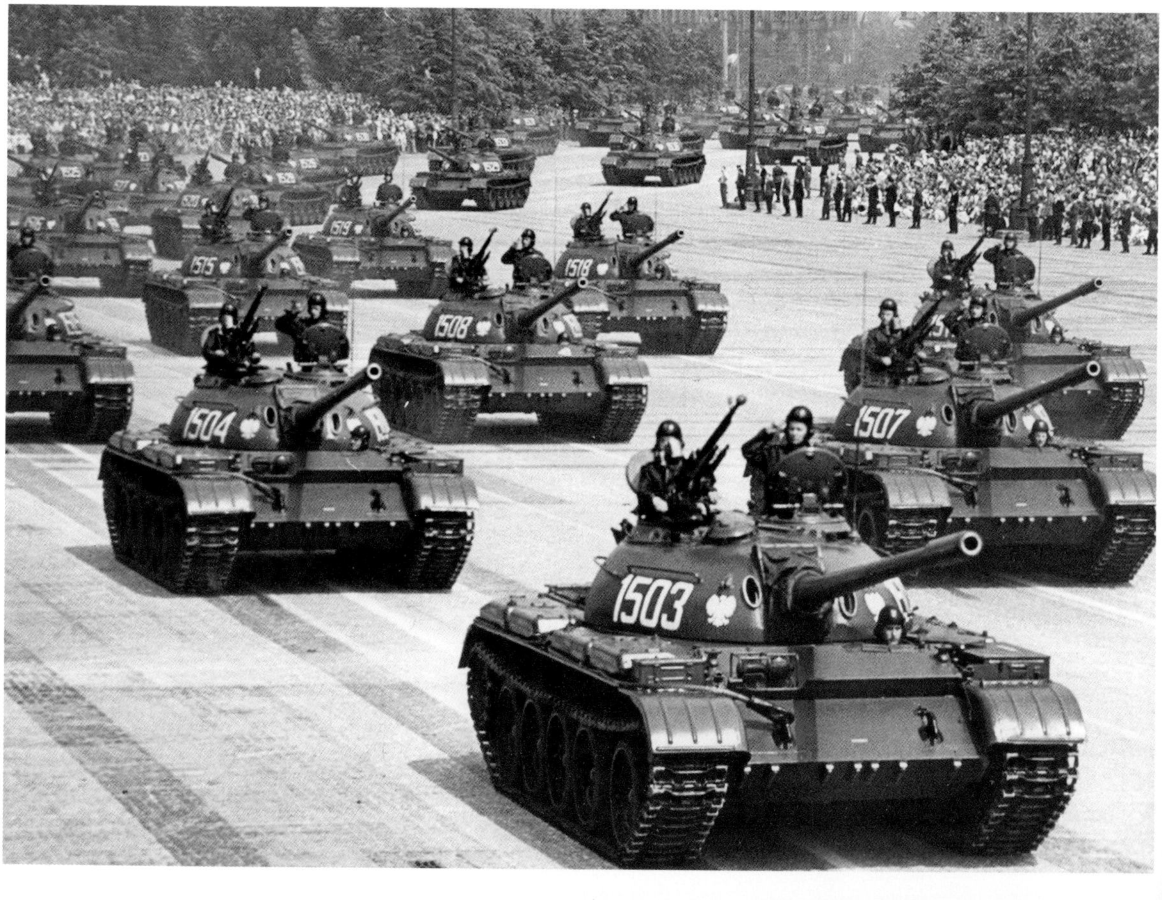
1503
1504
1507
1508
1518

(**Opposite, above**) Soviet industry borrowed its vertical-only gun stabilization system from the M4 series tank provided under Lend-Lease to the Red Army during the Second World War and added it to the T-54 series. Having acquired examples of captured American M26 and M46 medium tanks supplied by the Red Chinese Army, Soviet industry decided that bore evacuators made a lot of sense and decided to add them to the T-54 series. The resulting tank seen here became the T-55A version and first appeared in 1955. (*Author's collection*)

(**Opposite, below**) A picture of a Cold War-era Polish Army parade featuring T-54 series tanks. With the fitting of a two-axis stabilization system to the T-54 series, the designation T-54B appeared. The first production examples appeared in 1957. In 1959, the T-54B received both infrared night-driving and night-fighting systems. The Polish-built version of the Soviet T-54B had the designation T-54AM applied. (*Author's collection*)

(**Right**) In this overhead illustration of a T-54 series tank, various boxes line the vehicle's fenders. Three are armoured, each containing 21 gallons of fuel. The others are not armoured and are for storage of items such as tools. Inside there are two fuel tanks, one located alongside the driver and another in front of the transversely-mounted engine and transmission, to provide a combined total of 115 gallons. If required, two non-armoured 44-gallon drums can go onto the rear of the tank's hull. (*US Army*)

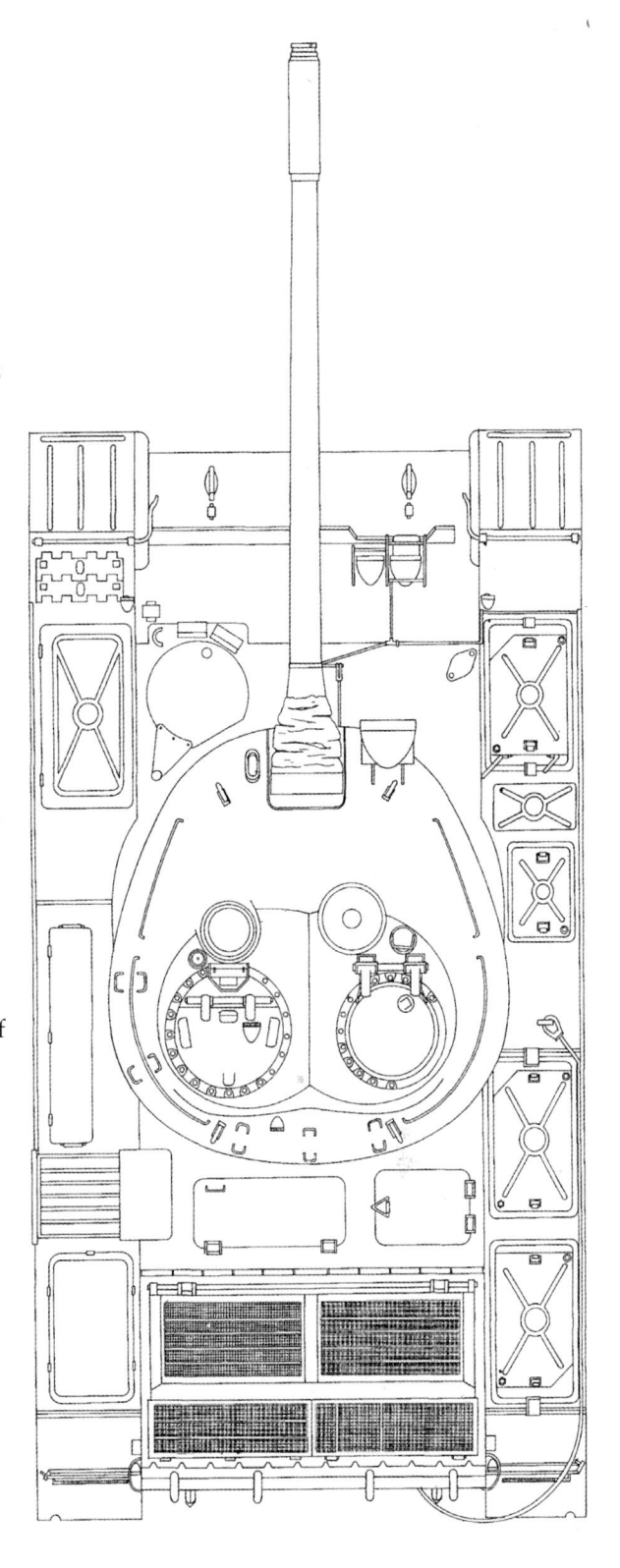

59

(**Above**) With the threat of NATO's tactical nuclear weapons, the Soviet Army tasked industry to provide the means for its tanks to withstand a nuclear weapon's blast. The answer was an upgraded version of the T-54B. Production of the tank began in 1958 as the T-55. The example pictured here has a large infrared searchlight for the gunner and a smaller one for the vehicle commander. (*Chris Hughes*)

(**Opposite, below**) The addition of new design features to the T-55 allows its crew to operate in a contaminated nuclear environment and survive the effects of biological and chemical weapons. This would result in the discontinuation of the turret exhaust ventilation dome as fitted to the T-54 series. The T-55 tank in the foreground lacks the ventilation dome. It had an atmospheric overpressure system to keep out dangerous elements from the interior of the T-55 tank. (*Pierre-Olivier Buan*)

(**Above**) The four-man crew of a T-55 series tank stands by a river's edge before preparing their vehicle for a crossing with the aid of its fording kit. As the Soviet Army was largely conscript, a typical Soviet tanker spent only two years on his vehicle. Cross-training, a standard feature of NATO tank crews, did not exist. The training proved far less rigorous than that of the NATO armies, with few chances for realistic training or the firing of main gun rounds. (*Author's collection*)

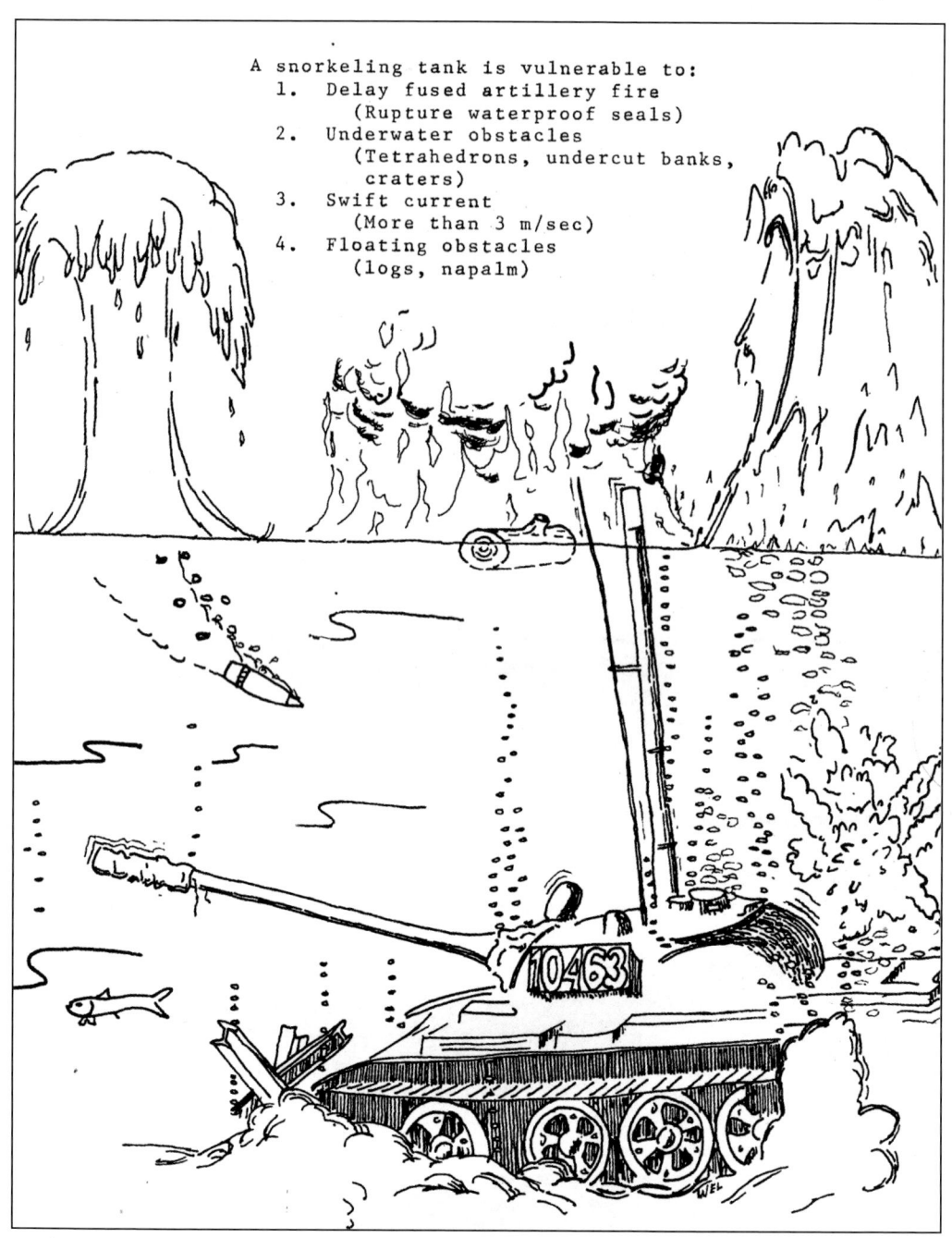

Lacking the divisional-level bridging assets of its NATO counterparts, the Soviet Army placed heavy reliance on its tanks having the ability to ford the numerous water obstacles of widely-varying widths and depths they would encounter in invading Western Europe. In a Cold War-era US Army report, this is an illustration of the various threats that Soviet tankers would encounter in attempting to cross a river defended by NATO. (*US Army*)

In this photograph taken inside a T-55 series medium tank, the 100mm main gun breech is visible with the gunner's position to the left. The vehicle commander would be located directly behind and slightly above the gunner's position, and the loader on the right side of the gun's breech. Unlike the optical rangefinder on NATO tanks, the gunner on the T-54/T-55 series has only a simple stadiametric sight. (*Hans Halberstadt*)

(**Above**) The driver's position on a T-55 series tank. Not an easy job, with a conventional clutch and brake system, and without any boosted controls. It requires brute strength to operate, and hence quickly becomes very tiring to drive for any length of time, especially over rough terrain. The driver can open his overhead hatch and raise his seat to look out over the front hull in a non-combat environment. The maximum speed on level ground is around 30mph. (*Hans Halberstadt*)

(**Opposite, above**) A T-55 series tank is seen here in the foreground, followed by a bridge-launching version. With the addition of a newly-developed radiation protective material consisting of a lead-impregnated plastic applied to the interior and exterior of T-55 tank series turrets including their hatches, the designation T-55A appeared. Those so modified first came off the assembly lines in 1963. (*Author's collection*)

(**Opposite, below**) A Czech Army T-55 series tank pictured at the Virginia Museum of Military Vehicles. Doubting the usefulness of the DShK(M) 1946 12.7mm machine gun against modern jet-powered ground-attack aircraft, the Soviet Army discontinued its use mounted on the loader's hatch of the T-55 series tanks. However, NATO's introduction of helicopter gunships beginning in the 1970s led to the Soviet Army having its T-55 series tanks modified to mount the 12.7mm machine gun again at the loader's hatch. (*Richard and Barb Eshleman*)

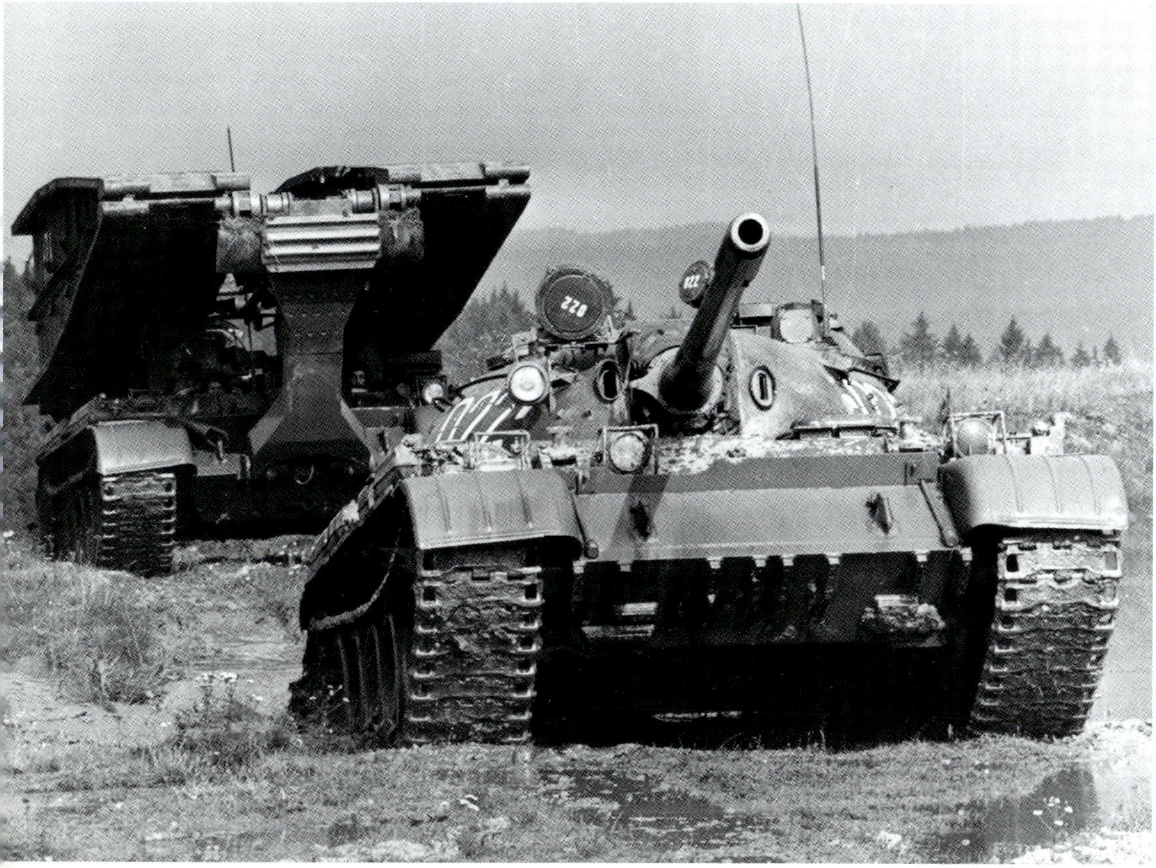
022

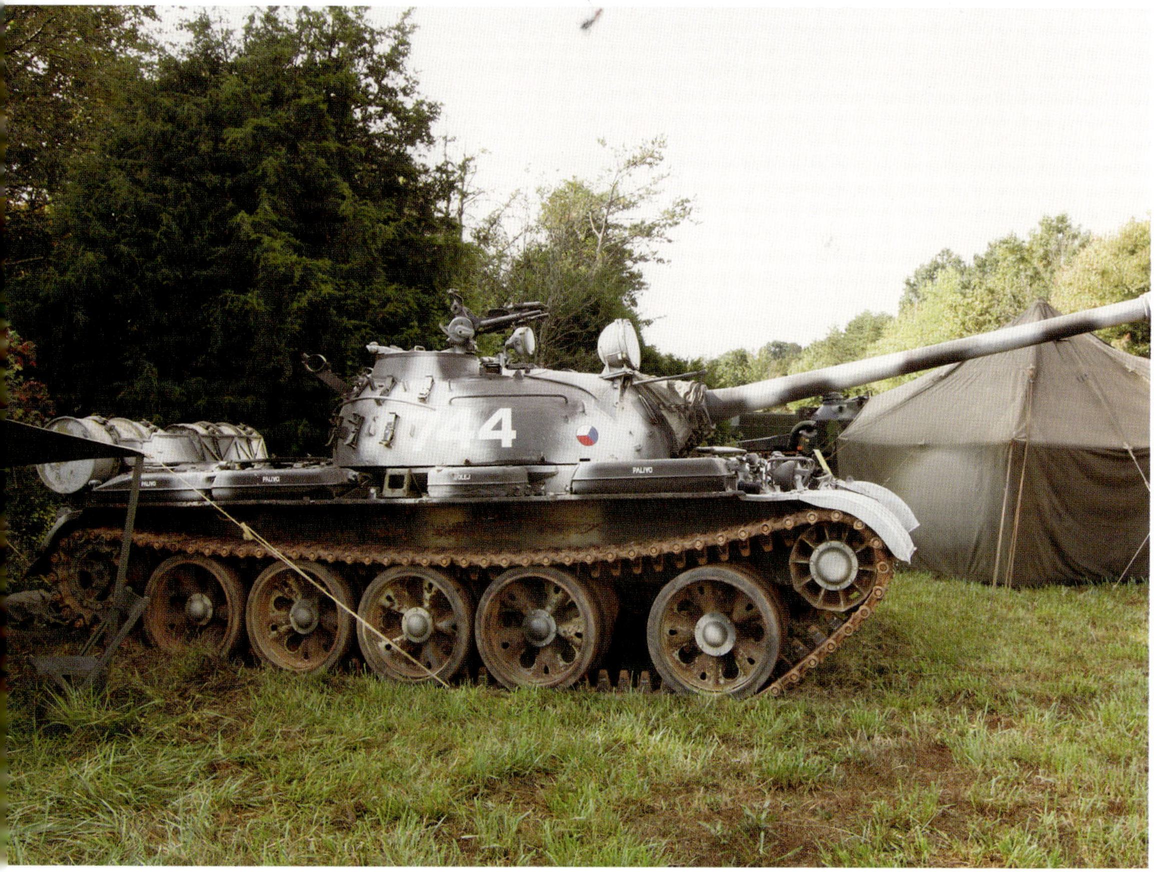
744
PALIVO

(**Above**) To keep its fleet of older-generation T-55 series tanks viable on potential Cold War battlefields, the Soviet Army began a programme in 1983 that involved adding additional armour to the front of the tank's turret and its glacis, as seen in this photograph. The Soviet code-name for the add-on armour was 'BDD'. Its popular but unofficial nickname of 'Brow' armour was because it reminded people of Vladimir Ilyich Lenin's thick eyebrows. Lenin was one of the Communist Party's founders. (*Dreamstime*)

(**Opposite, above**) Rather than conventional steel armour, both the add-on turret armour and the glacis BDD armour consisted of armoured steel boxes containing evenly-spaced steel plates encased in polyurethane. That arrangement is referred to as non-energetic reactive armour (NERA). According to Russian sources, BDD armour's addition made the T-55 series tanks so fitted immune to 105mm APDS and HEAT rounds. Pictured here is a T-55 tank fitted with BDD. (*Dreamstime*)

(**Opposite, below**) A Czech-built version of T-55 series tanks upgraded with the BDD armour arrangement seen here also featured additional improvements. These included a new fire-control system, with an attached laser rangefinder (LRF), visible in the box just above the gun shield. The LRF improved the tank gun's effectiveness greatly. At the rear of the turret roof, the vertical stalk contained a wind sensor and a laser illumination detecting set. These features were not seen on Soviet-built T-55 series tanks. (*Dreamstime*)

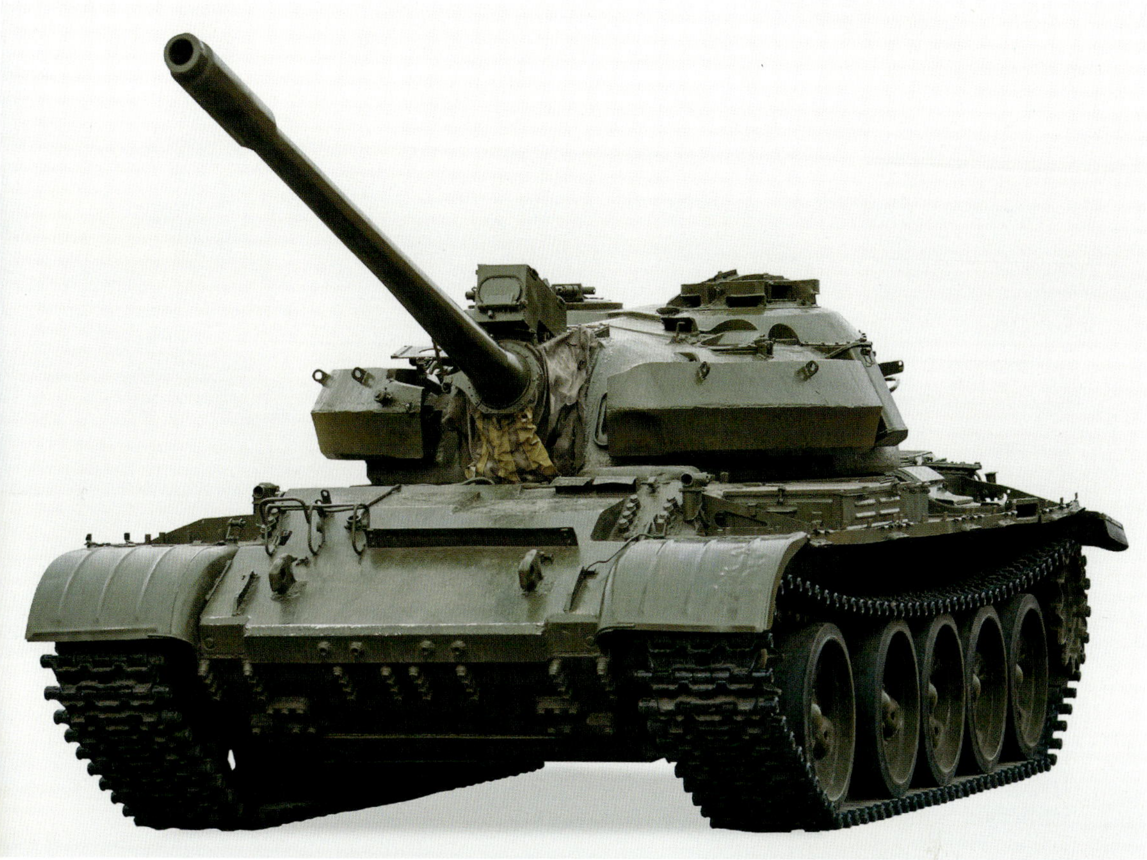

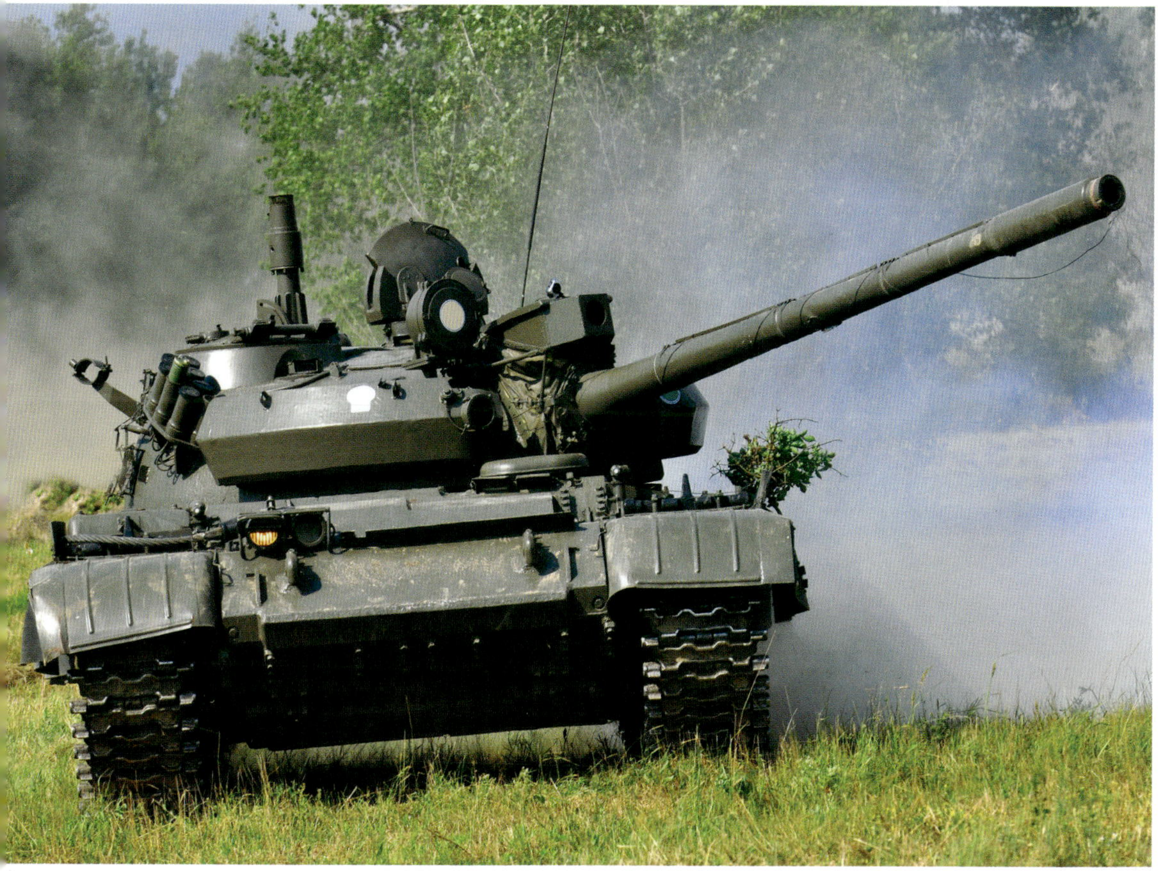

Pictured here is a three-man PT-76B Light Tank. The need for buoyancy dictates the tank's large boat-like hull. Reflecting its requirements for buoyancy and its primary role as a reconnaissance vehicle, armour protection on the three-man vehicle proved minimal. The armour provided defence only from small-calibre machine-gun fire and some artillery fragments. (*Chris Hughes*)

The PT-76 series depended on a water jet propulsion system that took in water at the front of the vehicle's hull and ejected it at the rear hull through two ports, both seen here covered by armoured flaps. In calm inland waterways, the vehicle's maximum speed came to 6mph. Also employed at one point by the Soviet Marine infantry, it did not have the buoyancy or sea-keeping ability to cross heavy surf. (*Richard and Barb Eshleman*)

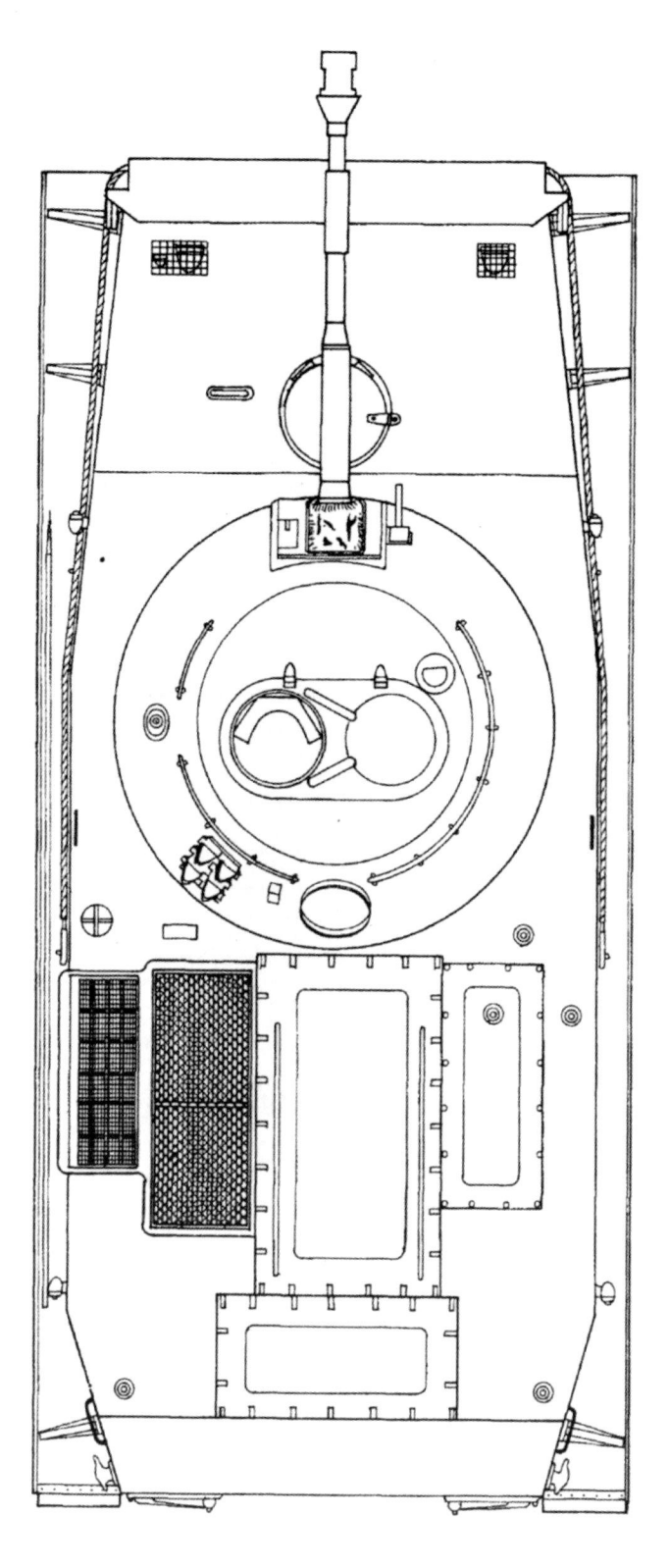

The 16-ton PT-76 series had a length of 23ft, and with the main gun forward an overall length of 25ft. Its width came in at 10ft. Its liquid-cooled diesel engine provided it with a top speed on level ground of 27mph and a range of 155 miles. The tank had storage for forty rounds, a mixture of hyper-velocity armour-piercing (HVAP), armour-piercing high-explosive (APHE) and a HEAT round for its 76mm main gun. (*US Army*)

The IS-4 proved to be a failed heavy tank project for the Soviet Army. Development began in 1944, with production approved in 1947. Like the previous Red Army heavy tanks, its main armament was a 122mm gun. Only 200 came down the assembly lines before the Soviet Army decided it lacked the mobility it desired for its heavy tanks. Most of the IS-4 tanks eventually had their turrets removed and emplaced as pillboxes as pictured here. (*Dreamstime*)

The T-10 was an immediate post-war-developed heavy tank placed into production for the Soviet Army. It looked much like the wartime IS-3 Stalin Heavy Tanks, and included their sharply-angled glacis. The 122mm main gun on the original version of the T-10 lacked a bore evacuator and featured a wartime-designed double-baffle muzzle brake, as seen in this illustration. (*US Army*)

Like almost all Soviet Army tanks during the Cold War, the T-10 went through a progressive series of upgrades, resulting in the designations T-10, T-10A, T-10B and T-10M. The 'A' and 'B' model T-10s had a bore evacuator fitted and retained the first model's double-baffle muzzle brake. With the advent of the T-10M, a new multi-slotted muzzle brake in the image's foreground replaced the original double-baffle muzzle brake. (*Dreamstime*)

Reflecting its increased length over the IS-3 Stalin tank, the T-10M tank pictured here has seven roadwheels on either side of the hull compared to the former's six. The original T-10 model also lacked a main gun stabilization system. The follow-on T-10A had a vertical-only stabilization system and the T-10B a two-axis stabilization system. All the models of the T-10 series had storage for thirty main gun rounds. (*Dreamstime*)

Like the previous Red/Soviet Army heavy tanks, the T-10 series received power from a liquid-cooled diesel engine. Top speed on level roads topped out at around 26mph. The internal fuel tanks of the T-10 series provided a range of about 143 miles, with the last iteration of the tank having a range on internal fuel tanks of approximately 217 miles. The addition of external fuel drums pushed up the vehicle's range. (*US Army*)

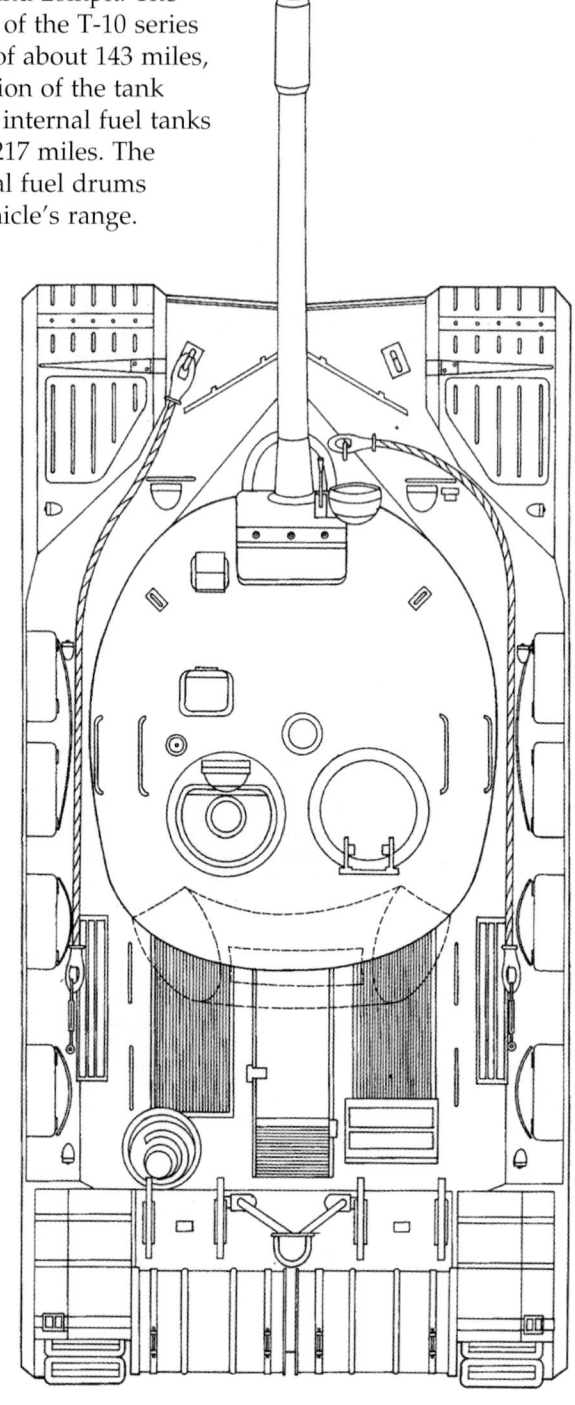

Pictured here is a 55-ton T-10M. All the different models had the same armour protection levels, with the front turret/gun shield around 10in (250mm) thick and the upper glacis 5in (120mm) thick. As on its medium tank, the Soviet Army eventually added infrared driving and sighting systems to the T-10M. The M model also received a new and more powerful version of the 122mm main gun. (*Dreamstime*)

Chapter Three

Keeping Pace

With the US Army's sharp downsizing following the Second World War came a shortage of tank development funding. With no money to replace the wartime M26, in 1948 the US Army decided that the next best option involved modernizing its M26s. This included the original wartime-built M26s and the slightly upgraded post-war M26A1s.

The M26 series' biggest shortcoming was its 500hp liquid-cooled GAF engine, a version of the Ford GAA engine that powered the M4A3(76)W Sherman tank. Well aware that the engine provided insufficient power for heavier tanks such as the M26 series, in July 1943 the US Army initiated a development programme for the ideal tank engine. Nothing came of it until 1946.

The ideal tank engine proved to be a 12-cylinder, V-type, four-cycle, air-cooled, gasoline-powered model originally designed for aircraft, boasting 740 gross hp. After some additional tweaking, the engine managed to produce 810 gross hp. Designers coupled the engine to a new cross-drive transmission. The term 'cross-drive' referred to the transmission's orientation in the hull; the axis of the transmission's drive shaft was perpendicular to the tank's direction of travel.

M46 Medium Tank

Both the up-rated ideal tank engine and an improved cross-drive transmission went into a modified M26 hull. The US Army liked what it saw, approving it for production in July 1948 with the designation Tank, Medium, M46 and officially nicknamed 'General Patton'.

Between 1948 and 1951, 1,170 examples of the approximately 48-ton M26 series tank were reworked into the M46 configuration. The original plans had called for all 2,202 M26s to be upgraded. The vertical gun shield had a thickness of 114mm (4.5in) and the glacis 102mm (4in), sloped at 46 degrees.

The excitement generated by the M46 appears in a passage by US Army Sergeant Dale E. Mille, in the September–October 1952 issue of *Armor* magazine:

> Driving the M46 in combat after training on the M4 is like stepping from a Model T Ford into a new Cadillac ... I think the M46 is a dream to drive compared with the old M4. You can drive all day and not become tired. And that means a lot when you have long missions over rough terrain and need to be on your toes in enemy action or watching for mines.

As the last 360 production examples of the M46 featured modifications based on continued testing and user input, they received the designation M46A1. External differences between the M26 series and M46 series mostly revolved around the rear engine compartment and engine exhaust configuration.

Problems

The first M46s arrived in Korea in August 1950, supplementing approximately 300 M26 and almost 700 M4 series tanks in the theatre. Like the M26, the M46 spent most of its time in Korea as an infantry support weapon, engaging in such activities as indirect fire, bunker-busting and reconnaissance. The eventual number delivered reached around 200 vehicles in 1951. By the end of the Korean War, most M4 and Pershing M26 units had been re-equipped with the M46.

The M46's additional power proved a welcome addition for many tank crews. However, like the M26, the M46 proved unequal to the Korean terrain, with the

How an American Tank Comes About
Randy R. Talbot, US Army Command Historian (Retired):

It begins with a requirement to fill a gap or need identified by either the commanders in the field or Department of the Army. The Army, in turn, sends the requirement to the appropriate Commodity Command. For military vehicles, the Tank-automotive and Armaments Command (TACOM) at the Detroit Arsenal have managed them since 1942.

The requirement then goes to the Research and Development Engineering Center to begin concept development, design or an engineering solution to meet the requirement. The concept is sent back to the Army for assignment to the appropriate Program Office (Ground Combat Systems or Combat Support/Combat Service Support).

The program office selects a Program Manager and builds a team of acquisition (contracting), logistics, engineering personnel and administrative staffing. With a staff of experts, the Program Managers and engineering center develop a system for production.

Working with the local Acquisition Center, the Program Manager issues a Request for Proposal (RFP) to industry. Throughout the Cold War, most tank programs took place at the Detroit Arsenal Tank Plant (Chrysler), with some work done at American Locomotive, Ford and the Delaware Tank Plant. Contractors submit proposals for review, and this includes meeting all the requirements and specifications from the original requirement through the engineering and development. A selection is made, and a contract is awarded to begin production. The Program Manager monitors production and works through funding, warranty, spare parts, tools and logistics, and fields the system to the force.

Once fielded, the Program Manager works with the logistics center to provide support and sustainment needed for the system until the system is retired from the fleet. The logistics center is responsible for storage for future foreign military sales and assists with the sale.

most trouble-prone aspect of its design proving to be the new cross-drive transmission. Adding to the problems of M46s in Korea, the US Army's logistical system could not keep up with its spare parts requirements or provide the trained manpower to maintain and operate the vehicles.

M47 Medium Tank

With the perceived threat of a tank-led Soviet invasion of Western Europe arising while the Korean War raged, it became clear to the US Army that it needed many more tanks in a hurry. Building brand-new M46 tanks made no sense as they were reaching the point of obsolescence.

Because of the long time frame involved in designing and building a new tank, the US Army decided to take a shortcut. They took the turret of an experimental tank armed with the M36 90mm gun (and a new but unproven state-of-the-art fire-control system) and mounted it on the M46 chassis. In November 1950, this makeshift solution became the Tank, 90mm Gun, M47, even before a single prototype appeared for testing.

In 1952, the approximately 51-ton M47 received its official nickname of the 'Patton II'. Later, the official nickname was changed to 'Patton 47'. The tankers themselves typically referred to them merely by their numbers to identify what type of tank they had. This practice went back to the M26 series and continued up through to the M60 series.

Fielding of the M47 began in June 1952. Where the M46 suspension had five-track return rollers, the M47 had only three. Like the M26 and M46, the M47 depended on an electric-hydraulic-powered turret traverse and gun elevation system. Also like the M26 and M46, the M47 lacked a main gun stabilizer system.

Ballistic protection offered by the M47's turret exceeded that of the M46, as the armour was both thicker and better sloped, with the turret gun shield at 114mm (4.5in) thick and sloped at 60 degrees. The glacis plate was 102mm (4in) thick and also inclined at 60 degrees. The ventilation blower seen in the M46's hull roof between the driver and bow-gunner positions disappeared because the new turret had one in its turret bustle.

Some early-production M47s went off for testing. Despite the US Army's hope that the tank would prove combat-ready, it wasn't. The M46 chassis was not the problem, but the new turret's advanced fire-control system with its stereoscopic rangefinder proved problematic.

> ### New Classification System
> The designation of Tank, 90mm, M47 for the vehicle rather than a medium tank reflected a US Army change in terminology in November 1950. The former weight bracket method of classifying American tanks as light, medium or heavy was no longer viable due to changing concepts in the development and tactical employment of tanks. However, the M26 and M46 kept their original designation as medium tanks until leaving US Army service.

> **HEAT Rounds**
>
> The requirement for an advanced fire-control system on the M47 and other American tanks came from the US Army's reliance on High-Explosive Anti-Tank (HEAT) rounds as its key tank-killing ammunition from the 1950s into the 1960s.
>
> HEAT rounds were available for 76, 90, 105 and 120mm tank guns. HEAT also proved to be the preferred tank-killing round for Soviet T-54/T-55 series tanks in the 1950s up through to the 1960s.
>
> During the early Cold War years, HEAT's popularity revolved around its ability to penetrate thicker steel armour than existing kinetic energy (KE) rounds. The latter depended on their mass (and mechanical properties including hardness and density) combined with their velocity at the moment of impact with the target (striking velocity) to penetrate steel armour. In the 1950s and 1960s, KE rounds were intended for firing at enemy tanks' more vulnerable flanks or rear armour.
>
> Because HEAT rounds are slower than KE rounds, they have a very curved trajectory in flight compared to KE rounds' much flatter trajectories. Hence, HE rounds required a more sophisticated fire-control system for maximum accuracy.
>
> A vital attribute of HEAT is that its target-defeating potential is not affected by range. Unlike KE rounds, the HEAT target effect is caused by its exploding projectile rather than by the speed at which it strikes a target.

Fifteen significant modifications had to occur before the supposedly superior M47's fire-control system could even match the much cruder stadiametric rangefinders in the gunner's optical sight of the M26 and M46 tanks. The required fire-control upgrades were quickly made to those M47s already built and then applied to examples coming off the assembly lines.

Production of the M47 continued until November 1953, with a total of 8,527 vehicles. Most went to US Army armoured units stationed in Western Europe, replacing their M26 and M46 series tanks; the US Marine Corps fielded the M47 until 1959. The M47 remained in service with some Army divisions until the early 1960s.

M48 Medium Tank

Even before the first production example of the M47 came off the assembly lines, the US Army expressed an interest to American industry for a more thickly-armoured 90mm gun-armed replacement tank. Plans called for the new tank to use the same air-cooled gasoline engine and transmission (referred to as a power pack) as fitted to the M47.

Instead of using the M47's hull and turret, the US Army designers decided they wanted a new elliptically-shaped version of both. This was based on developments for an experimental heavy tank which eventually became the M103. With the new hull's planned adoption, the assistant driver/bow gunner's position was eliminated, bringing the crew down to four for the M47 replacement tank, which eventually became the M48 in April 1953, officially nicknamed the 'Patton 48'.

The problem with gasoline engines appears in a July–August 1953 issue of *Armor* magazine in an article by Colonel Rothwell H. Brown titled 'The Coming War – A Concept: The Answer – Armor':

> The present operating range of our series of medium tanks is a source of very deep concern. Even with jettison-type gas tanks, I doubt very much if our present medium tanks, under combat conditions, will have an operating radius of 90 miles. This is too limited. In addition, it will impose an almost insuperable resupply problem on all agencies supporting armored units.

Tank Details

The initial version of the 49-ton M48 fitted with wider tracks was a bit heavier than its predecessor, and rolled off the factory floor in early 1953. Its gun shield had a slope of 30 degrees and a thickness of 114mm (4.5in). The glacis plate had a slope of 60 degrees and a thickness of 110mm (4.3in).

The M48 came with the first analogue ballistic computer for a tank. It mathematically accounted for such variables as the vehicle's cant (if on a slope) and the operational parameters of the type of main gun round fired. None of the M48 series tanks had a main gun stabilizer system, making accurate firing on the move impossible.

The output from the M48 ballistic computer went to a ballistic drive unit that allowed the tank's main gun and optical sights to move independently of each other to apply superelevation, especially in the case of HEAT. It caused the tank's main gun to move the required amount above the line sight for a given round to strike a target at a given range (superelevation angle). The M47 had a ballistic drive but not a ballistic computer. The gunner operated the vehicle's rangefinder. With the M48, the vehicle commander operated the tank's rangefinder.

At the beginning of October 1954, the 52-ton M48A1 started coming off the production lines.

Problems Appear

The rush with which the US Army attempted to field the early M48 series tanks resulted in so many teething problems that they were unfit even for training duties. The difficulties included both the power pack as well as the suspension system. This led to a series of Congressional investigations starting in the late 1950s and running into the early 1960s.

The Government Account Office (GAO) stated in a 1960 report: 'In our opinion, the vehicle deficiencies are attributable primarily to the practice of contracting prematurely for volume production despite identified serious defects for which there is no assurance that effective correction can be made and of relying upon subsequent modifications to correct the defects.'

Engine Description

In the January–February issue of *Armor* magazine is an article titled 'Road Test M48'. From that article is the following passage:

> The M48 is powered by a Continental V-12 air-cooled engine of about 825 horsepower. The cylinders are individually replaceable units. Overhead valves with rocker arm assemblies are actuated by a camshaft along each bank. Two mechanical fans provide cooling air around cylinders and oil coolers. Power is transmitted to the final drives through a cross-drive transmission, which is a combined transmission, steering and braking unit. The brakes are of the wet, multiple disk type. The engine lies beneath a six-foot square grating which makes up part of the rear deck. Care must be taken in walking on this deck while the engine is running, since during rapid deceleration, three- or four-foot sheets of flame sometimes sweep across the deck from the exhaust.

The US Army blamed many of the problems identified by GAO on the tank crews, citing inattention to the proper vehicle maintenance. It also insisted that the early M48 series tanks 'could have been effectively used without modifications'. The GAO doubted that statement, as training units' experience had clearly shown that the tanks remained too unreliable for employment in a combat situation.

New Versions

The 52-ton M48A2 replaced the M48A1 on the production lines in December 1955. It retained its predecessor's 90mm main gun. According to the GAO reports, the M48A2 did offer a degree of improved reliability but not much.

The M48A2 featured a new air-cooled gasoline-powered engine fitted with a fuel injection system, improving its operational range on roads. The new gasoline engine contributed 4 to 14 per cent of the M48A2's improved range; the rest came from larger fuel tanks. It also received a new transmission. The M48A2 had a new all hydraulically-operated turret traverse and gun elevation system, a design feature that remained in use until the M60 series. A big advantage was that it was around 30 per cent faster than electrical systems.

The M48A2 featured an enlarged rear engine deck to aid in cooling the gasoline-powered engine. The purpose was to minimize its infrared (heat) signature. The reworked rear engine deck arrangement remained a design feature of all M48 follow-on models, with some modifications. Correction of some design issues with the 57-ton M48A2 resulted in the revised designation of the M48A2C.

Upgraded and modified M48A2s were widely deployed to both the US Army and US Marine Corps, fully replacing the M47 Patton in combat units. It was also exported to NATO allies and foreign governments.

By the time the M48 series production ended in 1959, a total of 11,703 examples had been manufactured. Follow-on versions of the M48 series came from converting the US Army's existing inventory of M48 through to M48A2C tanks into new versions rather than building brand-new tanks.

Diesel-Engine-Powered

The US Army's long aversion to employing diesel engines in its vehicles began to change in 1955. In 1960 they decided to explore upgrading some of their M48A1s with a diesel engine. That eventually led to the following year's approval to fit 600 M48A1 tanks with an air-cooled diesel engine, as well as some new design features from the M60 series.

The reworked M48A1s became the 53-ton M48A3, with the US Army's first examples appearing in 1963. The decision was made to retain the M48A1's 90mm main gun due to large stockpiles of 90mm ammunition being on hand.

By 1965, the US Army expressed an interest in arming the M48A3 with a 105mm main gun. That did not occur as many of them were then serving in South Vietnam, and the diversion of available funding to higher-priority programmes meant that no upgrades took place.

Some 419 examples of the M48A1 were reworked into M48A3s by 1964 and went off to the Marine Corps. The Marines retained the M48A3s in service until 1974.

In 1967, another 578 M48A1s went through the upgrade programme into the M48A3 configuration for use by the US Army and Marine Corps. They featured some changes, including enlarged vehicle commander cupolas.

Vietnam War Interlude

Both US Army and Marine Corps' M48A3s would see extensive use during the Vietnam War (1965–75). A few US Army M48A2Cs also served, but were not popular due to their flammability and limited range.

Rangefinder Problems

The M48A2C's coincidence rangefinder was more straightforward and easier to use than the more complex stereoscopic rangefinder on the M47 and previous M48 series tanks. Like the latter, the coincidence rangefinder's accuracy could be affected by weather changes and varying temperatures.

The reason for replacing the stereoscopic rangefinder was that there had been many unresolved problems associated with it, including the extensive training needed to operate them effectively. Among other issues, 20 per cent of the US Army's tankers could not use the stereoscopic rangefinder due to its vision requirements.

A GAO report from 1960 mentions another issue that plagued the stereoscopic rangefinders: 'The rangefinder in many of the M48 tanks are not being used by operating personnel. We were informed [by the US Army] that the equipment is too complicated and is beyond the intellectual capabilities of the personnel who must be trained to use it.'

Retired US Army officer James Walker recalls the stout defensive works the enemy had built: 'The VC [Viet Cong] had dug their bunkers with the firing slits just above ground level, making them nearly invisible. Though the HEP round did not silence them, the tank driver put 52 tons of [M48A3] tank onto the bunker, crushing it and its hapless occupants beneath.'

The M48A3's thick hull armour made them popular with American tankers during the Vietnam War as, excluding suspension damage, they were generally invulnerable to enemy mines. However, their thick turret and hull armour

> **M48A3 Impressions**
> Retired US Marine Corps officer Kenneth W. Estes describes the M48A3 tank on which he spent time early in his military career:
>> I first came into contact with the M48A3 medium tank in 1970, at the Marine Corps' Tank Officer Course. In our tank-infantry training, it performed well with excellent cross-country speed and agility. I would come to know it well by the sound of its suspension, which usually was more pronounced than its diesel engine.
>>
>> In particular, its venerable 90mm cannon brought considerable power and effect to the battlefield. Thanks to its developmental past as an anti-aircraft gun, now coupled to a very robust and effective analog fire-control system, it could fire projectiles with great accuracy beyond 2,000 meters, of a great variety never again seen in fighting vehicles.
>>
>> With very few shots fired in training, a tank crew could hit moving or static tank-size targets at least to 2,500 meters with rarely a second round required, thanks to the very wide coincidence rangefinder and the excellent connections the tank commander had with his gunner.
>>
>> Driving the M48A3 was especially simple and efficient. The Continental diesel engine started easily, eliminated the short-legged reputation of the gasoline-fueled M48s, and brought outstanding reliability in the field. The steering and controls remained so smooth that we found ourselves almost reaching for the non-existent turn signal handle because it drove so much like an automobile, so smooth was its steering, braking and automatic shifting. Only when in reverse did the steering cause a surprise or two.
>>
>> On operations, as heavy as the tank was, the power pack and suspension took it easily over most terrain from fording high-surf beaches to climbing boulder-strewn mountains that I encountered in the United States and a Mediterranean deployment.
>>
>> We were told in 1971 that our guns were no longer rated effective against the new tank armor systems and we would have to give up the 90mm for the new 105mm which we never found so user-friendly. Even when we received the latest model M1A1 series tanks, there remained some old-timers who swore 'we never should have given up the '48s'!

sometimes failed to protect them from the enemy's shaped-charge warhead rocket-propelled grenades (RPGs).

90mm Tank Ammunition

The most commonly employed round during the Vietnam War by M48A3 tank crews was canister, designed solely for use against enemy personnel within several hundred yards. When fired, the projectile's casing split open as it exited main gun's muzzle and spewed 1,281 steel pellets in a conical pattern.

In South Vietnam, the canister round's success led to rapid development and fielding of the improved M580 Anti-Personnel Tracer (APERS-T) round, unofficially nicknamed the 'Beehive'. It contained 4,100 small steel flechettes and proved even more deadly than the canister rounds. Retired US Marine Corps armour officer Gene Berbaum recalls after firing such rounds: 'It was not uncommon to see enemy personnel pinned to stripped trees by the flechettes.'

NATO M47s

Under the Mutual Defense Assistance Program (MDAP), thousands of Patton tanks went to NATO and friendly non-NATO countries' armies. The M46 and M46A1 that previously went to different NATO armies did not remain in service very long before many M47s became available in the early 1950s.

Of the 8,576 examples of the M47 built, most spent their service careers in NATO army service. At one point in time, the Italian Army boasted an inventory of more than 2,000 M47 tanks. The French and Belgian armies received approximately 800 M47s each. Both the Turkish and Greek armies also received the M47; more than 1,300 for the Turks and about 300 for the Greeks.

The West German Army took into service 1,100 examples of the M47 under MDAP, with the initial delivery in January 1956. It proved to be the first tank of the newly-formed West German Army. German tankers considered the M47 obsolete, but it was the only tank available in sufficient numbers to outfit their rapidly-expanding armour branch. The last M47s were pulled from West German Army service in 1968.

With a choice between the American M48 and the British Centurion tank, the West German Army decided on the former. As a result, they took into service roughly 200 M48A1s, more than 1,000 M48A2s and almost 500 M48A2C tanks, all powered by air-cooled gasoline-powered engines.

Delivery of the first M48A1s to the West German Army began in 1957. Over time, they modernized their inventory of M48 series tanks, making it the West Germany Army's mainstay tank through the mid-1970s. Their initial upgrades of their M48A2 and M48A2C tanks, such as fitting of white light/infrared searchlights, resulted in the suffix letter 'G' being added to their designations.

Between 1978 and 1980, 650 of the West Germany Army M48 series tanks received the British-designed 105mm tank gun L7 as well as other improvements, but not a diesel engine. These, therefore, became the M48A2C G A2. In this configuration, they survived until the end of the Cold War in West Germany Army service with reserve forces, referred to as the Territorial Army.

NATO M48s

In 1963 Norway received thirty-eight examples of the original version of the M48 and returned them to the United States in 1982. The Turkish Army began receiving M48 series tanks under MDAP, as well as some surplus West German Army M48s, for a combined total of around 3,000 examples by the 1960s. The Greek Army acquired about 800 examples of the M48 series in the same period.

The M41

Following the Second World War, the US Army began looking for a replacement for the wartime-designed and built M24 Light Tank, officially nicknamed the 'Chaffee'. As initially envisioned, the new light tank was to feature a stereoscopic rangefinder. That later changed to a new British-designed fire-control system, which included a two-axis (azimuth and elevation) stabilization system and a coincidence rangefinder, as well as an automatic lead computer.

Because the British-designed fire-control system had not reached maturity in the US Army's opinion, it did not receive consideration. The US Army, therefore, switched back to a stereoscopic rangefinder. The outbreak of the Korean War resulted in the US Army wanting to rush its prototype light tank design into production. Hence, the requirement for an optical rangefinder no longer existed.

The simplified light tank eventually became the 26-ton M41 and later M41A1, with the first examples coming off the factory floor in mid-1951. Armed with a high-velocity 76mm main gun, a total of 3,729 examples were manufactured by 1954. Its thickest armour was the gun shield at 32mm (1.2in), with the glacis plate at 25mm (1in). The M41 series last saw service with the US Army National Guard in the early 1970s.

The four-man M41 series tanks were gasoline-engine-powered and rode on a torsion bar suspension system. Eventually the M41's engine carburettors were

> **The Army's New Light Tank**
> From the May–June 1951 issue of *Armor* magazine is the following extract: 'The T-41 [M41] Walker Bulldog is the first completely new tank to be built by the Army since World War II,' said Secretary of the Army Frank Pace recently, marking the occasion of the first production model to roll off the assembly line at the Cleveland Tank Plant of Cadillac:
>
>> It is a fast, maneuverable vehicle, classed as light because of its 26-ton overall weight, and its cavalry and reconnaissance role mission. Its punch is a new high-velocity 76mm gun. On the basis of present knowledge we think it will outfight, outgun and outmaneuver anything of its class in the world, and its armor provides maximum crew protection for vehicles of its class.

removed and replaced by fuel injection to improve range, resulting in the M41A2 and M41A3 designations. The M41 series originally received the official nickname of the 'Little Bulldog' but eventually became the 'Walker Bulldog'.

NATO M41s

Among the NATO armies, the West German Army received the largest number of M41 series tanks, totalling 602 examples, with the first delivered in 1956. All were the M41A1 version, with the last examples remaining in service until 1969.

The West Germany Army considered the M41 obsolete due to its short operational range and because its main gun could not defeat Soviet Army T-54/T-55 medium tanks. Yet, like the M47, it proved available at the right time in the numbers required. Belgium got 135 M41s and had them in their inventory from 1958 until 1974. Denmark took into service fifty-three M41s beginning in 1956.

M103 Heavy Tank Series

Early in the Cold War, it was clear that the US Army would require a modern heavy tank to offset the many Soviet Army heavy tanks. The proposed development of a new gasoline-engine-powered heavy tank designated the T43 in 1948, armed with a 120mm main gun, seemed to be the answer.

Unfortunately, the outbreak of the Korean War in June 1950 found the T43 as still only a wooden mock-up. A plan to speed up its development met with resistance. Some thought the effort required to build as many heavy tanks as would be needed to stop a Soviet Army invasion of Western Europe was beyond the national war economy's ability. Others in the US Army preferred 90mm gun-armed tanks firing a newly-developed HEAT round.

Eventually, the US Army decided to develop the T43 on the fast-track for fielding as it had with the M41 and M47 by skipping normal pre-production testing process. In January 1952, the US Army ordered eighty examples of the T43. With a strong interest from the Marine Corps, that number rose to 300 examples of a modified version, designated the T43E1, in December 1952.

Problems Galore

Testing of a pilot T43E1 and a production example in 1954 found that the fire-control system did not meet US Army standards, and serious problems existed with the main gun ammunition, among other issues. Therefore, the US Army in Europe and the Marine Corps rejected the tank in 1955, leading to all of them going into storage.

The US Army came up with a list of ninety-eight modifications for correcting the T43E1 problems in 1955. Production was approved the following year. With these proposed changes, the T43E1 became the M103 in April 1956. The approximately 62-ton vehicle never received an official nickname. Funding became available for seventy-two of the US Army's T43E1 tanks for the conversion process into the M103 configuration, all of which went to Western Europe in 1958.

> **Heavy Tank Dimension Comparisons**
> Like American medium tanks of the 1950s, the M103 series had a height of around 11ft, with a turret roof-mounted machine gun. The length came in at 37ft 2in, and the width at 12ft 2in.
>
> In comparison, the IS-3 and the T-10 had a much lower silhouette with their height of 8ft, not counting turret roof-mounted machine guns. Both had a length of around 32ft; the IS-3 had a width of 10ft 3in, with the T-10 coming in at 11ft 7in.

The results were not encouraging, as seen in a passage from a 1960 GAO report. According to statements by GAO representatives:

> We were informed at one using company that they had no manuals that state how the vehicles are to be utilized, that the vehicle had a good gun, that the power pack was inadequate, that the 15-ton weight differential with the M48 made the M103 extremely slow, and that the M103 could not keep up with the infantry [APCs]. We found 15 out of 18 of the company's vehicles were in need of engine and transmission replacement.

Design Corrections

A more extensive upgrade programme for the T43E1 resulted in the T43E2 configuration. However, the US Army did not fund its production and considered it only a standby design for possible future use. The Marine Corps liked what they saw and authorized funding in 1957 for converting 219 of its T43E1 tanks to the T43E2 standard. The T43E2 then became the M103A1. Completion of the conversion took until 1959.

In Ken Estes' book titled *M103 Heavy Tank 1950–1974*, he describes the powerful recoil of the tank's 120mm main gun:

> The real challenge came upon firing, though, as the recoil of the powerful 120mm cannon pulled the tank back on its suspension, in spite of the considerable weight of the vehicle. This rocking uniquely caused the gunner to lose sight of the target upon firing, as the sight picture jumped completely above the target. This effect required the gunner to both reacquire the target and sense the tracer or impact of the round, as the sights and tank rocked back level, to determine any corrections to aim, if necessary.

Rather than spending the money to convert its M103 inventory to the 62-ton M103A1 standard, the US Army borrowed seventy-two of the Marine Corps' M103A1s for deployment to Western Europe in place of its original M103s.

A much-improved diesel-engine-powered M103 series tank labelled the M103A2 entered Marine Corps' service beginning in 1963. With enlarged fuel tanks and its diesel engine, the M103A2's maximum range went up from around 80 miles to an impressive 300 miles.

Besides a diesel engine, the 64-ton tank incorporated many components from the M60 tank. The Marine Corps retired its 208 M103A2 tanks in 1972, as it had by then adopted the M60 tank.

Fire Control and Ammunition

None of the M103 series tanks had a stabilizer system. The M103 depended on an electric-hydraulic-powered turret traverse and gun elevation system. In contrast, the M103A1 and M103A2 had an amplidyne-powered (electromechanical amplifier) turret traverse and gun elevation system, which proved unpopular.

The M103 and M103A1 had stereoscopic rangefinders and the M103A2 a coincidence rangefinder, with all connected to ballistic drive units. The A1 and A2 models also had ballistic computers. All M103 versions had a gun shield sloped at 45 degrees that ranged in thickness from 102mm to 254mm (4in to 10in). The glacis plate had a slope of 60 degrees and a thickness of 127mm (5in).

The original plans called for the M103's 120mm gun to fire High-Velocity Armor-Piercing (HVAP) or High-Velocity Armor-Piercing Discarding Sabot (HVAP-DS) rounds. Because these rounds would lead to serious bore erosion issues, the decision was made to rely on a new HEAT round as the vehicle's main tank-killing ammunition. In theory, it could penetrate up to 14in (1.16ft) of steel armour. The M103 series also carried an Armor-Piercing Capped (APC) round, as well as a High-Explosive (HE) round for non-armoured targets.

> **This is Going to Hurt**
>
> In the July–August 1983 issue of *Armor* magazine appears the following passage in an article titled 'Improving Combat Crew Survivability' on the behind-the-armour effects generated by a HEAT projectile including:
>
>> The production of an expanding cone of fragments originating from both the armor and the penetrator. The fragments are in a wide range of sizes, from dust to large chunks, with velocities from a few hundred to several thousands of feet per second. In a normal (perpendicular) attack, the cone may typically have an included angle of 90–110 degrees. The fragments can be likened to the subsurface burst of an explosive grenade within the vehicle with the quantity of fragments being a direct function of the size (caliber) of the armor-defeating mechanism and the diameter of the tale [sic] made by the penetrator on the interior wall.
>>
>> The internal explosion overpressures may range from as little as a third to as much as three or more atmospheres (e.g. 5-50 pounds per square inch with durations up to 100 milliseconds), which can result in trauma ranging from eardrum damage to major injury. The lungs and other body cavities are particularly affected by excess overpressure. The suddenly developed pressure may also throw the occupants about the interior of the vehicle's crew compartment with possible injuries resulting from collisions with hard objects within the vehicle.

AMX-13 Light Tank

The American government agreed in 1948 to help France rebuild its industrial base, which had been devastated during the Second World War, and its armed forces. As the French government proved to be keen on retaining its pre-war overseas colonies, the French Army identified a requirement for a light tank transportable by existing transport aircraft.

The American wartime-supplied M3/M5 light tanks were obsolete and the post-war-supplied M24 light tanks too heavy for existing transport aircraft. As their replacement, the French Army began taking into service, starting in July 1951, the first version of the French-built AMX-13. The three-man tank, riding on torsion bar suspension, received power from a liquid-cooled gasoline engine. Maximum armour thickness was 25mm for the turret front, sloped at 45 degrees.

The 16-ton AMX-13 boasted a 75mm main gun derived from the German wartime Panther tank main gun, mounted into a novel two-man oscillating turret with a rear turret bustle autoloader holding twelve main gun rounds in two six-round rotating magazines. The gun fired a full-calibre, heat-treated steel shot capable of penetrating 170mm (6.7in) of armour sloped at less than 90 degrees at 1,094 yards (1,000m). The gun's combat range topped out at 1,203 yards (1,100m).

The AMX-13 autoloader provided the tank with a very high initial rate of fire; the downside was that once empty, the tank had to retire from the battlefield. The crew then reloaded the autoloader from outside the tank, from rounds stored within the hull.

Between 1951 and 1962, the French armaments industry built around 1,200 examples of the AMX-13, all armed with the 75mm main gun. During its production run, the tank went through a series of progressive improvements; these were identified by added numbers and suffix letters to modified vehicles.

Oscillating Turrets

A two-piece oscillating turret had some advantages: as they are typically smaller and more compact than a conventional one-piece turret, they could mount a more powerful gun and allow simpler inline autoloaders. However, the disadvantages were many, including weight, complexity and the inability to have a gun stabilization system.

The gap between the two parts of an oscillating turret weakened a tank's frontal armour protection and made it impossible to protect the crew from Nuclear/Biological/Chemical (NBC) weapons. An oscillating turret is also less precise in its movements than a conventional one-piece turret.

The French armament industry attempted to develop a medium tank, designated the AMX-50, fitted with a 120mm gun-armed oscillating turret in the early 1950s. That project eventually foundered and died in 1959. The US Army also considered oscillating turrets with autoloaders for both light and heavy tanks in the 1950s, but ultimately rejected the concept.

As the AMX-13 entered service with French Army armoured units, they replaced the wartime US M4 series and M26 medium tanks. Some went to reconnaissance units. With much thinner armour than the tanks it replaced, the AMX-13 needed to ambush enemy tanks rather than confront them head-on.

Seeing Action

The French Army had anticipated employing the AMX-13 in the First Indochina War (1946–54), but French forces departed the country before they were available. However, it would see service with the French Army during the Algerian War (1954–62) in an infantry support role.

Also seeing use during the Algerian War was an AMX-13 hull fitted with the M24 Light Tank turret. Its official designation was the 'AMX-US', unofficially nicknamed the 'AMX-13 Chaffee'. These consisted of hulls from the earliest production examples of the AMX-13.

After the Algerian War, 150 examples of the AMX-US had their main guns and gun mounts removed and became driver training vehicles. They remained in use until the early 1980s. A 90mm gun-armed model of the AMX-13 would last in French Army service in ever decreasing numbers until the early 1980s.

New Centurion Models

Based on early combat experience gained during the Korean War with the Centurion Mk 3, British industry began developmental work in late 1952 on a series of improvements to the tank. This led to the manufacture of brand-new Centurion Mk 5s, starting in 1955 and ending in 1958, with 221 examples completed. There was no Centurion Mk 4.

Most of the British Army's fleet of Centurion Mk 3 tanks eventually found themselves upgraded to the Mk 5 standard. An external identification feature of late-production Mk 5 tanks was the addition of a bore evacuator at the 20-pounder barrel's midpoint.

The Mk 3 and early-production Mk 5s lacked an evacuator, and sported only a muzzle-end counterweight. Sub-variants of the Mk 5 included the Mk 5/1 and the Mk 5/2. Maximum armour thickness of the Mk 5 models came in at 195mm (7.7in) on the gun shield, with the glacis plate coming in at 127mm (5in).

In the footsteps of the 56-ton Centurion Mk 5 tanks, there appeared the Mk 6 version. All were up-gunned and up-armoured Centurion Mk 5 tanks. There appeared only one sub-variant, the Mk 6/1.

As improved design features appeared for the Centurion tank series, they were applied to early-production examples during refits. To distinguish between different model configurations, they received new mark number designations and suffixes to identify sub-variants.

A total of 755 new-built examples of the 57-ton Centurion Mk 7 drove out of the factory doors between 1954 and 1960. The Mk 7 had two sub-variants: the Mk 7/1 and Mk 7/2.

Centurion Tank Memories

Former British Army senior non-commissioned officer Rob Griffin describes his experience with the Centurion:

> My association with the Centurion began at a very early age, when as a junior soldier in the then Junior Leaders Regiment, Royal Armoured Corps, which allowed young people to join the army at the tender age of 15, but not as front-line troops but boys in training. I served there for three years, most of which was monotonous doing schoolwork, drill and other basic military training. We eventually were allowed to start our proper training, which covered gunnery, radio and driving. It is the gunnery and driving that led to my association with the Centurion.
>
> We had been shown the Centurion and allowed to clamber all over it in the early part of training to ensure we were kept enthusiastic till we came to use it. The gunnery course lasted for around fourteen weeks. We learned all about the systems used on the Centurion, including the longest name for the smallest part, 'screw retaining intermediate firing needle withdrawal lever' which was about ¼" in size.
>
> Lots of time was spent on the indoor CIM (Classroom instructional Model) with a shell construction to represent a Centurion turret; by means of hydraulics the complete loading and firing of the 20-pounder could be replicated; also a single-shot cut-down .22 rifle was linked to the gun so that the gunner could practise the gunnery techniques. We were also allowed to practise commanding, a brilliant piece of kit that survives, albeit in a much more technical shape, for the Challenger 2.
>
> The time came to put all this into practice, and we spent about a week at the ranges at Lulworth Cove in Dorset, where we put into practice all we had learned and also learned the joys of 'ammo-bashing', the evolution required to unbox the ammunition from its transit containers. My abiding memory of this period is as a loader, having just done my spell and loaded around ten rounds of 20-pounder ammo. I was about to climb out when my instructor told me to stay in and load for the next gunner, and this I did; by now, the rounds were feeling twice their weight. Still, eventually, the shoot ended, and I managed to clamber out, feeling drained; you have to remember that we were still developing, and those rounds were heavy but fun all the same.
>
> The next phase was driving, and we were to learn to drive 'A' (armoured) vehicles before even attempting a car licence. So, one pleasant sunny day, we arrived at the tank park at Bovington, armed with waterproof jackets and clutching what the army laughingly called a packed lunch, and there in front of us sat the Centurion we were to use because we were going to be allowed to drive. It seemed to have grown in size and appeared very intimidating. Still, no time for nerves; we clambered

> aboard. The instructor ran through all the checks and refreshed our minds on driving techniques; remember this is a crash gearbox, and all changes involved double-declutching (raising and depressing the clutch twice to aid the gear selection). That 'I wonder who is going to be first was soon solved with the words "Griffin into the driver's seat".' Gingerly I took my place, and following the instructions started up; gingerly I let the clutch out and successfully stalled; after a few choice words from the instructor I tried again, and this time we set off, gradually I managed to get into top gear, and happily drove around till it was time to change drivers. Many happy days were spent like that, and for most, the weather was kind, but even when it was not, we did not care; we were young and having fun. Centurion training was great fun and the most enjoyable part of the training syllabus.

In a never-ending quest to improve the Centurion tank's operational range, the Mk 7 version's rear engine compartment was lengthened to make room for additional fuel storage, doubling its operational range.

A total of 108 new-built Centurion Mk 8 tanks came down the assembly lines between 1955 and 1960. Sub-variants included the up-armoured Mk 8/1 and the up-gunned Mk 8/2.

Other NATO Users

Out of a total of 4,423 new-built Centurion series tanks constructed between 1945 and 1962, approximately half went to the British Army, with the other half going for export.

NATO armies that either purchased or received the Centurion tank series included Canada, which acquired the first of 274 examples of the Mk 3 configuration beginning in 1952. Additional orders would bring 374 more Centurions to Canada, with the Mk 5 model becoming the most numerous in service by the 1970s.

Most of the Canadian Centurion tanks would spend their entire careers based in West Germany until pulled from service in 1977, with the last examples remaining in Canada retired in 1979.

Using MDAP funds, the American government bought 216 Centurion Mk 3 tanks from Great Britain for the Danish Army in 1952. The reason was to aid Great Britain in offsetting a severe trade deficit that existed at that time, as well as stimulating British heavy industry.

With the same MDAP funding arrangement, the American government initially bought from the British government in 1953 a total of 435 examples of the Centurion Mk 3 for the Dutch Army. Another batch of 592 vehicles went to the Dutch Army beginning in 1956. A second order for seventy Centurion tanks was placed in 1959. The Dutch Army retired the majority of its Centurion tank inventory in the 1980s.

Conqueror Heavy Tank

In response to the threat posed by the Soviet Army's fleet of IS 3 heavy tanks, the US Army had pushed along the development of its M103 heavy tank armed with a 120mm main gun. The British Army followed suit. Their end product was the Conqueror, armed with a 120mm gun. Its official designation was Tank, Heavy No. 1, 120mm Gun, FV214 Conqueror Mk 1; a slightly modified version became the Mk 2. It, like the Centurion, rode on a Horstmann-type suspension system.

Production of the 71-ton Conqueror began in 1955 and concluded in 1959 with 185 examples completed. Power came from an up-rated version of the liquid-cooled gasoline engine that powered the Centurion tank series. It had a fuel injection system to boost its output. The tank's gun shield had a thickness of 250mm (10in).

Like the American M103 and M103A1 tanks, the Conqueror's operational range proved woefully limited at less than 100 miles. Unlike the American M103A2, the four-man Conqueror never received a more fuel-efficient diesel engine. The Conqueror also proved a bit larger than the M103 series, with a width of 13ft 1in, a length of 38ft and a height of 10ft 5in. The vehicle commander's cupola was fitted with a .30 Browning machine gun that could be traversed 360 degrees and fired from within the turret.

Like the American M013 tank, the Conqueror used multi-part separately loaded ammunition due to the weight of its main gun rounds. They ranged from 78lb for its High-Explosive Squash Head (HESH) rounds to 64lb for its APDS rounds. Unlike the M103, which had two loaders, the Conqueror had a single loader. Spent cartridge cases were ejected from a hatch on the tank turret's side by an electromechanical device.

The Conqueror was intended to engage Soviet Army heavy tanks at long range from defensive positions. The vehicle commander had a 360-degree rotating fire-control cupola that included a coincidence rangefinder that allowed the vehicle commander to take control from the gunner if he so chose to line up and engage targets when the tank was stationary, or line up a follow-on target for the gunner. On much more modern tanks, it became known as a 'hunter-killer sight'.

The Conqueror had a stabilization system to protect the heavy gun's trunnions (support bearings), but it did not provide the ability to fire on the move. As a more complex tank than the Centurion series, the Conqueror called for highly-trained crewmen, especially the vehicle commander and gunner, to achieve maximum effectiveness. However, they were always in short supply during the tank's service due to British Army personnel turnover.

With the advent of the new L7, the British Army fitted or retrofitted it to Centurions in 1959. As it had the same penetrative capabilities as the 120mm gun on the Conqueror, on a lighter platform there was no need for the Conqueror and all were retired by 1966. Like the American M103 series, there were no other Conqueror users, with most going off to firing ranges and a handful to museums.

How Would a Soviet Invasion Unfold?

In a US Army Center for Military History publication by Donald A. Carter titled *Forging the Shield: The US Army in Europe, 1951–1962* is the following passage on how the US Army leadership in Europe saw the beginning of the Third World War before the advent of tactical nuclear warheads:

> They believed that Soviet battle doctrine in the post-war period would reflect the lessons the Red Army had learned while fighting the *Wehrmacht* on the Eastern Front during World War II. A study of Red Army tactics during that conflict and reports from current Communist military exercises indicated that once the Soviets went on the offensive, they took advantage of their numerical edge in artillery and tanks to overwhelm their opponent. Massed artillery and mortars, often more than 300 tubes per 1,000 yards of front, bombarded enemy positions prior to an attack. Assault forces spearheaded by large numbers of tanks then struck defensive positions at several points across a broad front. Infantry divisions, organized like their Western counterparts on a triangular basis, would advance on fronts as narrow as 2 miles with two regiments forward and one in reserve ... A second division followed the leading wave, sometimes at a distance of less than 750 yards.
>
> When the first echelon began to slow down, the second reinforced or passed through as the circumstances required. Additional armored formations followed in subsequent waves, seeking to build on success until a breakthrough occurred. When it did, mechanized forces or cavalry pushed through the breach to attack the defenders' rear while less maneuverable infantry expanded the breach and mopped up along the main battle line.

Charioteer

The Centurion Mk 3 suffered from slow delivery, and the Conqueror had not yet entered service. As a stopgap measure, to strengthen its armoured units in West Germany, the British Army had industry fit it with a newly-designed turret armed with the 20-pounder gun to a modified Cromwell hull. It was named the 'Charioteer'. The official designation was the FV4101 Tank, Medium Gun, Charioteer.

The Charioteer's first production example entered British Army service in 1952, weighing approximately 32 tons. Around 442 examples came off the factory floor by 1954 before the British Army cancelled the remainder of the order, initially envisioned as 630 vehicles. The Charioteer lasted in service with British Army reserve units until 1956 and was then sold to a small number of non-NATO countries.

During the Korean War, an upgraded M26 Medium Tank designated the M26A1 appeared as pictured here. The suffix letter 'A' following a vehicle designation indicates a substantial change to a design, such as fitting a new engine, main gun or so forth. The M26A1 featured a new 90mm main gun with a lighter-weight single-baffle muzzle brake and bore evacuator. (*Dreamstime*)

The engine exhaust muffler is visible on the upper portion of the rear engine compartment plate of the M26A1 pictured. To its right is the rectangular box for a telephone. It allows those outside the tank to communicate with the vehicle commander, who can remain under armor. In the raised position is the tank's travel lock, which typically lies flat on the top of the engine compartment. (*Dreamstime*)

The M26 series tanks proved badly underpowered due to their 500hp liquid-cooled gasoline-powered engine which was a derivative of that used in the M4. American industry produced a more powerful 810hp air-cooled gasoline-powered engine to correct that deficiency. That engine went into the reconfigured engine compartment of an M26 seen here, resulting in the new designation of the M46. It received the official nickname of the 'General Patton'. *(TACOM)*

The M46 exhaust ran through the top centre grill of the engine deck roof and out pipes extending sideways to mufflers mounted on either fender as seen in this picture. This was unlike the engine exhaust on the M26 series, which ran through an exhaust muffler affixed to the tank's engine compartment rear plate. Despite its official nickname of the 'General Patton', most American tankers referred to it as the 'forty-six'. *(TACOM)*

(**Above**) A young US Army officer is seen here standing on an M46 medium tank at a NATO training base during a firing exercise. He appears to be overseeing a group of what appears to be Italian tankers, based on their uniforms. The M46 retained the turret and forward hull structure of the M26 series. The tank received power from a new smaller, more powerful, compact air-cooled gasoline-powered engine, combined with a new cross-drive transmission. (*Public domain*)

(**Opposite, above**) The outbreak of the Korean War gave rise to the American fear that it was a precursor to a Third World War in Western Europe. In response, the US Army rushed a stopgap medium tank into service. Seen here, it was designated the M47. It consisted of a modified M46 chassis fitted with a new turret design featuring a state-of-the-art fire-control system. It had a cylindrical blast deflector, which also served as a muzzle brake. (*Pierre-Olivier Buan*)

(**Opposite, below**) The most prominent design feature of the M47 tank, its pronounced rear turret bustle, is evident in this picture. It contained the vehicle's radios, stowage for four main gun rounds, and an electrically-powered ventilation blower. The blower's uppermost portion protruded through the vehicle's rear roof under a circular armoured housing. The first production example of the M47 came off the factory floor in June 1951. The vehicle's initial nickname, the 'Patton II', later changed to the 'Patton 47'. (*Dreamstime*)

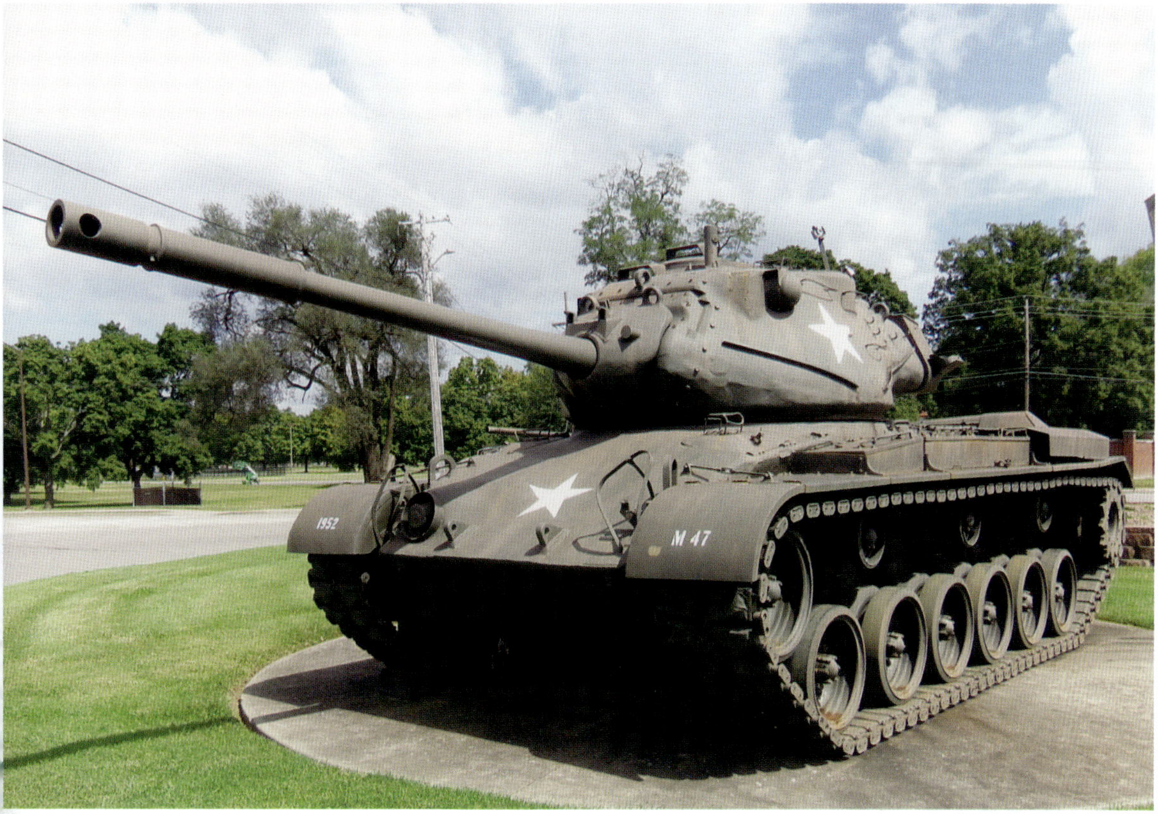
1952
M 47

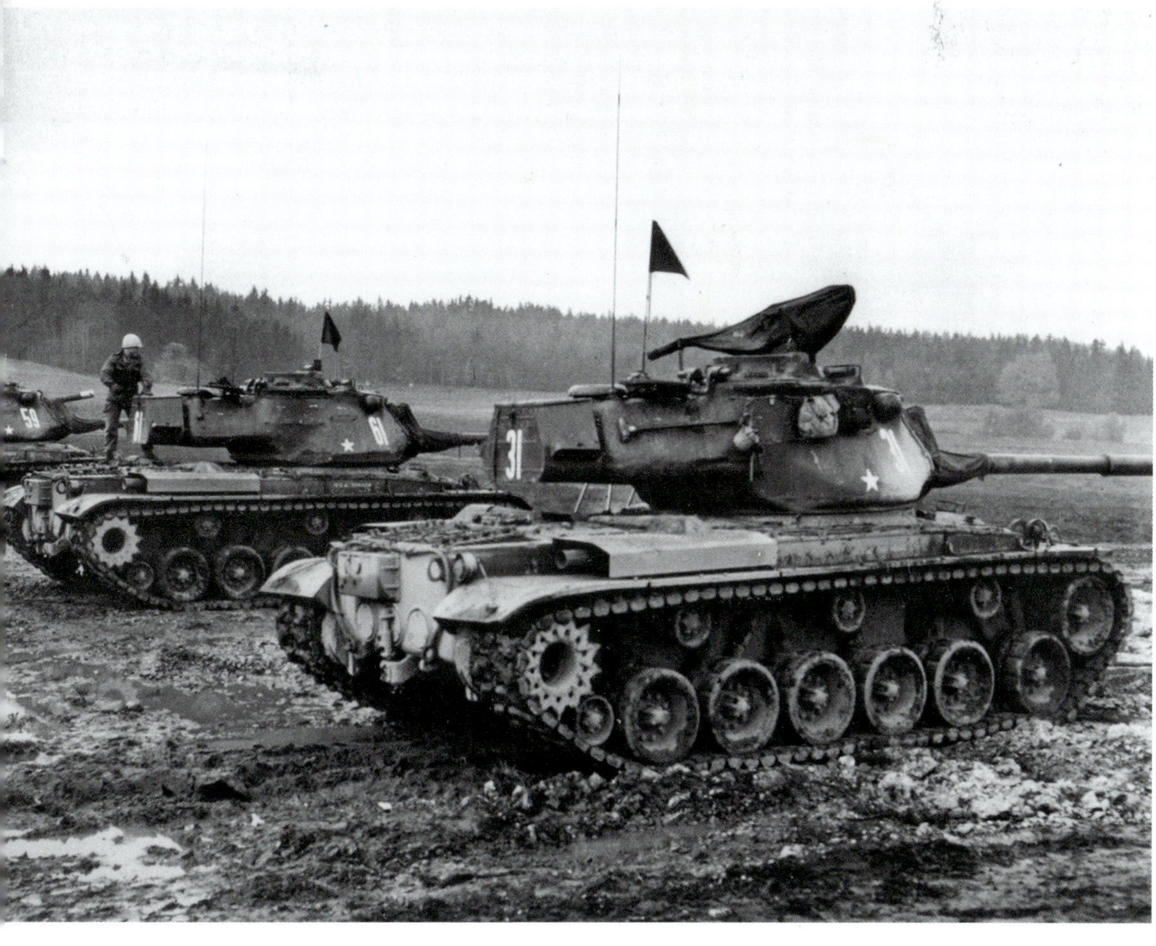
59
61
31

Late-production M47s came with a T-shaped blast deflector, shown here. As originally conceived, plans called for an armoured blister on either side of the turret containing a fixed forward-firing .30 calibre machine gun. That later changed to an armoured box on the vehicle's front fenders, each holding a fixed forward-firing .30 calibre machine gun. Test results were unsatisfactory and the idea was dropped from consideration. (*Dreamstime*)

Even as the US Army had the interim M47 rushed into production, it expedited the next version of its Patton medium tank series into production in 1953. This had a new elliptically-shaped cast-armoured turret as seen in this picture. The vehicle received the designation of the M48. Rather than the three return rollers on either side of the M47 hull, initially the M48 came with five return rollers on either side of its hull. (*Patton Museum*)

The follow-on to the M48 proved to be the M48A1. The most noticeable design feature of the tank was the enclosed vehicle commander's M1 cupola armed with a .50 calibre machine gun pictured here. On the previous M48, the vehicle commander could fire the pedestal-mounted .50 calibre machine gun from within the tank's turret, but he had to expose his head and upper torso to reload the weapon. (*Patton Museum*)

(**Above**) The US Army approved production of the M48A2 in 1955. It retained the 90mm main gun of previous versions. It featured a new raised rear engine deck seen here with a vertical rear hull plate featuring two large louvred doors. These replaced the complicated grill work seen on the M48 and M48A1 upper rear engine compartments. (*TACOM*)

(**Opposite, above**) A 1964 US Army gunnery manual illustrates a representative direct-fire control system for an M48 series medium tank. Unlike the optical rangefinder on the M47 tank operated by the gunner, the vehicle commander operated it on the M48 series. Until the M48A3 tank, the vehicles employed a stereoscopic rangefinder, which required great depth perception. Beginning with the M48A3, the US Army switched to the easier-to-use coincidence rangefinder, which proved more tolerant of some vision challenges. (*US Army*)

(**Opposite, below**) The West German Army took many M48 series tanks into service, including the M48A1, M48A2 and the M48A2C. The smoke grenade-launcher assemblies on the turret side were a German addition and not seen on US Army M48 series tanks. (*Dreamstime*)

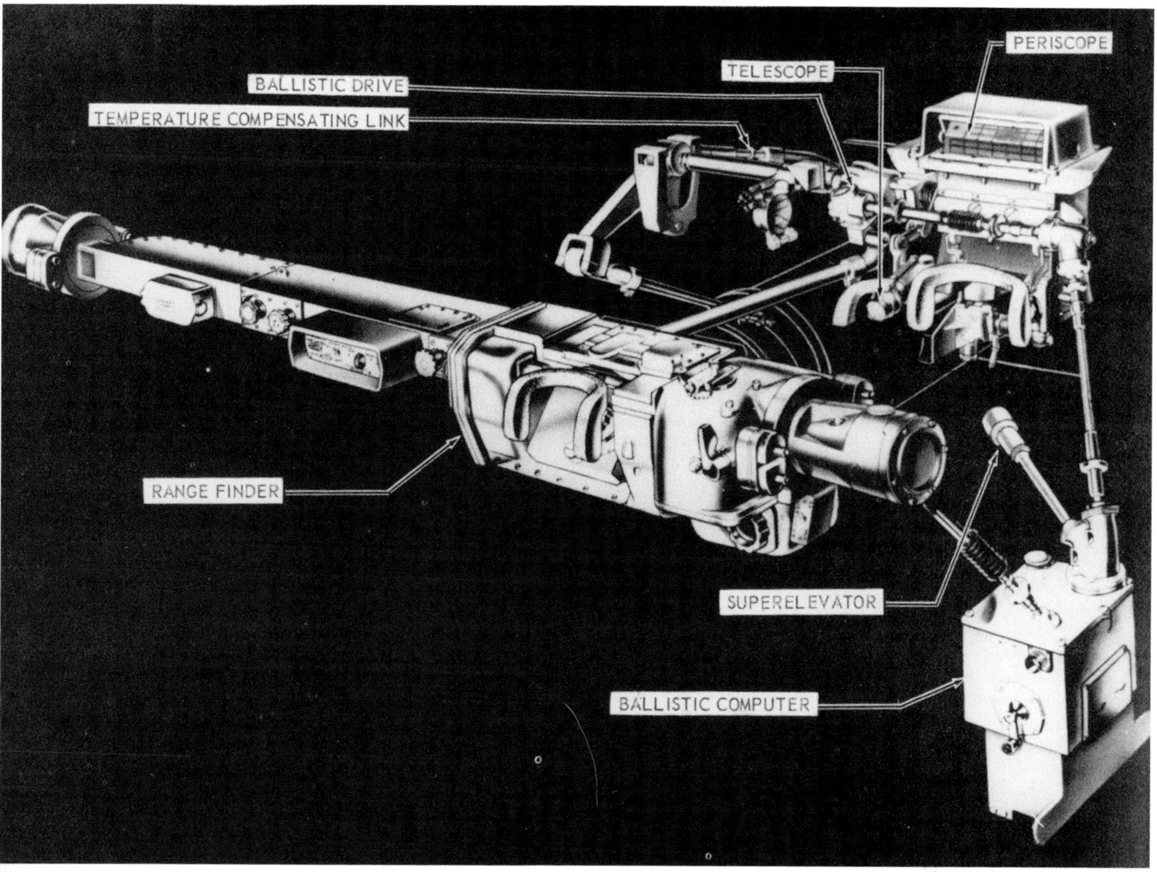
PERISCOPE
TELESCOPE
BALLISTIC DRIVE
TEMPERATURE COMPENSATING LINK
RANGE FINDER
SUPERELEVATOR
BALLISTIC COMPUTER

632
635

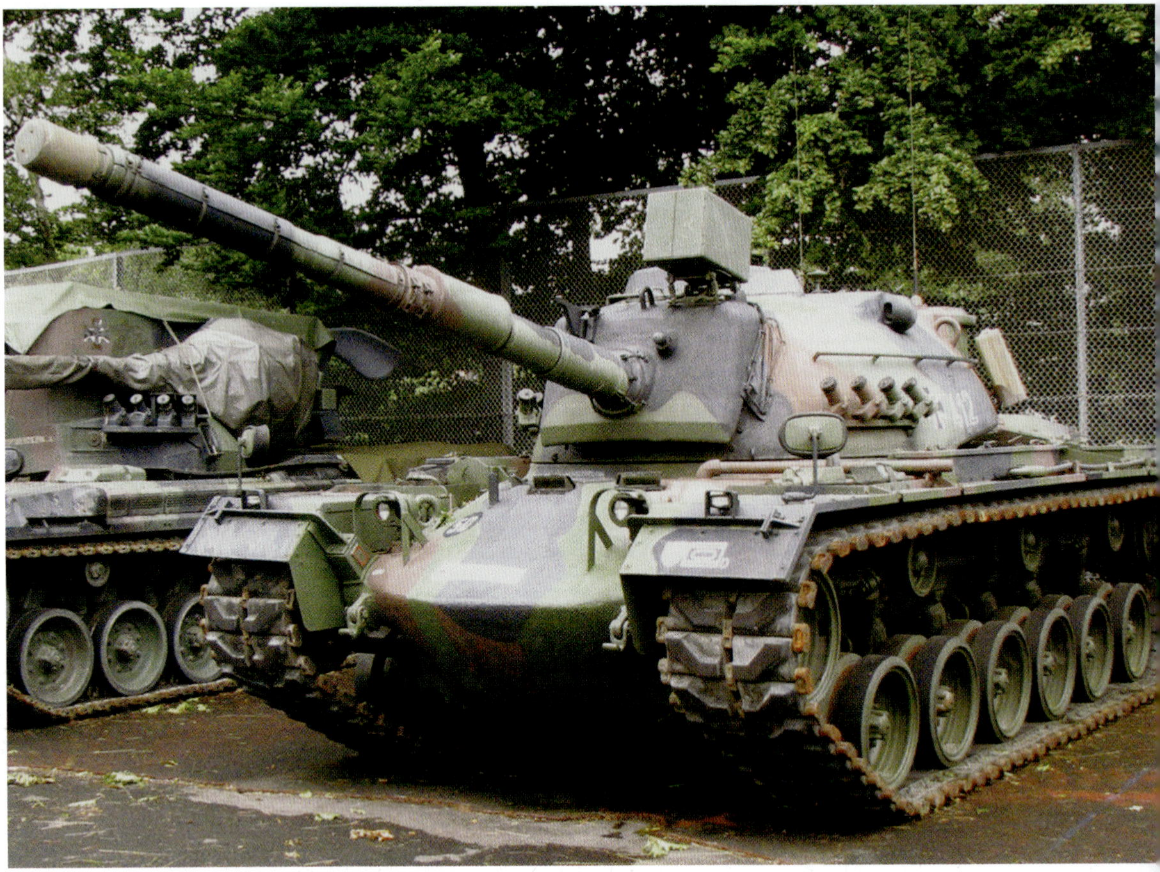

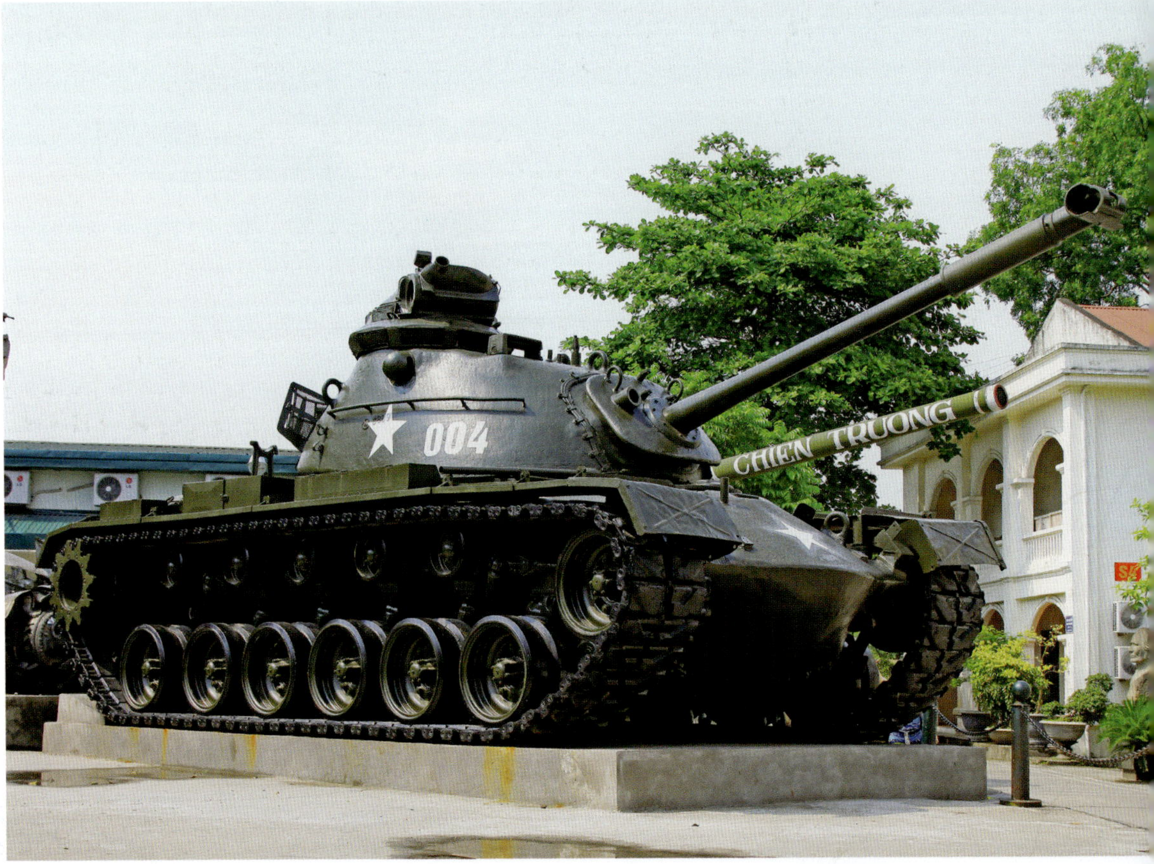
004
CHIEN TRUONG

(**Opposite, above**) Seen here at the German Army Museum is an M48A2C Medium Tank. The box-like object over the gun shield is the infrared/white light searchlight. Between 1978 and 1980, German industry upgraded 650 examples of the approximately 1,700 M48 series tanks taken into service by the West German Army. The resulting improvements, seen here on the vehicle designated M48A2 G A2, include a 105mm L7 main gun with bore evacuator as well as a new thicker cast-armour gun shield. (*Frank Schulz*)

(**Opposite, below**) On display at a Vietnamese military museum is a former American M48A3 Medium Tank that would have last seen service with the former South Vietnamese Army. Unlike the previous versions of the M48 series, the M48A3 came with an air-cooled diesel engine. It did, however, retain the 90mm main gun of its predecessors. (*Dreamstime*)

(**Above**) The US Army light tank companion to the M47 and M48 series medium tanks was the 76mm gun-armed M41, pictured here in West German Army service. The thinly-armoured tank had a four-man crew and received power from an air-cooled gasoline-powered engine. Like the US Army's medium tanks, it had an electric-hydraulic turret traverse and elevation system. It did not have a stabilization system and hence no fire-on-the-move capability. (*BMV/g*)

The M41 series light tanks, which included the A1, A2 and A3 versions, had a pronounced rear turret bustle, as is evident in this photograph. It held the vehicle's radio and an electrically-powered turret blower, with the exhaust vent on the turret's rear roof under an armoured dome. The vehicle's gasoline-powered engine provided the tank with a maximum speed on level roads of 45mph. *(Dreamstime)*

The Danish Army was among the many forces that received the M41 series light tanks via American military aid during the Cold War. In the 1980s, the Danish Army decided to upgrade its M41 light tanks. The 76mm main gun remained, but the vehicle now had a laser rangefinder and mounted a halogen searchlight above the gun shield. A diesel engine replaced the original gasoline-powered engine. Reflecting these changes, the Danish Army designated the reworked tanks the M41 DK-1. *(Dreamstime)*

To deal with Soviet Army heavy tanks, the US Army pushed forward what eventually became the M103 series of heavy tanks. All were armed with the 120mm main gun seen here, fitted with a bore evacuator but no muzzle brake/flash deflector. Due to the weight and size of the separately-loaded main gun rounds requiring two loaders, the maximum firing rate decreased to five rounds per minute. The M103 had no fire-on-the-move capability. (*Patton Museum*)

(**Above**) By the mid-1950s, the US Army began to lose interest in the problem-plagued M103 Heavy Tank. It would fall to the Marine Corps to push continued development of the M103, resulting in the M103A1 and finally the M103A2 pictured here. The M103 and M103A1 had gasoline-powered engines and the M103A2 a diesel engine. The A2 version of the M103 featured an enlarged rear engine compartment, like the one that appeared on the M48A2 medium tank. (*Ian Wilcox*)

(**Opposite, above**) A view of the interior of an M103A2 turret with the gun, gun mount and gun shield removed. The large circular metal objects on either side of the turret are trunnions, allowing the main gun to elevate and depress. At the centre rear of the turret is the folded-up vehicle commander's seat, with main gun round stowage on either side. The M103 had stowage space for thirty-three main gun rounds. The A1 and A2 versions had stowage space for thirty-eight main gun rounds. (*Hans Halberstadt*)

(**Opposite, below**) In the immediate post-war period, the French Army depended on a wide variety of American-supplied tanks from the Second World War and those acquired post-war. Despite these tanks, French industry proved keen on providing the army with a new light tank that could travel by existing French cargo aircraft. That light tank proved to be the 75mm main gun-armed AMX-13 seen here during its early trials. (*Public domain*)

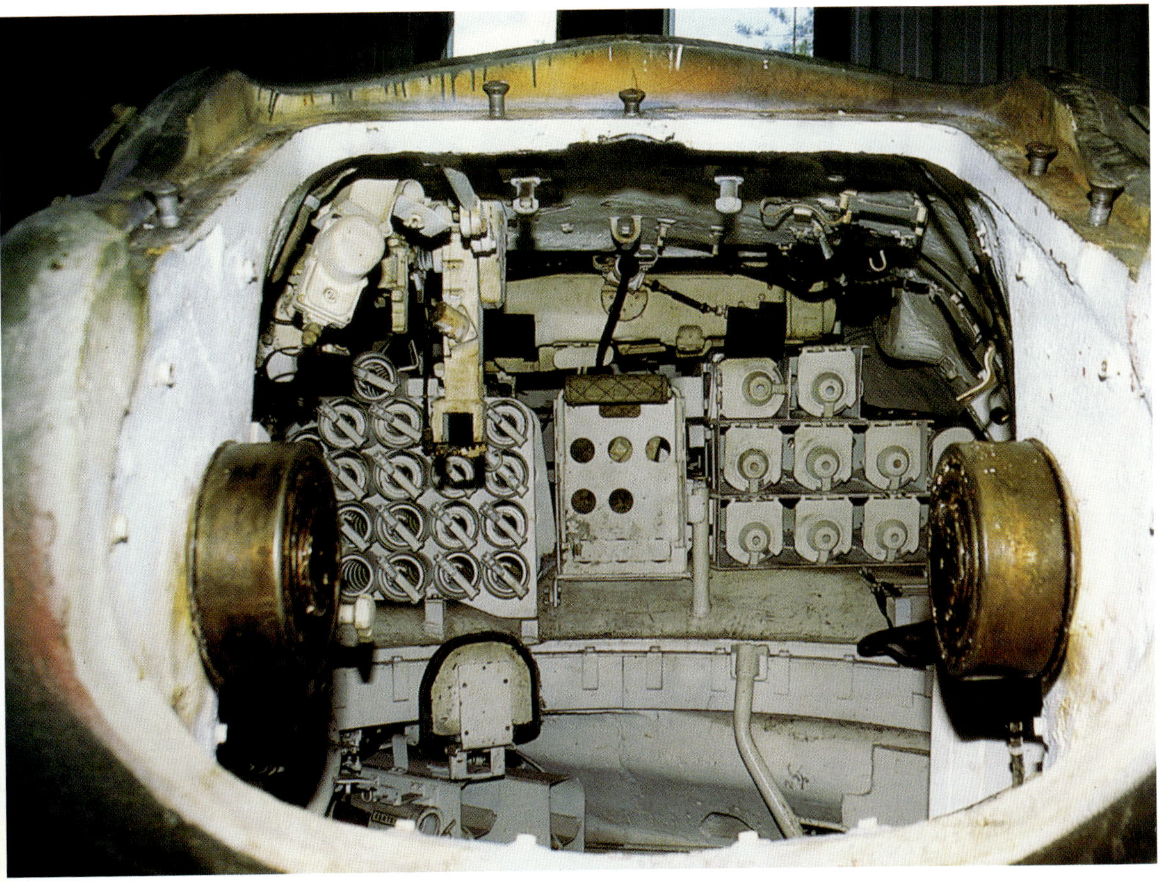

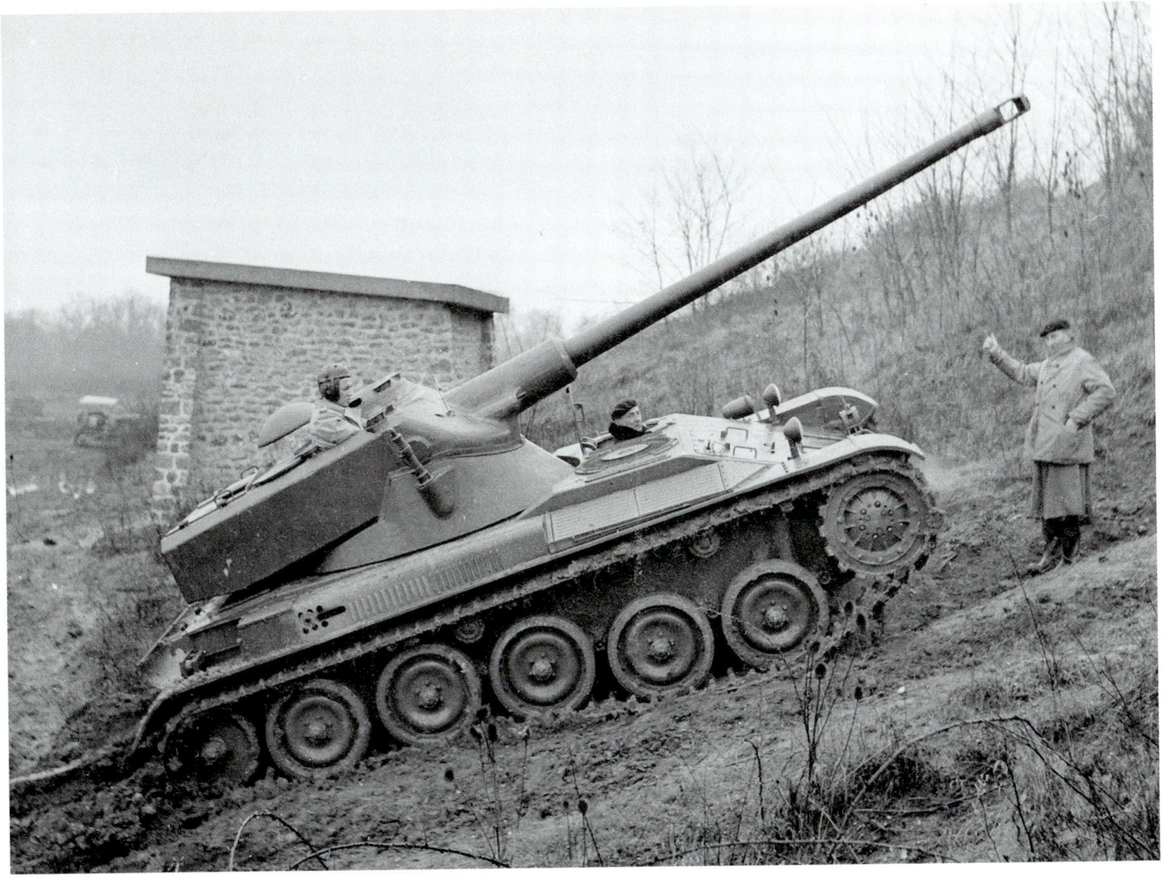

(**Above**) The AMX-13 seen here proved novel in concept when placed into production in 1952. It had a two-piece oscillating turret, with a twelve-round automatic loader in the tank's rear turret bustle and a front hull-mounted gasoline-powered engine. The automatic loader reduced the crew down to three men. The vehicle commander and gunner sat in the turret and the driver sat in the front hull alongside the engine. (*Pierre-Olivier Buan*)

(**Opposite, above**) As the 75mm main gun on the AMX-13 became outdated by new generations of better-armoured Soviet Army medium tanks, the French Army began looking for an affordable solution. One answer was to arm some of their AMX-13 tanks with a new French-designed and built SS-11 wire-guided anti-tank missile as seen here on this museum vehicle. The SS-11 first appeared on French Army helicopters. (*Pierre-Olivier Buan*)

(**Opposite, below**) Wire-guided anti-tank missiles at the time of the SS-11's introduction in 1956 were reasonably large. When mounted on the front of the AMX-13 turret, they were vulnerable to artillery fragments as well as small-arms fire. That pushed the French Army to adopt a 90mm main gun-armed AMX-13 seen here beginning in the early 1960s. That gun came with a thermal shroud and a single-baffle muzzle brake. (*Pierre-Olivier Buan*)

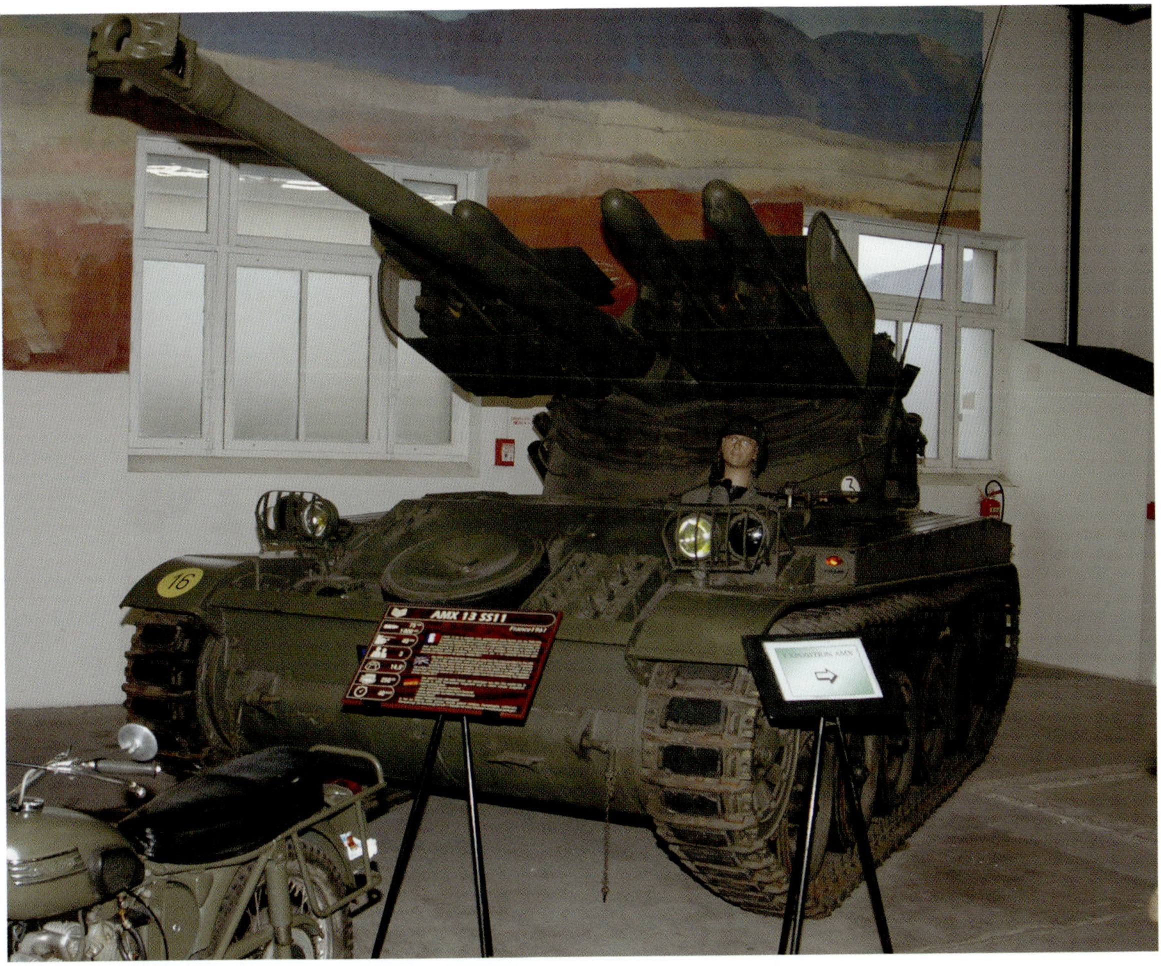
AMX 13 SS11

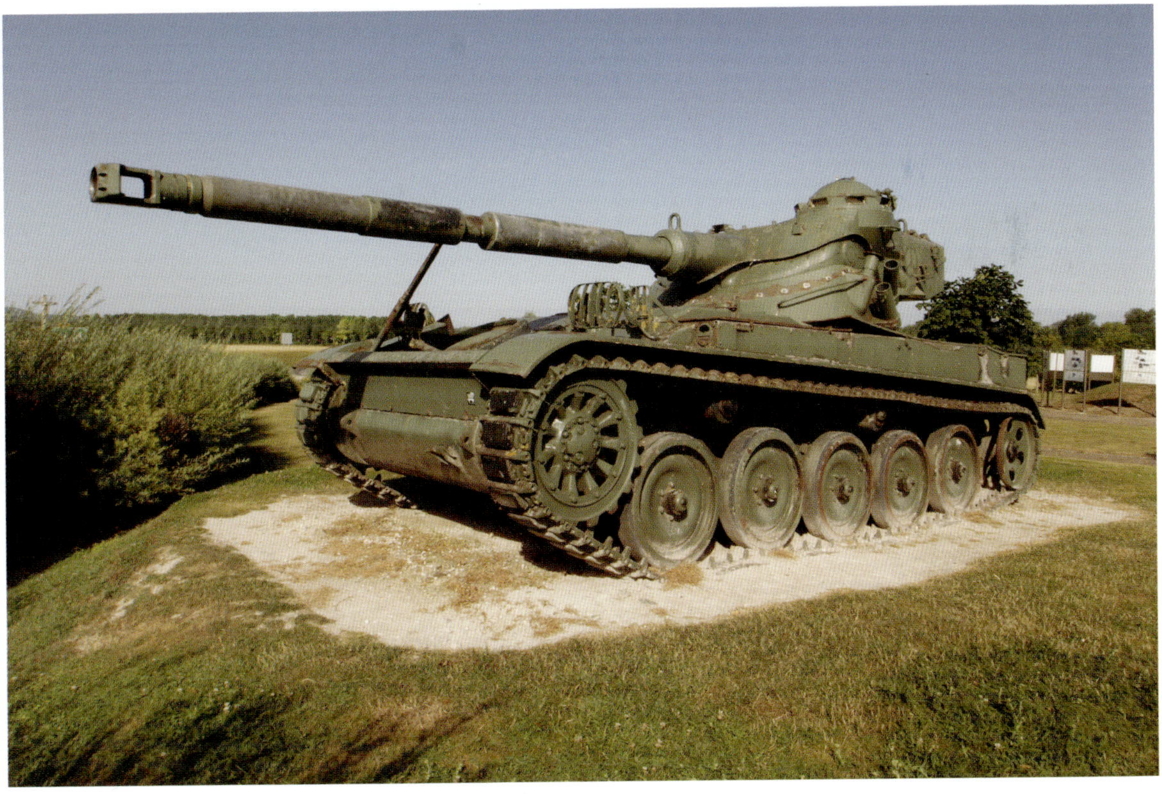

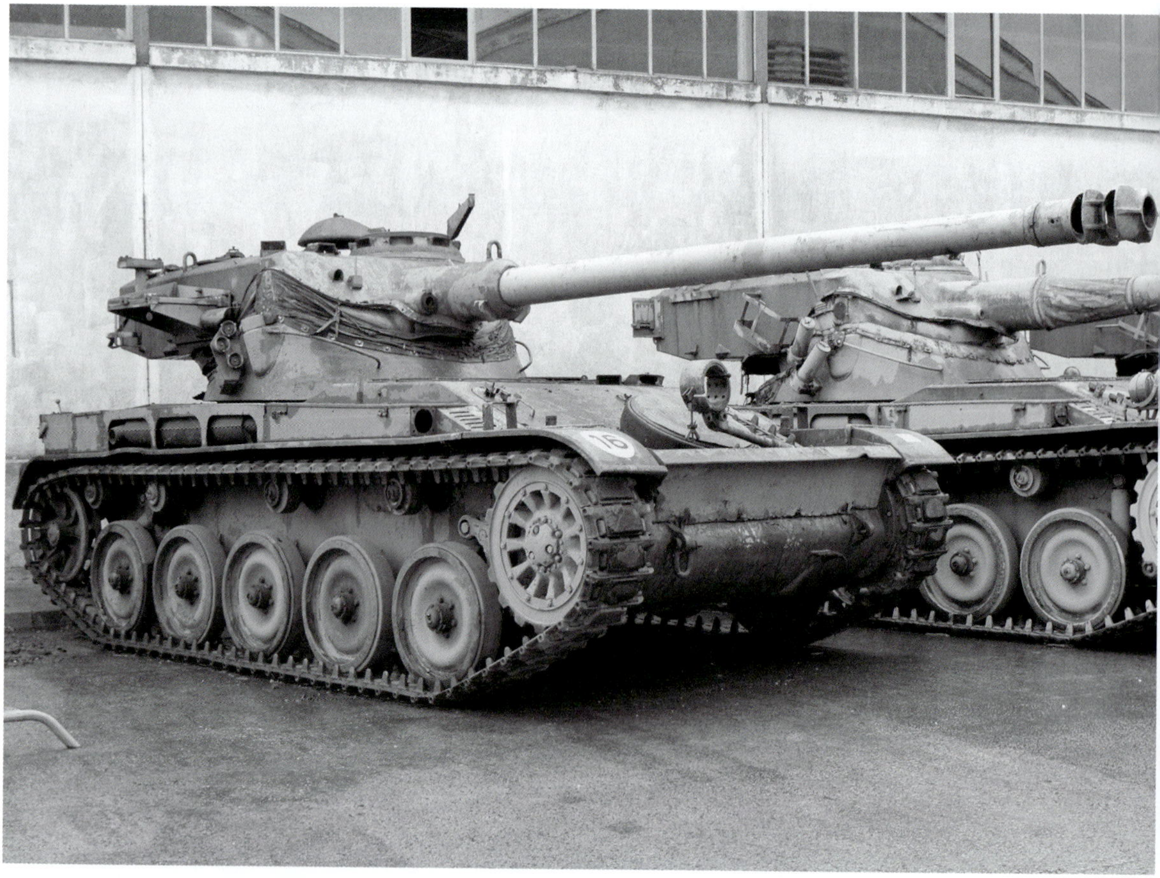
16

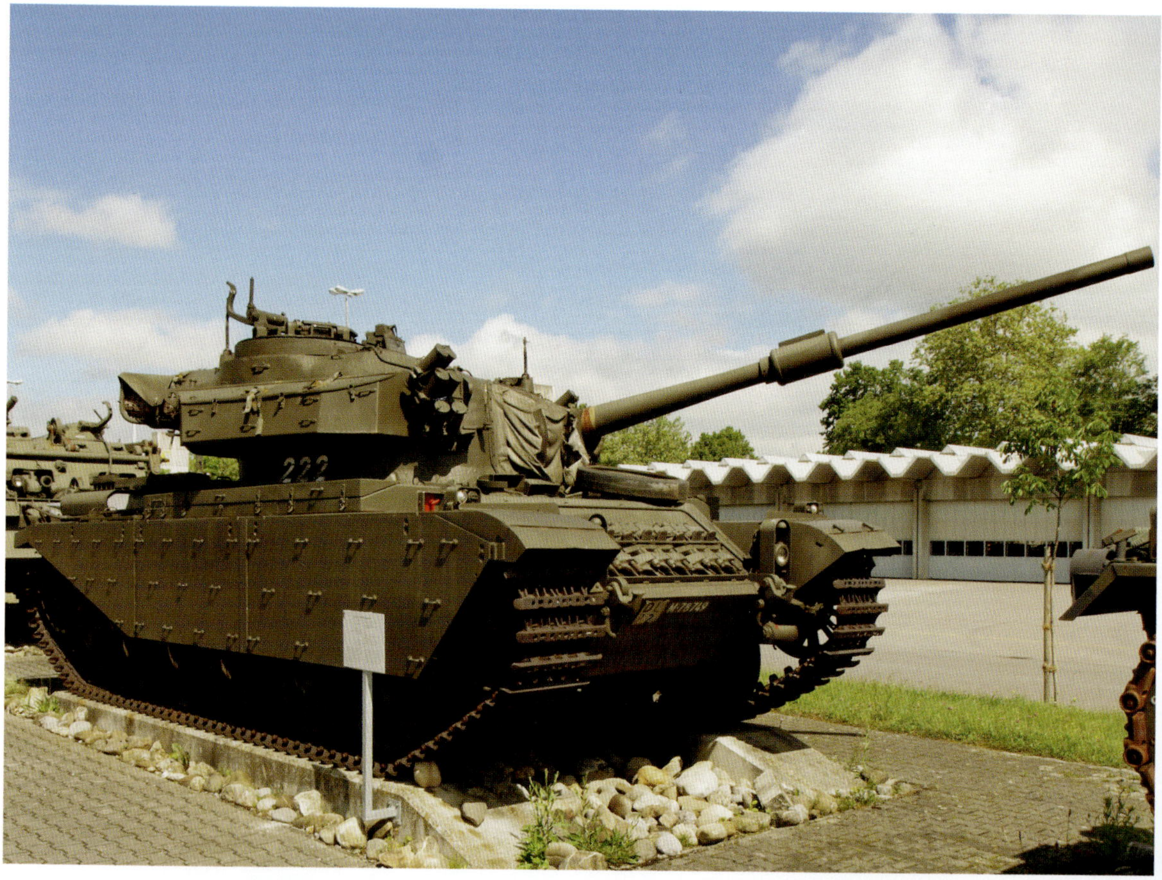
222

(**Opposite, above**) The last up-gunning of the AMX-13 fitted the tank with a French-designed and built 105mm main gun as pictured here. The weapon featured a double baffle muzzle brake to reduce recoil. The French Army eventually passed on the project. French industry then offered the up-gunned tank for export. The only NATO army to adopt it was the Dutch Army, which acquired 131 examples in 1962. (*Christophe Vallier*)

(**Opposite, below**) On display at a museum is a former Swiss Army Centurion Mk 5 armed with a 20-pounder. The gun on this example has what was described as the B-barrel, as it features a bore evacuator midway on its barrel. Running along the top of the bore evacuator are three thin vertical metal ridges not seen on the bore evacuator of the later British-designed 105mm main gun labelled the L7. (*Dreamstime*)

(**Above**) The short operational range of the earlier models of the Centurion series, a problem shared by gasoline-engine-powered American light, medium and heavy tanks of the 1950s, drove several experiments to increase their range. One involved the tanks towing gasoline-filled wheeled trailers. The more practical solution came when a British firm lengthened the tank's rear hull to enlarge the vehicle's fuel tanks, resulting in the Mk 7 pictured here. (*Tank Museum*)

The British Army Conqueror was the counterpart to the American M103 series of heavy tanks. It used a 120mm main gun, the same as on the American heavy tank. The British Army's Conqueror tanks spent all their service careers in West Germany between 1957 and 1966. In case of the outbreak of a Third World War, their role was to engage and destroy Soviet Army heavy tanks. This allowed the Centurion tanks to engage Soviet Army medium tanks. *(Tank Museum)*

Seen here on display at the now-closed Military Vehicle Technology Foundation (MVTF) is a former British Army Conqueror tank. Its 71-ton weight prevented it from using many West German roads, and bridges were tactical handicaps. Its maximum speed of only 21mph added to several reliability problems, while its electrical system and an automatic spent case ejection system did not endear the vehicle to its crews. *(Chris Hughes)*

The Charioteer was a stopgap tank for the British Army in the immediate post-war period to stand in until enough Centurion tanks came off the assembly lines. It consisted of a modified Second World War Cromwell chassis fitted with a lightly-armoured turret armed with the 20-pounder 83.2mm main gun. Some 442 of these rolled off the factory floor, and all were pulled from service by 1956. Most would eventually go off to non-NATO armies. *(Dreamstime)*

Chapter Four

The Odds Get Worse

During the Hungarian Revolution (October/November 1956), a captured Soviet T-54A found its way into British embassy grounds in Budapest. The onsite British military attaché (a former tanker) examined the vehicle and numerous wrecks before the Soviets reclaimed their property. His findings made it clear to the British Army that the 20-pounder (83.4mm) main gun on their Centurion tanks could not penetrate the thick, sloped frontal armour of the T-54A tank.

The British Solution

Having anticipated a requirement for a more powerful main gun for the Centurion series, British industry had already begun developing a new rifled 105mm tank main gun in the early 1950s, designated the 'L7'. The weapon's initial firing trials took place in July 1956. Its performance demonstrated that it would have no problem in punching holes in the T-54A's thickest armour.

The 105mm gun was designed from the beginning to fit the Centurion's existing 20-pounder gun mount. British industry began a programme in 1959 of up-gunning existing Centurion tanks during refits and new production vehicles with the 105mm main gun. The gun's primary tank-killing rounds were APDS and HESH/HEP. British Centurion tanks did not use HEAT rounds as the HESH was considered multipurpose.

With the addition of the new 105mm main gun, in conjunction with an up-armouring programme, the Mk 5 Centurion became the Mk 6, and with the 105mm main gun, the Mk 7 and Mk 8 respectively received the designations Mk 9 and Mk 10.

The Centurion Mk 9/1 proved to be the first in the series equipped with infra-red (IR) sighting and driving systems as standard equipment. Earlier versions of the Centurion series were similarly retrofitted.

The Centurion Mk 10 proved to be the last new-built Centurion model, with 155 examples completed between 1959 and 1962. Progressively improved follow-on Centurion models, the Mk 11, 12 and 13, consisted of reworked examples of earlier production vehicles.

The American Solution

The British discovery that its 20-pounder main gun lacked the penetrating power to defeat the frontal armour on the T-54A made it clear to the US Army that its 90mm tank gun was also obsolete.

> **Ranging Gun**
>
> The British Army began fitting its Centurion tanks with a .50 calibre (12.7mm) coaxial ranging gun in 1966. Its ballistics matched the tank's main gun rounds; the gunner would observe the tracer element to see if the rounds impacted the selected target. If so, he would follow it with a main gun round.
>
> An article that appeared in *Armor* magazine listed the advantages with a ranging gun: '... takes into account such factors as crosswind and trunnion cant, which the optical rangefinder does not. It is also easier to use when light is poor or when the target – such as bushes hiding an anti-tank weapon – does not have sharp contours.'
>
> The ranging gun was only good up to 1.5 miles. British APDS rounds of the era had a maximum effective range of about 1 mile. As HESH rounds had an effective range of 2 to 2.5 miles, the ranging gun proved less useful. However, British tankers believed that most Third World War tank-on-tank engagements would occur at ranges of about 1 mile; hence this was not a significant handicap.

The US Army had developed and tested various calibre tank guns during the 1950s, including an American-designed and built 105mm gun as a possible replacement for its existing 90mm tank gun. However, none received approval for production. Upon testing the British 105mm L7 tank gun in 1958, it became apparent to all concerned that it was far superior to anything in development for the US Army.

The impressive showing by the British 105mm L7 gun prompted its adoption by the US Army in a modified form, designated the M68. That gun went into the then developmental XM60, standardized as the 105mm Gun, Full-Tracked Combat Tank M60 in March 1959. Its tank-killing rounds included an APDS and HEAT round.

The first production examples of the M60 came off the factory floor in 1959, entering US Army service the following year. By the time production concluded in 1962, a total of 2,205 examples had come off the assembly lines.

The US Army saw the M60 as a main battle tank (MBT), defined in a 1965 Army Dictionary (AR-320-5) as the following: 'A tracked vehicle providing heavy armor protection and serving as the principal assault weapon of armored and infantry troops.'

M60 Details

Derived from the previous M48 Patton tank series, the much-improved 51-ton M60 never received an official US Army nickname, despite many unofficially calling it a Patton tank, or even the Super Patton.

The initial turret design of the M60, derived from a modified version of that fitted to the M48A2, included hydraulic-operated turret traverse and gun elevation system.

American 105mm KE Rounds

During the 1973 Yom Kippur War, the Israeli Army discovered that the M392 APDS-T rounds provided with their American-supplied M60 series tanks had a problem. The rounds, instead of penetrating, glanced off the Soviet T-54/T-55 tanks' low-slung, rounded cast-steel turrets despite their theoretical ability to penetrate the armour.

American designers quickly came up with a new APDS-T round labelled the M392A2. It had a ballistic cap covering the projectile's tip, which pivoted the penetrator as it struck the target. This tilting action caused the penetrator to strike the surface at a right angle, directing the kinetic energy to penetrate the armour instead of glancing off.

By the 1970s, the US Army replaced the M392 series of 105mm APDS rounds with the much more potent M735 series APFSDS rounds, with a tungsten heavy alloy penetrator rather than high-hardness steel.

In the 1980–81 time period, the US Army began fielding the M774 105mm APFSDS round with a penetrator made of depleted uranium (DU). Due to issues with its accuracy, the M774 did not last long in service.

In 1983, the US Army introduced the new M833 105mm APFSDS round with a DU projectile. At first it suffered from accuracy problems at longer ranges, corrected by the late 1980s.

The last APFSDS round for the 105mm gun on the M1 series appeared in 1989 and bore the designation M900. The Soviet Army introduced a 125mm APFSDS round with a DU penetrator in 1990.

A US Army report on tank main gun ammunition, dated June 1980, discussed the reason for switching from tungsten to DU: 'With the advent of spaced armor targets ... it was quickly discovered that a tungsten carbide penetrator was susceptible to break-up against even a thin (e.g. 10mm) front plate and could be rendered ineffective against the remaining plates in a spaced array.'

DU offered a couple of important advantages as a tank-killing round. It is pyrophoric, which means it self-ignites when exposed to oxygen. Hence, it can cause explosions without having an explosive element. Tungsten penetrators became blunt as they cleaved through armour, resulting in their tip crushing into a mushroom shape, which impedes penetrator progress. DU, on the other hand, has a self-sharpening property as it passes through armour.

A prominent external design feature of the initial iteration of the M60 was the 105mm main gun, which lacked a muzzle brake, and was fitted with a bore evacuator centred on the length of the barrel. The M60's gun mount did not have a stabilization system.

An important and yet not visible design feature of the four-man M60 was its more reliable and fuel-efficient air-cooled diesel engine carried over from the M48A3.

Other Details

The US Army had initially planned to use lightweight siliceous-cored (glass) armour (sandwiched in between layers of steel armour). As a result, the M60 had a wedge-shaped glacis 93mm (3.7in) thick and sloped at 65 degrees.

Siliceous-cored armour (a form of ceramic armour) offered superior protection from the HEAT rounds which were the primary tank-killing round of the T-54/T-55 series' 100mm main guns. What ended consideration of siliceous-cored armour on the M60 was cost and the inability to manufacture enough for the number of tanks expected to be built. In addition, field-repaired panel castings suffered a loss of kinetic energy protection and led to termination of the project.

From a declassified US Army report dated November 1958 titled 'Evaluation of Siliceous Cored Armor for the M60 Tank' is the following passage on the advantage of siliceous armour:

> Under proper conditions, the stopping power of glass exceeds that of armor steel on a thickness basis, and in many cases, glass is more than twice as good as steel on a thickness basis. The development of siliceous cored armor is an effort to utilize this phenomenon of glass in a practical manner.

The original turret design for the M60 featured a low-profile machine-gun-armed vehicle commander's cupola. Also envisioned for the initial configuration M60 turret was a hydraulically-operated spent cartridge case ejector mechanism on the tank's left turret wall.

A New Version of the M60

Not pleased with the modified M48A2 turret's protection on the first version of the M60, the US Army had American industry develop a new elongated turret that presented a much smaller target profile from the front with increased

---

New Type of Protection

Ceramics are about four times harder than the hardest steel and can effectively defeat shaped-charge warheads. Modern ceramics also offer a reasonable degree of protection from KE projectiles.

Ceramics are too brittle as a stand-alone structure and must serve a secondary role when mounted on tanks. Another disadvantage with ceramics is that an entire panel will be destroyed on the first hit, leaving the tank vulnerable to a second hit in the same general location. However, the odds of striking the exact location with another round are not that high.

With the advent of composite armour, there appeared a new term: 'equivalent thickness'. It describes the degree of protection afforded by a composite armour array by comparing it to the thickness required of conventional steel armour to match its protective quality. The equivalent thickness of composite armour can vary depending on what type of round it is optimized to defend against, HEAT or KE.

> **Israeli Army Experience with the M60A1**
>
> Israeli Army combat experience in 1973 demonstrated that the M60A1 turret ring and chin armour was too thin, resulting in penetrations at those points. Therefore, the US Army had the armour in those portions of new-production M60A1 tanks thickened at the factory, a modification eventually applied to earlier production vehicles.
>
> Another Israeli Army combat lesson learned with the M60A1 was that the highly-pressurized hydraulic oil (unofficially nicknamed 'cherry juice') in the tank's traverse and elevation systems proved extremely flammable. Any enemy projectile that penetrated the turret and ruptured the hydraulic hoses caused horrible burns to the turret crews and often detonated onboard main gun rounds. The US Army's answer to the problem was development of a flame-resistant hydraulic oil.
>
> According to a US Marine Corps' study of the 1973 Yom Kippur War, the M48/M60 series tanks' propensity for catastrophic explosions meant that fewer than 20 per cent returned to duty after being disabled in combat. This was in sharp contrast to the British Centurion, of which 60 per cent returned to duty after being disabled, and 55 per cent of T-54/T-55 tanks.

ballistic protection, ranging from 127mm to 254mm (5in to 10in), with a slope of 60 degrees. The elongated turret also provided additional room for the tank's loader to handle the next-generation of longer tank-killing rounds. With this new turret, the M60 had the suffix 'A1' added.

Production of the M60A1 began in 1962 and continued until 1980, with 7,948 examples completed. In 1966 the tanks' original analogue electromechanical ballistic computers were replaced by new solid-state ballistic computers. The next big improvement, in 1972, was an add-on two-axis stabilizing system; the tanks thus upgraded became the M60A1-AOS (add-on stabilizer). It proved to be the first American tank with true fire-on-the-move capability.

Some 578 M60A1s went off to the US Marine Corps and another 874 were allocated for foreign military sales. In addition to the new turret design, the sloping front hull armour thickness on the M60A1 was increased to 109mm (4.3in), with the extra armour adding another 1 ton of weight to the tank.

A much-improved air-cooled diesel-powered engine went into the M60A1 starting in 1975 as the Reliability-Improved-Selected-Equipment (RISE) engine. This feature was backdated to earlier production M60A1s. Other upgrades included replacing the original white light/infrared searchlight with a passive night-fighting system. A passive night-driving system was also added. These features resulted in the designation of the M60A1 (RISE) Passive.

From a May 1980 US Army report by the Office of the Project Manager M60 is the following passage on the positive improvements to the tank series:

> Over the past several years, there have been major improvements made to the M60 series tanks. One of the most significant has been the AVDS

1790-2C/2D RISE engine. The tanks equipped with the RISE engine have been received with considerable enthusiasm by the field, and it is proving to be a very reliable engine. The preponderance of positive feedback from the user about the RISE engine, the Commander/Gunner Passive Night Sights, and the drivers' Night Viewer certainly indicates that the M60A1 RISE Passive tank is a highly satisfactory weapon system.

The only NATO army that took the M60A1 into service during the Cold War was the Italian Army: 100 came from the US Army inventory in the 1970s, with Italian industry building another 200 examples under licence. Following the Cold War, the American government supplied M60A1s to fellow NATO members Greece and Turkey.

> **Freaking Cold**
> Former US Army tanker Jerry Sodan of the 3/64 Armor, 3rd Infantry Division, West Germany, recalls the weather and keeping their M60 series tanks up and running:
>
>> To set the stage, the winter of 78-79 was brutal. I was born in upstate New York and lived there until I was 15 but don't remember ever experiencing cold like that. Anyway, we had the mission to be ready to go to war if the Warsaw Pact decided to test us. At the temperatures we had that winter diesel fuel would jell. To prevent this, we would go to the motor pool every four hours. The tanks were parked grill doors to grill doors in pairs. When you got to the motor pool the grill doors on each tank would be opened. Exhaust stacks and heat shields were removed then one tank would be started. The exhaust gasses would heat the other tank. This was a pretty good way to keep the tanks ready to go at a moment's notice.
>>
>> The tanks would alternate heating each other. If it were your turn to do the heating and your tank wouldn't start your partner would warm your tank until yours would start. If this happened, you'd then run your tank for at least fifteen minutes to warm the fluids, fuel and charge the batteries. Hopefully, it would start on its own the next time around and you'd be able to warm your partner's tank. I remember great white clouds of unburnt diesel not only from the engines but from the heater exhausts too. The fifteen minutes of engine warm-up would often extend to an hour or more due to starting problems. More often than not a lot of time was spent trying to simply unlock the loader's hatch to gain access to the tanks. We solved this with our trusty ZIPPO lighters. We quickly discovered if you heated the brass key for the series 200 padlock sufficiently to burn your fingers it would quickly open the lock. We also learned that ensuring each tank was warmed up sufficiently allowed us to spend minimal time out in that weather.

The Missile Detour

A 1958 US Army report by the Ad-Hoc Group on Armament for Future Tanks or Similar Combat Vehicles (ARCOVE) strongly recommended the US Army develop a missile-firing tank. At the same time, the study group urged curtailing any future development of 'conventional weapon programs, including hyper-velocity fin-stabilized penetrators and guns'.

The reasoning behind the ARCOVE recommendation is that existing fire-control systems lacked the accuracy necessary when engaging targets at longer ranges with KE rounds. The supposed answer was a 152mm combination gun/missile system launcher. Besides firing a guided anti-tank missile, officially nicknamed 'Shillelagh', it could fire a conventional caseless HEAT or HE round. The term 'caseless' refers to a solid mass of propellant being cast to form the cartridge's body in place of the standard metal (steel/aluminium) cartridge cases.

Some of the perceived advantages of the Shillelagh appeared in this passage from the November–December 1970 issue of *Armor* magazine:

> These new missiles, Shillelagh, for example, can be launched from lightweight, closed-breech tubes, with low trunnion reaction and little intrusion into the turret volume. Furthermore, the extremely high hit-and-kill probability achieved by the terminally guided HEAT missile removes the necessity for achievement of a high rate of sustained fire, eliminating the requirement for automatic ammunition handling.

Low-rate production of the Shillelagh began in 1964, with initial fielding in 1967. Early testing of the infrared-guided missile indicated an 80 per cent probability rate of first-round hits at ranges from 1,640 to 3,281 yards (almost 2 miles or 3 km).

ATGM Tank Disadvantages

In a US Department of the Army translation of an article titled 'Tanks and Tank Troops', a high-ranking Soviet Army officer listed some of the disadvantages of specialized ATGM vehicles, such as the M551 and the M60A2:

> Slow rate of fire, since the speed of an ATGM in flight is considerably less than that of conventional projectiles, as well as a comparatively small number of missiles carried on board, due to the fact that a missile is larger in size than an artillery shell.
>
> ATGMs have a single role – antitank; this is due to the fact that a considerable portion of the total weight (80-90 per cent) is taken up not by the warhead but by the systems which fly the ATGM to the target and control it in flight. For this reason, the missile carries only a shaped-charge warhead.
>
> Fire at inconspicuous targets (dug-in tank, ATGM, etc.) is not always effective, due to the possibility that the missile will strike the ground

> or emplacement parapet as a consequence of the fact that in flight an ATGM executes oscillatory movements with a certain vertical amplitude.
>
> The possibility of missile control disruption and loss during flight. This can occur because a guided missile requires that a line of sight be maintained between launcher and target. Shell bursts, smoke and dust on the battlefield can disrupt this line of sight.
>
> In addition, high cost (a Shillelagh ATGM, for example, costs 25 to 30 times as much as a 105 mm shell) and complexity of operation have had the result that ATGMs are at the present time not in widespread use on main battle tanks.

The downside was that the missile was not able to engage targets at less than 875 yards since its onboard guidance and control system could not acquire (locate and track) the missile's infrared emitter until it had reached a certain height in its flight path as the blast from the missile's launch obscured the optics' view of the target.

M551 Sheridan Tank

The US Army's plans called for the 152mm gun/missile system to the M41 Light Tank's replacement, the brand-new Armored Reconnaissance, Airborne Assault Vehicle (AR/AAV), XM551. The XM551 later received the official nickname of 'General Sheridan'. An article in the July–August issue of *Armor* magazine describes the Sheridan's missile in operation:

> The missile is unique in many ways. First, it is loaded like a normal round of tank gun ammunition. Second, the gunner engages a target just as he would when firing a conventional round. The gunner is simply required to keep the crosshair of his sight on the target, and the missile will fly to the point designated by the sight. On moving targets, the same procedure is followed, and the missile corrects its flight path to align itself with the gunner's crosshair as he follows his target; no lead is necessary.

To keep the four-man M551's weight down so that it could be both amphibious and air-deliverable, the M551 had an aluminium hull with a steel turret. It protected the tank only from heavy-calibre machine-gun fire and some artillery fragments; the tank's thickest armour was the gun shield at 32mm (1.3in).

The first production example of the approximately 16-ton M551 rolled out of the factory in 1966. Still, it did not enter US Army service until the following year due to unresolved design issues. A GAO report noted:

> Not one Sheridan as originally designed and produced was suitable for combat use without extensive retrofits ... and that hundreds of unissued tanks in depots that had passed the final military-civilian joint inspection were defective and not ready for deployment.

Into Action

Tests conducted in Panama showed the M551's electronics and caseless main gun rounds were not suitable for employment in damp and humid environments. Despite these findings, the US Army decided to ship some to South Vietnam between 1969 and 1970. It is hard to comprehend the reasoning behind that decision; the reason given was to impress Congress on its viability as an effective combat vehicle. That turned out to be a significant mistake.

Those M551s sent to South Vietnam had their anti-tank missiles and associated fire-control components removed. The enemy had not fielded any tanks in South Vietnam, and the US Army did not want to take the chance that the equipment might fall into the wrong hands.

As foretold, the M551 proved unreliable during its time in South Vietnam. It had severe issues involving both its mechanical and electrical systems, and its caseless combustible main gun ammunition swelled in the country's climate and made it both unusable and dangerous at the same time.

M551 crews during the Vietnam War lived in fear of their vehicles running over an enemy anti-tank mine or any large improvised explosive device (IED) because the M551's thin hull armour offered little or no protection. It typically resulted in a crewman's death and the vehicle's destruction, whereas the heavier M48 series would have survived. Eventually, add-on armour plates attached to the bottom hull were built and fielded.

US Army General Donn A. Starry wrote to a US Army colonel on 4 January 1980 regarding the fragile and dangerous threat posed by the M551's caseless main gun rounds:

> In my experience in Vietnam, while commanding the 11th Armored Cavalry Regiment, every Sheridan hit by an RPG [Rocket-Propelled Grenade] exploded and burned because the ammunition [rounds] broke up and detonated within fifteen seconds, destroying the vehicle and seriously injuring or killing the crew. In almost every case of a mine hit one or more rounds in the ready rack fractured, and in several, the detonation vented the hull and ignited the fractured cartridge cases.

Trying to Improve

Production of the M551 ended in 1970, with 1,662 examples of the four-man vehicle completed. With the addition of a laser rangefinder (LRF) in 1972 and other improvements, the vehicle became the M551A1. In 1977, the tank went through a Product Improvement Program (PIP).

Despite the PIP, problems persisted. These were of such an extent that in 1978 the US Army gave up on the vehicle and began pulling it from service. The only unit to retain them was a single battalion attached to the 82nd Airborne Division.

Those M551A1 tanks assigned to the airborne division came with new features. These included a British-designed smoke grenade-launcher, a Belgian-designed coaxial machine gun and a tank thermal sight (TTS); the tank then became the M551A1 (TTS) and remained in service until 1996.

Mock-Up Soviet Army Vehicles

In its final role, in 1981 330 M551A1 tanks went off to a US Army National Training Center (NTC) in the desert region of southern California. On arrival, they were modified in appearance with plastic and wood to vaguely resemble a variety of Soviet Army vehicles. In this guise, they were employed as training vehicles to replicate a Soviet Army Motorized Rifle Regiment against incoming US Army units for two-week training sessions. By 2004, the remaining number of M551A1s had outlived their service life and were finally pulled from service and scrapped.

> **M551 Impressions**
> Colonel (Retired) John D. Blumenson, Honorary Colonel of the 73rd Cavalry Regiment, recalls his impressions of the M551s under his command:
>
>> The M551 Sheridan was a great vehicle on which to serve, and I had the opportunity to do so in the 82nd Airborne Division. It was perhaps the most unique armored vehicle of the Cold War era as it was light, fast, heavily armed, lightly armored, could be transported by C-130 aircraft, dropped by air and swim.
>>
>> I told my drivers to drive it like a sports car. Because it was fast, nimble, and small for an armored vehicle, it could quickly maneuver between trees in ways that main battle tanks could not. Rolling across open fields, it could cruise at 25mph to 35mph and even faster on long downhills.
>>
>> Firing the main gun was a wild ride. The recoil of the 152mm main gun/launcher, which we referred to as the 'main gun', would lift the vehicle off the ground to its middle road wheel. Everyone had to hang on when the gunner announced, 'On the way'! An experienced gunner would keep his brow pressed against the gunner's periscope headrest to prevent getting a black eye from the recoil.
>>
>> When we would fire it during live-fire exercises, any ground troops lying prone to our flanks within about 15 meters would be bounced off the ground. And anyone standing on the back deck not hanging on to the bustle rack would likely be thrown off the vehicle, as happened to a friend of mine who was serving as a live-fire safety officer. We even once rigged a nice, cushioned spot for the Assistant Division Commander – Operations – in the bustle rack of my Sheridan to ride downrange with us on our Tank Table VII daylight pre-qualification run. When we returned from our run, I asked him how he enjoyed it. He replied with words to the effect that 'It will be a cold day in Hell before I do that again.'
>>
>> Serving in the 82nd Airborne Division provided us Airborne Tankers with ample opportunities to train with our habitually attached infantry

units, often conducting live-fire exercises. When firing the 152mm High-Explosive (HE) round, it looked like a mortar round impacting when it hit the target. We also fired High-Explosive Anti-Tank (HEAT) rounds, canister rounds (basically 152mm shotgun shells that contained thousands of razor-sharp dart-like flechettes), and the anti-tank Shillelagh missile.

We also conducted plenty of airborne operations. During my time in the division, our primary means of air deployment for the Sheridan was the Low-Altitude Parachute Extraction System known as a LAPES. Loaded onto a large aluminum 'sled' pallet and cushioned with lots of honey-combed cardboard, the LAPES was like dragster parachutes that would separate the rigged Sheridan from the back of a C-130 flying, ideally, a few feet above the landing zone. It usually worked. If dropped slightly, the impact could cause minor damage to the suspension or break loose items in the turret. If dropped above 15 feet, the sled pallet's forward edge could catch the ground and cause the vehicle to flip end-over-end, as happened on one exercise I was involved in. Needless to say, our paratroopers did not ride down with the vehicle!

M60A2 Tank

Fitted with a new specially-designed turret and armed with the 152mm Gun/Missile-Launcher, the M60A1 became the Tank, Combat, Fully Tracked: 152mm, Gun/Launcher M60A2. The 57-ton tank never received an official US Army assigned nickname. Unlike the early-production M60A1 tanks, it came with a two-axis stabilizer system. It also proved to be the first US Army tank fitted with a laser rangefinder (LRF).

The US Army saw the M60A2 only as an interim vehicle until the next generation Main Battle Tank-1970 (MBT-70) entered service. Due to countless design issues, never resolved, and the costs associated with fixing those problems, Congress killed the joint American-West German MBT-70 programme in 1969.

Production of the four-man M60A2 started in 1973 with the eventual goal of replacing all the US Army's M60A1 tanks. However, an endless stream of problems with the 152mm Gun/Launcher System and its combustible caseless ammunition, as had occurred with the M551, quickly soured the US Army on the tank.

A US Army officer wrote in the January–February 1975 issue of *Armor* magazine an article titled 'M60A2 in Perspective: A Message to the Armor Community' about the need to embrace the tank:

> The essence of my message is that the M60A2 is a good tank and it can be maintained. The purpose of this is simply to spark some degree of enthusiasm for and confidence in the tank. The attitude toward the tank of those who find themselves in an A2 unit is of key importance in the success of that unit in effective maintenance and operations.

Such was the disdain for the M60A2 before it even entered service, but crews seemed to have some skewed affection for the A2, referring to it as 'The Deuce' or the 'Starship'.

US Army General Donn A. Starry wrote to another US Army general on 9 March 1979: 'I know of no compelling logic to keep the A2 in our inventory. It is now a questionable target servicer, has always been a maintenance nightmare, and should be considered for removal as soon as possible.'

Only 540 examples of the M60A2 came out of the factory by 1974 before production was cancelled. Those that did enter service were pulled from Army use

> **The Elephant**
> Former US Army M60 series tanker Jerry Sodan, 3/64 Armor, 3rd Infantry Division, then stationed in West Germany, recalls an amusing moment:
>
>> In the spring of 1979, 3rd Battalion, 64th Armor was preparing for its annual visit from the Inspector General [IG]. Any of us old soldiers can easily remember the countless hours preparing for this visit. Everything, and I mean everything, had to be accounted for, expertly maintained, taken apart, polished, spit-shined, gone over with a fine-toothed comb, and then and only then reassembled. This applied from the individual soldier's socks, to weapons in the arms room, to the individual tanks in the motor pool. All this and still being ready to go to war if the balloon went up. Charlie Company was an enormously proud unit. We had exceptional officers, senior NCOs, tank commanders and troops.
>>
>> Part of the process in preparing for the IG was a Basic Issue Items (BII) layout and ammunition inspection by the battalion commander. Our motor pool was laid out in a herringbone design, the tank pads were arranged along the main axis with grassy areas between each tank pad. I commanded C-23, and my roommate commanded C-25. As I remember, the ammo inspection went very well on C-25. All the lead seals on the machine-gun ammo were in place and intact. The main gun ammo as well was in an excellent (go to war) state. The next thing to be inspected was the BII of C25. It went well until the battalion commander noticed a white plastic garden chain attached to the tie-down eye on the left side of C-25. It was about 10 feet long and went to this giant wooden stake which had been driven into the ground. The battalion commander had heard the stories of how 2nd Platoon was full of jokers and a few rather unhinged individuals. With a smile on his face, he faced the young sergeant tank commander and asked 'Sergeant XXXXX, what the hell is the stake and chain for?' Sergeant XXXXX glanced at the unit crest, which featured an elephant, on his own shoulder and stated 'Well ya see Sir, I've been in this circus for 39 months now and I'll be damned if that elephant is gunna get away from me now.' Needless to say, the battalion commander was impressed and stated, 'Good job sergeant.'

by 1982, with their specially-designed turrets going off to target ranges and the hulls converted for other roles, such as bridge-launchers.

An article titled 'American Tank Development During the Cold War: Maintaining the Edge or Just Getting By?' that appeared in the July–August 1998 issue of *Armor* magazine, by Dr Robert S. Cameron, the US Army Armor Branch historian, includes the following passage: 'The priority given to the Shillelagh's development also slowed work on conventional gun designs. When the gun/missile system failed, the Army found itself without an effective conventional substitute other than the M68 105mm gun.'

The British were able to see the T-54A when one presented itself to the Embassy in Budapest in 1956. The British realized that the frontal armour thickness on the Soviet Army's T-54A Medium Tank made it immune to the 20-pounder (83.4mm) main gun of the Centurion tank. This led to the vehicle's last up-gunning, beginning in 1959. They chose the British-designed and built 105mm L7 as seen on the Centurion Mk 13 tank pictured here. Infrared searchlights and infrared driving lights began appearing on the Centurion series in 1965. (*Public domain*)

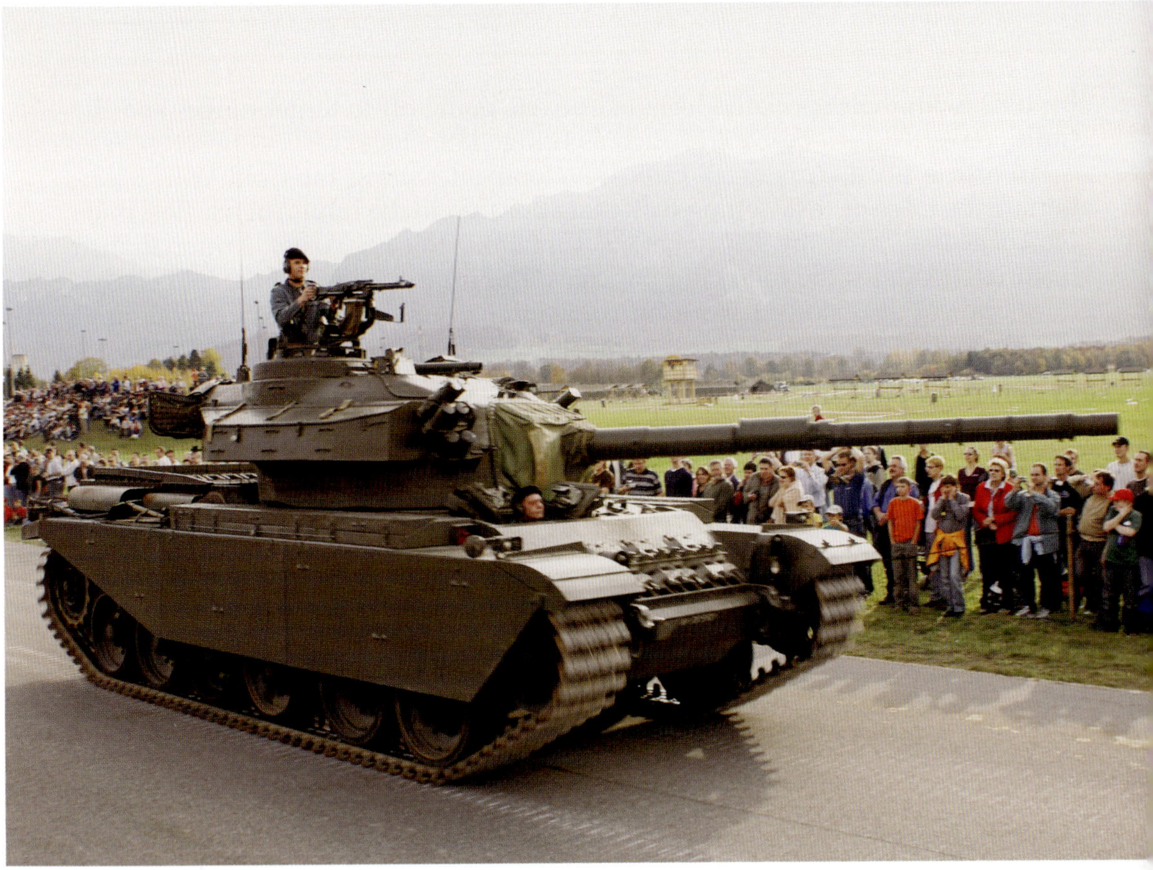

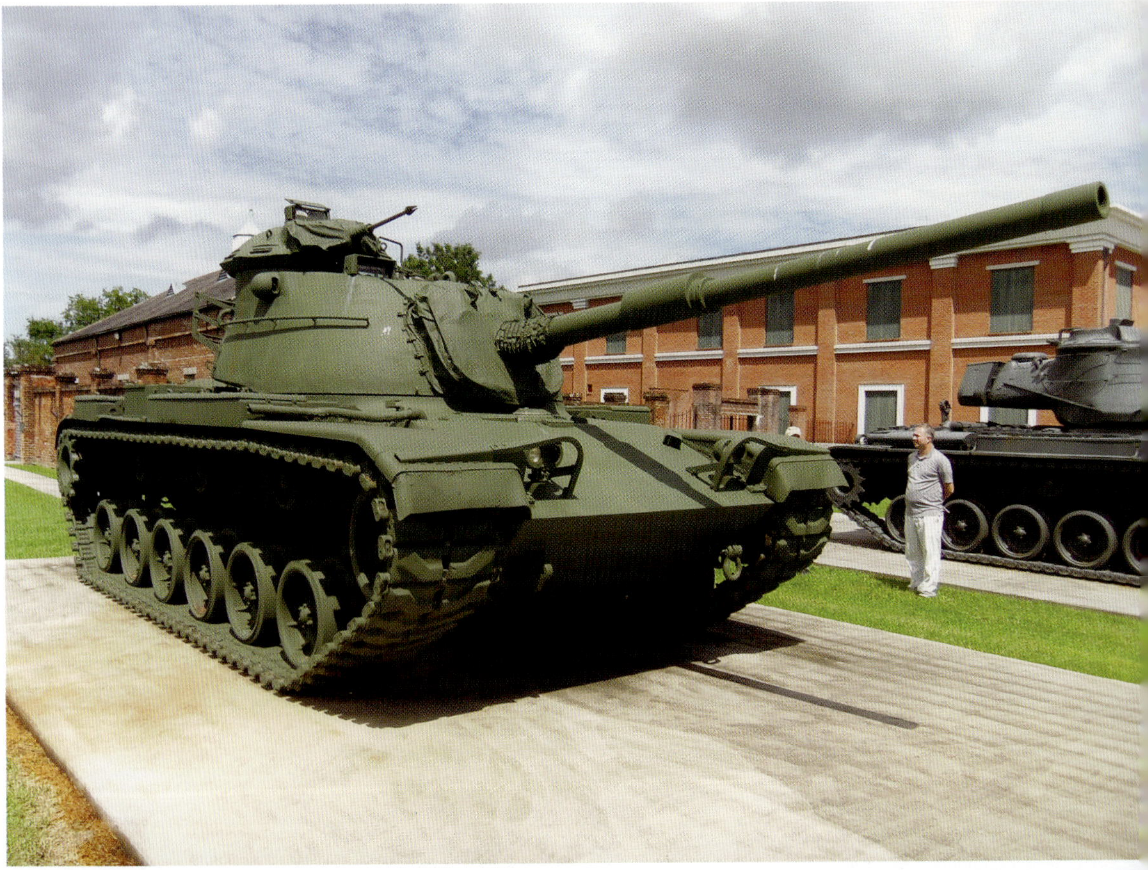

(**Opposite, above**) The Centurion was a popular tank among both NATO and non-NATO armies, and is typified by the 105mm gun-armed Centurion pictured here. Centurions in British Army service numbered thirteen progressively improved models, from the Mk 1 through to the Mk 13. The first British Army Centurion to feature the 105mm L7 main gun was the Mk 5/2. The last new-built Centurion was the Mk 7. The Mk 6, 9, 11, 12 and 13 were all reworked examples of earlier-production models. (*Public domain*)

(**Above**) This upgraded Dutch Army Centurion Mk 5/2 is armed with a 105mm L7 main gun and is riding on steel tracks fitted with rubber pads. This was in contrast to most users, including the British Army, which used all-steel tracks. The Dutch Army acquired approximately 1,000 early-production Centurions in the 1950s, with American assistance. Some 362 went on to be eventually upgraded with the 105mm L7 main gun. (*Public domain*)

(**Opposite, below**) The US Army began consideration of a replacement for the M48A2 in the early 1950s. A novel vehicle, the T-95 tank seemed to hold a lot of promise. Unfortunately, it proved to be a technology dead end. In its place, the US Army decided to go with a modified M48A2 featuring a diesel-powered engine and the new British-designed 105mm L7 gun. That tank became the M60 seen here with a rounded turret like that of its predecessor. (*Pierre-Olivier Buan*)

Production of the M60 began in 1959. Even before the first production example of the M60 rolled off the factory floor, the US Army had tasked industry with a more elongated turret seen here that increased the turret's front ballistic protection level. The turret also proved roomier than the original turret design. In this configuration, the tank became the M60A1. (*TACOM*)

From a US Army gunnery manual, a ghosted illustration shows the crew's position on the M60 and the M60A1. Going back to the Second World War M4 series of medium tanks, the vehicle commander and gunner (sitting in front of and below the vehicle commander) reside on the main gun breech's right-hand side. The loader is to the left of the breech, typical of Cold War NATO tanks. (*US Army*)

The M68 is a modified licence-built version of the British-designed and built 105mm L7 gun. This picture shows the breech end of the American-built 105mm main gun (designated the M68) located in the turret of an M60A1. From the breech's rear face to the muzzle, the M68 is a little over 18ft long. Like all previous American-designed and built Cold War medium tanks, the breechblock was semi-automatic with a vertical sliding wedge. *(Hans Halberstadt)*

An M60A1 is shown here preparing to board a West German ferry during a training exercise. The vehicle commander on the M60A1 had a 10-power coincidence type rangefinder for sighting targets and acquiring their range. The gunner had a periscope sight that contained both daylight and infrared sights. As a back-up, the gunner also had an articulated telescope fitted to the gun's right side. *(US Army)*

A Training Practice, Discarding Sabot (APDS) round is shown here. Blue denotes a training round. The combat version of the complete round weighed about 40lb and the projectile portion around 13lb. The cartridge case is aluminium. Between the hull and the rear turret bustle the M60A1 had stowage for sixty-three main gun rounds, three more than the original M60 model. (*DOD*)

(**Opposite, above**) Looking into the front hull of an M60A1 with its turret removed, the main gun round stowage arrangement on either side of the driver's position can be seen. The T-bar tiller replaced the M47 driver control lever (wobble stick) and the M48 series squared-off steering wheel. For the M48 and M60 series (with the transmission in neutral), full deflection of the steering wheel/T-bar tiller allowed the tank to pivot in place, with its tracks moving in opposite directions. (*Dreamstime*)

(**Opposite, below**) The shock-mounted radio rack in an M60A1 turret bustle is visible in this photograph. Directly below it are two stowage containers for 105mm main gun rounds. The standard VHF-FM tactical vehicular combat net radio in the M60A1 formed part of the AN/VRC-12 series and depended on transistor technology. The radio set had a maximum range of between 25 and 30 miles. In the early 1990s, the US Army began replacing its transistor radios with digital radios. (*Hans Halberstadt*)

MAIN PWR
INT ACCENT
RADIO TRANS
CDR + CREW
CDR ONLY
LISTENING SILENCE
POWER CKT BKR
INT ONLY
OTHER
RETRANS
INSTALLATIO SWITCH
POWER
ANT
BAND
CALL
SQUELCH
VOLUME

(**Above**) An M60A1 during a NATO training exercise in West Germany. Located in front of the tank's gun shields is the AN/VSS-1 Xenon searchlight. It provided both white and infrared illumination. Besides main gun rounds, the M60A1 also carried 900 rounds of .50 calibre machine-gun ammunition for the vehicle commander's cupola and 5,950 rounds for the tank's 7.62mm coaxial machine gun. If forced to dismount in combat, the crew had eight hand grenades and a single .45 calibre submachine gun. (*DOD*)

(**Opposite, above**) The US Marine Corps expressed interest in re-equipping its inventory of M60A1 tanks with explosive reactive armour (ERA) in 1986. For whatever reasons, it soon lost interest and reduced its order to only a battalion's worth (fifty-four tanks) in 1989. Pictured here is a Marine Corps' M60A1 with ERA during a training exercise. The first-generation ERA adopted by the Marines offered protection against shaped-charge warheads but not kinetic energy rounds. (*DOD*)

(**Opposite, below**) The ERA kit for the Marine Corps' M60A1 consisted of ninety-one tiles: forty-nine M1 tiles and forty-two M2 tiles. They were attached to the tank's hull with mounting hardware employing retaining clips and machine bolts. The M1 tiles were 11.5in by 11.5in. The M2 tiles came in at 11.5in by 17.5in. Both the M1 and M2 had a thickness of 2in. Some of the tow cables and other external features of the M60A1 had to be relocated to make room for the tiles. (*DOD*)

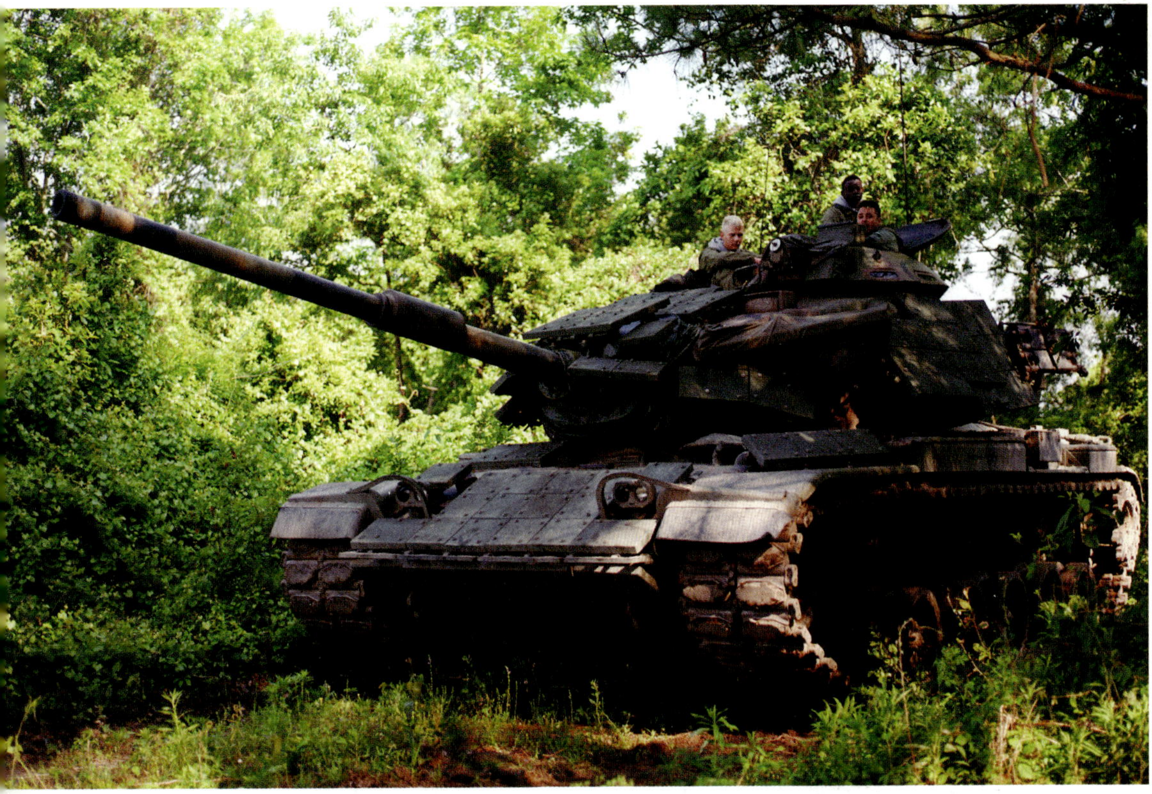

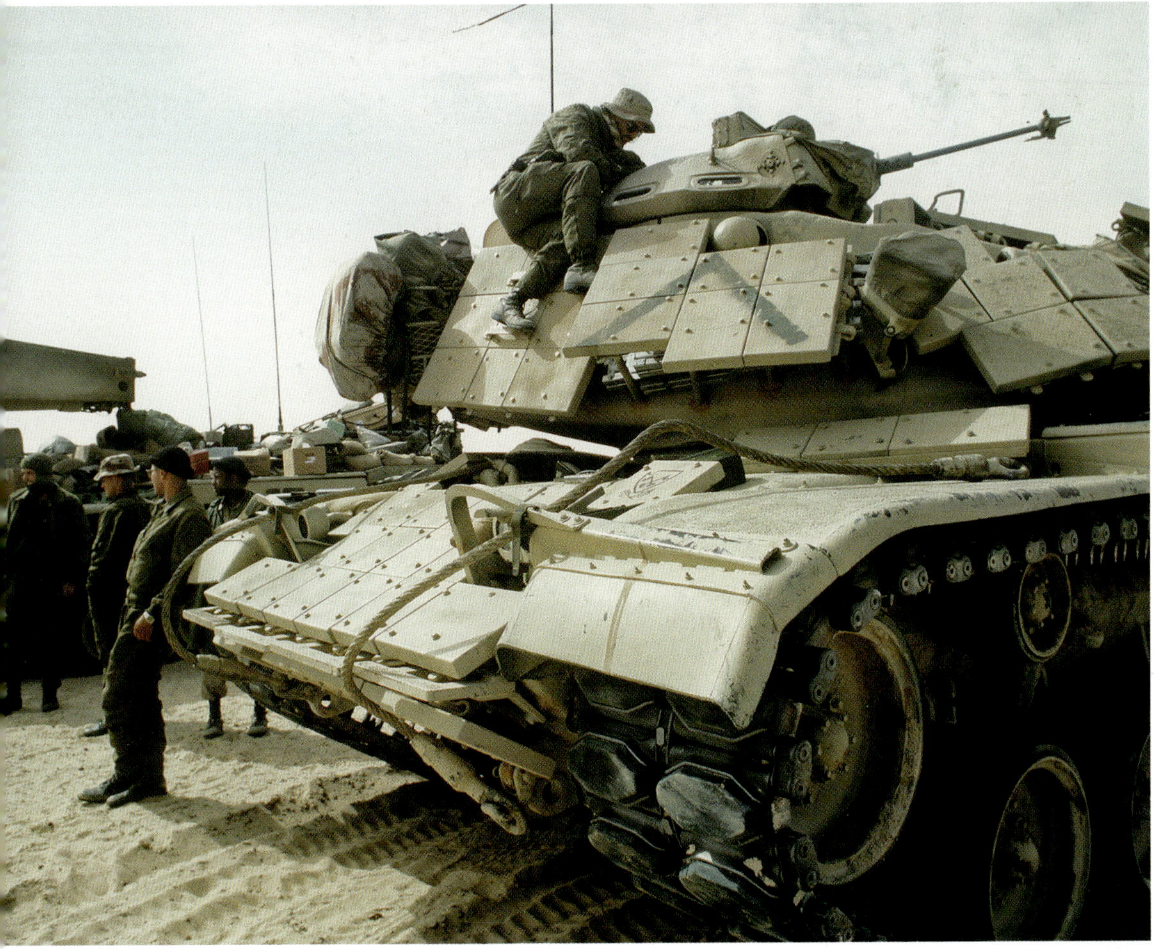

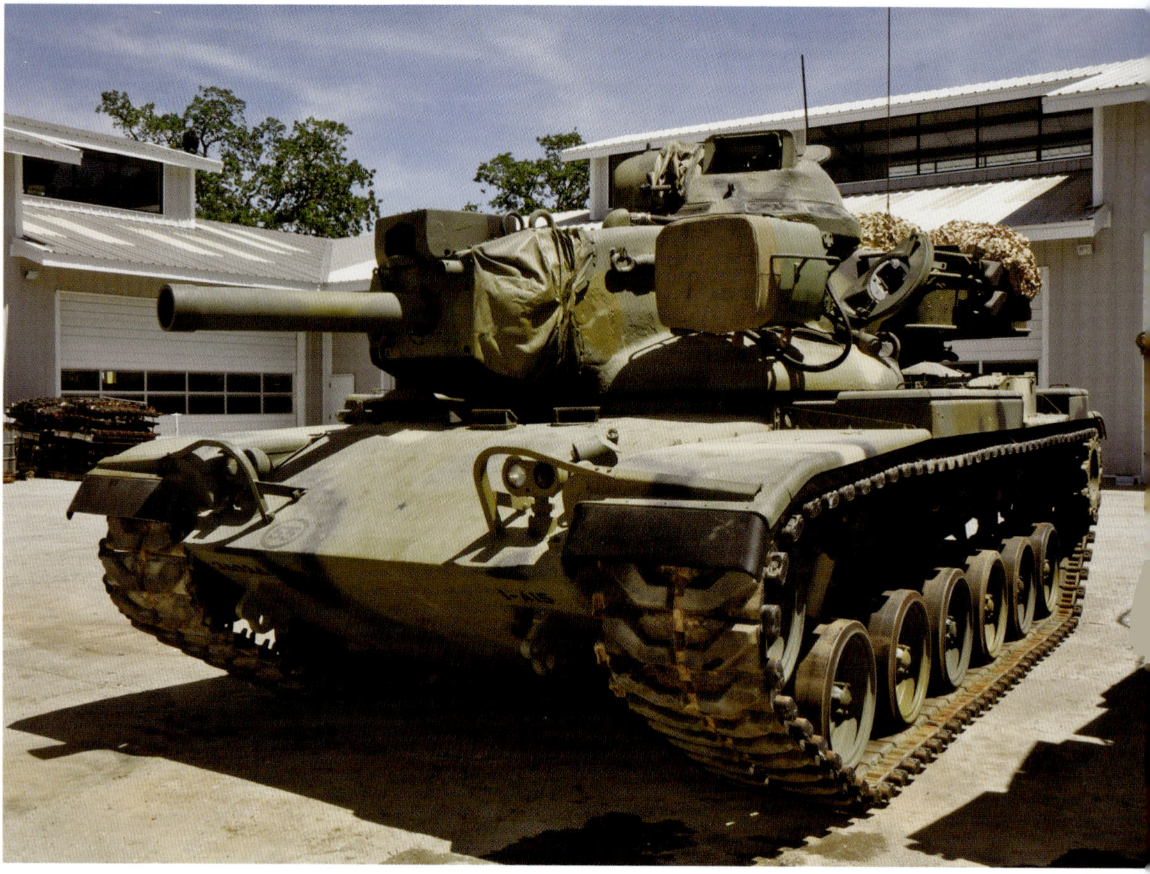

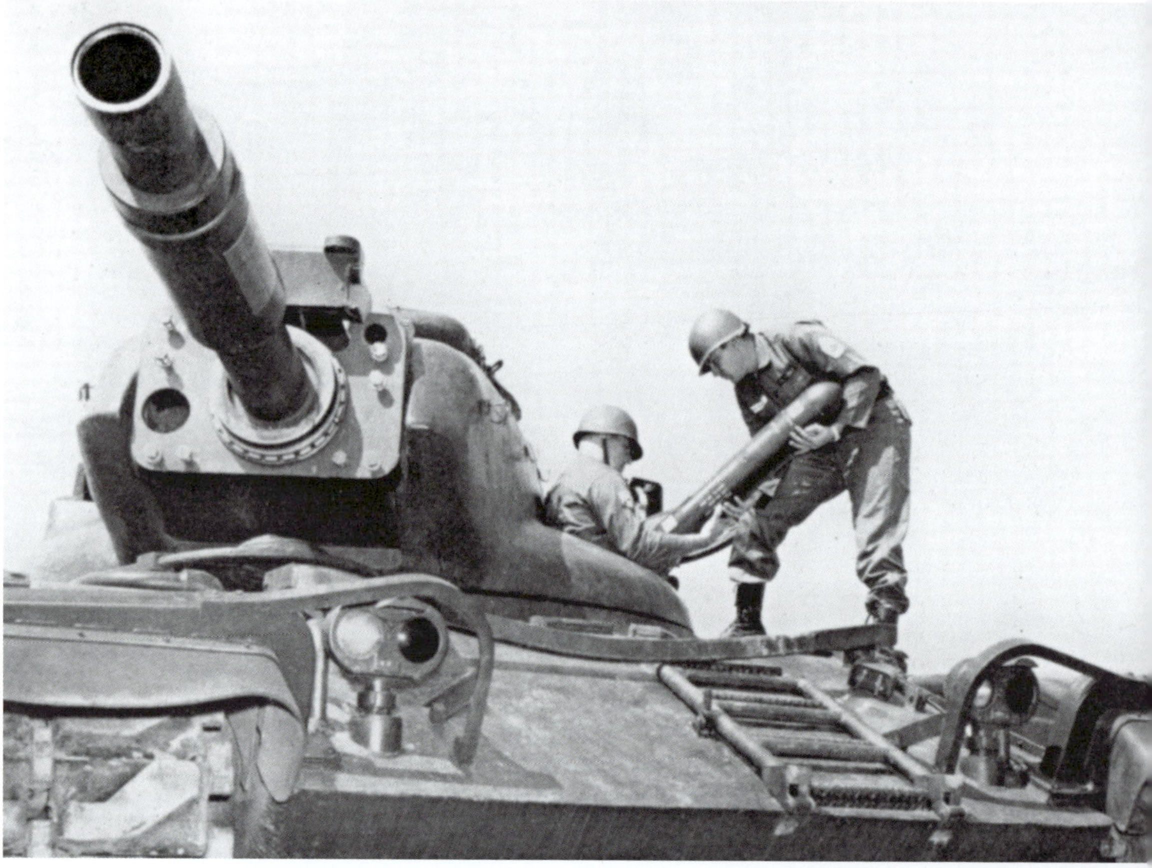

Ammunition Stowage Diagram Labels:

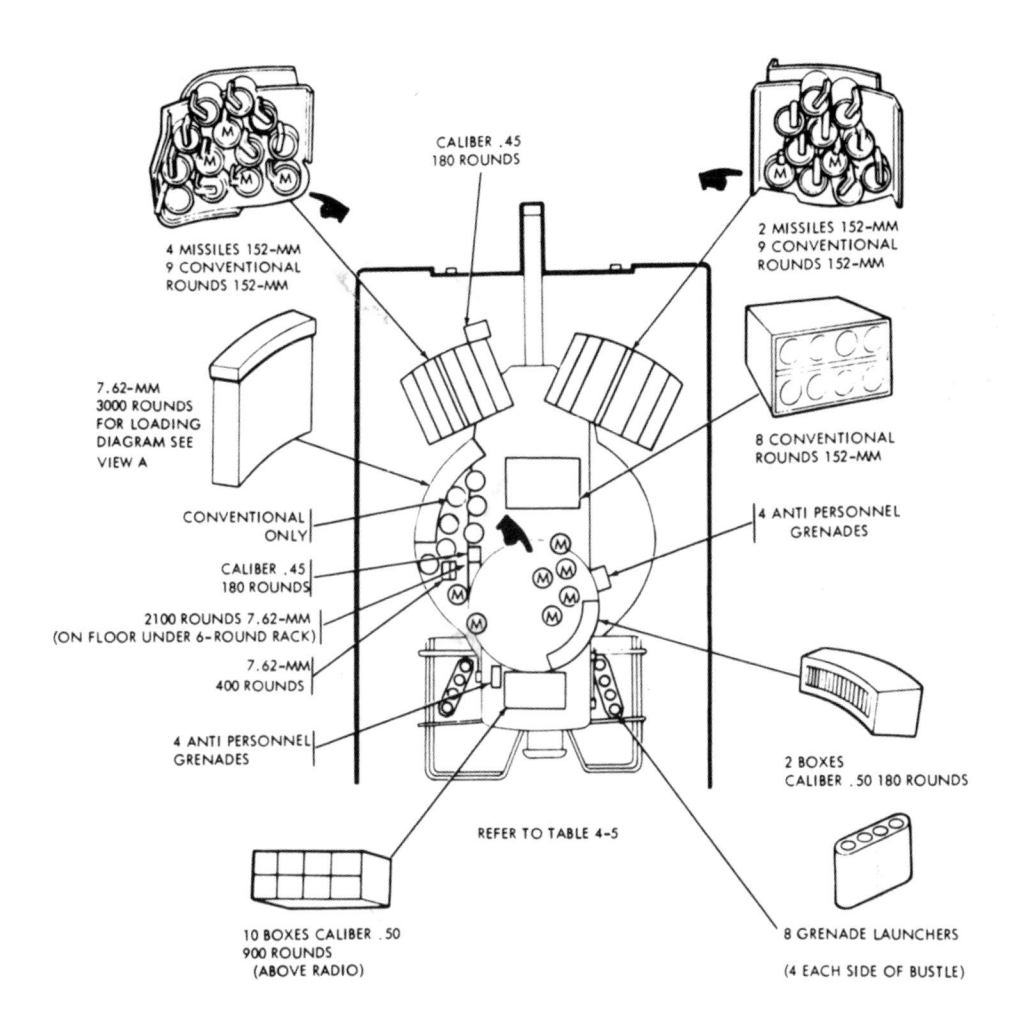

- CALIBER .45 180 ROUNDS
- 4 MISSILES 152-MM / 9 CONVENTIONAL ROUNDS 152-MM
- 2 MISSILES 152-MM / 9 CONVENTIONAL ROUNDS 152-MM
- 7.62-MM 3000 ROUNDS FOR LOADING DIAGRAM SEE VIEW A
- 8 CONVENTIONAL ROUNDS 152-MM
- CONVENTIONAL ONLY
- CALIBER .45 180 ROUNDS
- 2100 ROUNDS 7.62-MM (ON FLOOR UNDER 6-ROUND RACK)
- 7.62-MM 400 ROUNDS
- 4 ANTI PERSONNEL GRENADES
- 4 ANTI PERSONNEL GRENADES
- 2 BOXES CALIBER .50 180 ROUNDS
- REFER TO TABLE 4-5
- 10 BOXES CALIBER .50 900 ROUNDS (ABOVE RADIO)
- 8 GRENADE LAUNCHERS (4 EACH SIDE OF BUSTLE)

(**Opposite, above**) A 1958 study panel recommended that the US Army should field a tank capable of firing a long-range anti-tank missile and conventional rounds. This led to the fielding of the M60A2 tank (pictured in 1974, seven years after the US Army first standardized the vehicle). The delay in fielding the tank was caused by design issues centred around its 152mm gun/missile-launcher system designated the M162. (*Chris Hughes*)

(**Opposite, below**) The crew of an M60A2 is shown here loading a Shillelagh anti-tank missile into their tank. The gunner sat on the right side of the 152mm gun/missile-launcher and the loader on the opposite side. The vehicle commander sat behind and just above the weapon's breech at the rear of the turret. He had excellent visibility from his .50 calibre machine-gun-armed rotating cupola. The M60A2 depended on a large, unprotected infrared/white searchlight fitted to the turret's left-hand side. (*Patton Museum*)

(**Above**) From a US Army manual, the ammunition stowage arrangement of the M60A2. Stowage was available for seven Shillelagh anti-tank missiles and fifteen conventional 152mm main gun rounds in the M60A2 turret. In the hull, there was stowage for eighteen conventional main gun rounds and six missiles. For the vehicle commander's machine gun, the M60A2 carried 1,080 .50 calibre rounds. The coaxial 7.62mm machine gun had 5,500 rounds stowed. (*US Army*)

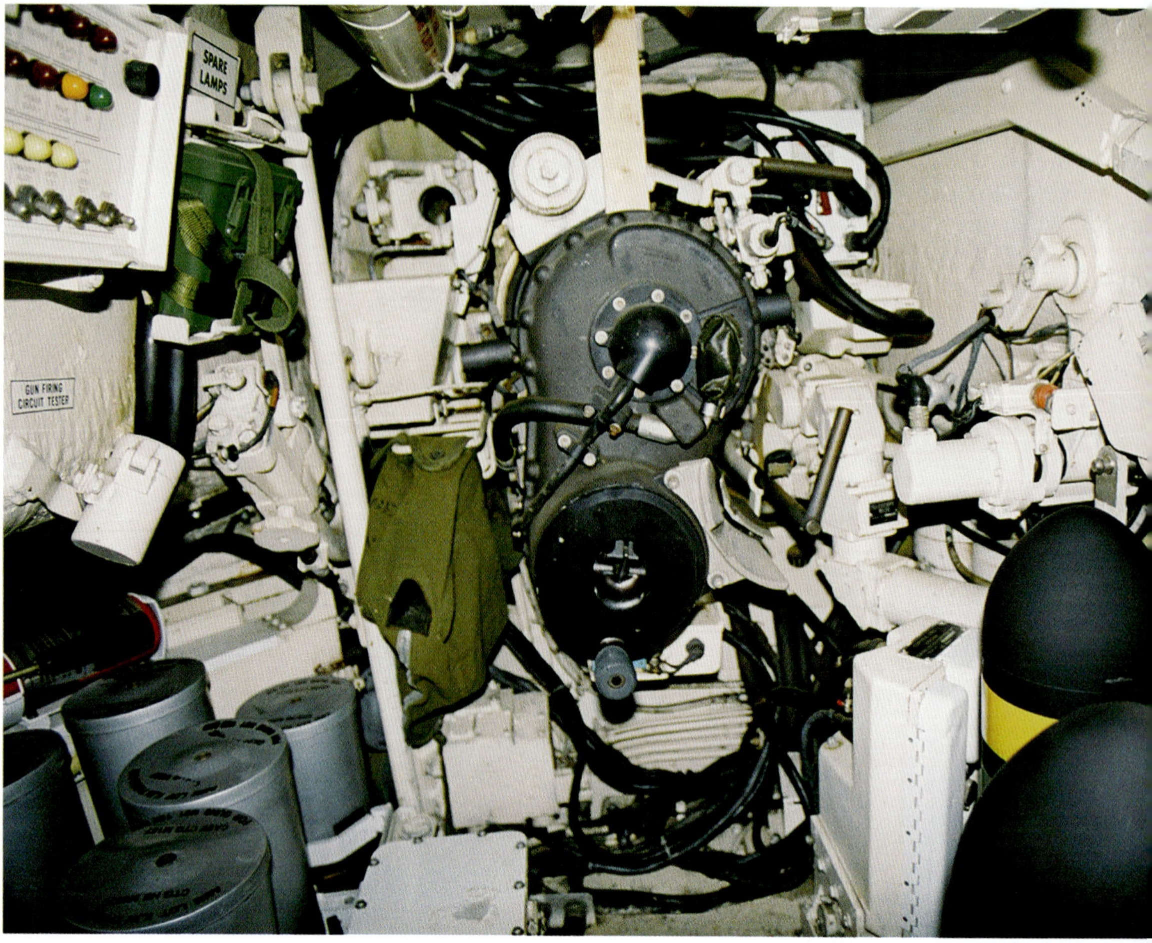
SPARE LAMPS
GUN FIRING CIRCUIT TESTER

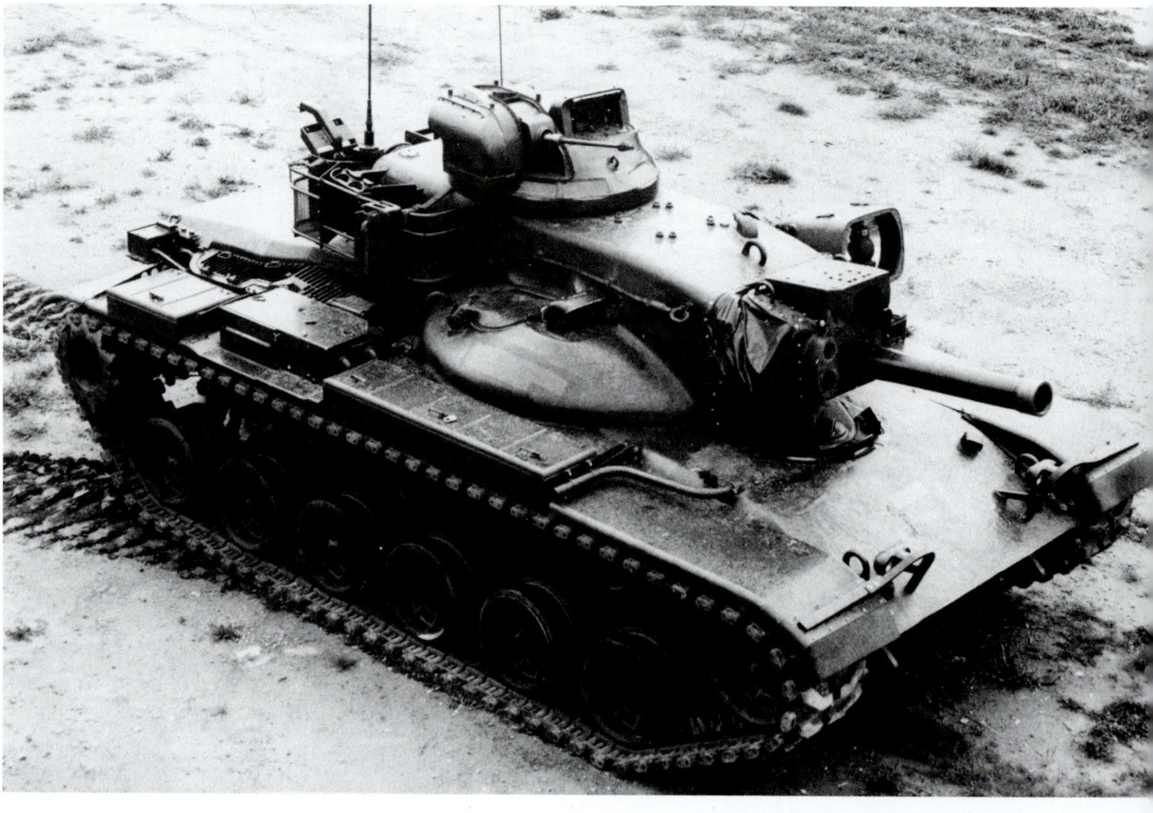

(**Opposite, above**) Looking forward from the vehicle commander's position in an M60A2, the breech of the semi-automatic separable chamber, electrically-operated 152mm gun/missile-launcher appears. The Shillelagh missiles came with an infrared tracking and command system and weighed about 61lb. The caseless conventional 152mm rounds, which included a HEAT, HE and canister, weighed between 40lb and 50lb. (*Chris Hughes*)

(**Opposite, below**) The early-production examples of the M60A2 came with a bore evacuator, dispensed with on later-production vehicles as seen here. In place of the bore evacuator, the M60A2s appeared with a Closed Breech Scavenging System (CBSS). The 152mm caseless ammunition tended to leave a smouldering residue in the barrel upon firing that caused breathing problems for the turret crew when it opened. The CBSS fired compressed air down the barrel before the breech opened. (*TACOM*)

(**Above**) The frontal profile of the M60A2 turret provided a small target for enemy tanks. The downside was that its narrow width did not allow for the inclusion of an optical rangefinder. Another issue was the tank's limited night-fighting ability. The Shillelagh anti-tank missile in its original configuration had a maximum range of approximately 2,000 yards. The tank's image intensifier had a range of only 656 yards and the Xenon searchlight 1,094 yards. (*Pierre-Olivier Buan*)

As the replacement for the M41 light tank, the US Army ordered in 1960 what they referred to as the Armored Reconnaissance, Airborne Assault Vehicle (AR/AAV). It also became the Tank, Combat, Full Tracked, 152mm Gun/Launcher XM551. An example appears here during early trials. It was officially assigned the nickname of 'General Sheridan'. (*Patton Museum*)

Pictured is the night launch of a Shillelagh missile. The missile had a muzzle velocity of 260 feet per second upon firing. When the missile's rocket booster ignited at a preset distance, muzzle velocity rose to around 1,060 feet per second. The rear end cap of the missile remained in the weapon's breech until being ejected when it opened after firing. The missile flew a line-of-sight path employing an infrared (IR) tracking and command system. (*Patton Museum*)

A view of the flotation screen erected on a production M551. The armoured aluminium hull sides of the M551 had lightweight flotation cells containing polystyrene foam to aid the vehicle's buoyancy. Once in the water, the vehicle's tracks propelled the tank at a maximum speed of 3.6mph in calm inland waterways. There were two bilge pumps, one in the crew compartment and the other in the engine compartment. (*Patton Museum*)

Early in its development, the US Army saw the M551's ability to fire the long-range Shillelagh anti-tank missile as its key selling-point. It overcame the biggest problem with previous light tanks. Due to their weight and inability to absorb a lot of recoil, they could not mount a large enough main gun to deal with enemy medium tanks. Rather than the electric-hydraulic turret traverse system of the M60 series, the M551 series had an all-electric turret traverse system. (*Dreamstime*)

(**Above**) The vehicle commander's cupola on the M551 had ten vision blocks and a pintle for the mounting of a .50 calibre machine gun. To improve protection for the vehicle commander when operating the .50 calibre machine gun, an open-topped armour box appeared during the Vietnam War. Some nicknamed it the 'Chicken Plate'. It remained in use until the vehicle left front-line service. The .50 calibre machine gun shown here is fitted with a starlight scope. (*Hans Halberstadt*)

(**Opposite, above**) Besides the Shillelagh anti-tank missile, the M551A1 shown here could also fire conventional 152mm rounds. Unlike the recoilless firing of the anti-tank missiles, the firing of the large-calibre conventional rounds lifted the front of the tank a foot and a half off the ground and threw the crew around the vehicle's interior. The shock also tended to disrupt the tank's fragile electrical system and sometimes ruptured the weapons' recoil system. (*Dreamstime*)

(**Below**) Unable to resolve the M551's numerous design issues with the tank's 152mm gun/missile-launcher, the US Army threw up its hands and eventually pulled most of its fleet of M551s from service by 1980. A battalion of the upgraded vehicle designated the M551A1 TTS remained in service a while longer with the 82nd Airborne Division as shown here. The vehicle had stowage space for nine missiles and twenty rounds of conventional 152mm ammunition. *(DOD)*

An M551 series tank before being loaded into an aircraft. Dragging an M551 out of an aircraft fuselage for a low-velocity air-drop (LVAD) required two modified 28ft-diameter cargo parachutes. Once ejected from the rear of the fuselage, the tank needed eight large 100ft-diameter parachutes to descend. To cushion the vehicle when impacting the ground, stacks of crushable aluminium honeycomb material lined the bottom of the platform upon which the tank sat when it landed. (DOD)

About 300 M551 series tanks went off for modification as Opposing Forces (OPFOR) vehicles. Before arriving at the National Training Center (NTC) located at Fort Irwin, California, all the 152mm gun/missile-launchers came off the M551s. Pictured here is a disarmed M551 at the NTC intended to resemble a Soviet Army BMP-1, including the Sagger anti-tank missile above the gun shield. (US Army)

Chapter Five

Keeping Up

The appearance of the M60A1 tank proved an unpleasant surprise to the Soviet Army, as the M60A1's 105mm main gun could easily penetrate the thickest armour on T-54/T-55 tanks. Even worse, the M60A1's thick frontal armour made it immune to the T-54/T-55 series' tank-killing rounds.

In response, Soviet industry began producing the 115mm main gun-armed T-62 medium tank in July 1962. The tank weighed approximately 40 tons. Its thickest armour was the gun shield/front of turret, topping out at 230mm (9in), with the tank's 60-degree sloped glacis coming in at 100mm (4in).

Like the M60, the four-man T-62 was not a brand-new tank, but rather an evolutionary development of what went before. Both the US and Soviet armies saw their respective tanks as interim vehicles, awaiting new state-of-the-art tanks that would offer a big leap forward in battlefield capabilities.

The T-62 rode on the lengthened version of the T55's diesel-engine-powered chassis, with a newly-designed turret. The T-62's most critical new design feature was that its 115mm main gun was not rifled but a smoothbore able to fire a new APFSDS at very high velocity. The US Army did not field an APFSDS round until the 1970s, eight years later.

A passage on the 115mm main gun's APFSDS round appears in a 1977 US Army manual:

> This round travels one mile every second. Its accuracy gives the T-62 tank crews a better than 50/50 chance of hitting a fully-exposed, frontal, stationary tank in the open with the first round at ranges to 1,800 meters [1,968 yards], or a moving target traveling in the open at constant speed at ranges to 1,000 meters [1,094 yards].

US Army 1977 Gunnery Manual Warning

About the enemy, two things are certain:

1. His equipment is good, and in spite of some differences in sophistication and quality, probably as good as ours.
2. He will outnumber us; he believes in using masses of men and equipment to overwhelm his foes.

Winning the first battle or battles of the next war is essential.

In order to win, US tank crews must outmaneuver the enemy and outshoot him at least 5 to 1.

During the 1973 Yom Kippur War, the APFSDS round fired by the Egyptians' T-62 tanks demonstrated that it could penetrate the frontal armour of the M60A1 at normal combat ranges. The M60A1 APDS rounds could also do the same to the T-62 at normal combat ranges.

Other rounds fired by the T-62's 115mm main gun included HE-Frag and HEAT. Like the T-55's gunner, the T-62 gunner had a stadiametric rangefinder in his optical sight, as well as an infrared (IR) sighting system.

In an article in the 1976 November–December issue of *AFV-G2 Magazine* titled 'Modern Soviet Medium Tanks: An Appraisal, Part 2', the magazine's editor James G. Steuard explained the advantages and disadvantages of smoothbore tank guns:

> By using a smoothbore gun tube, a much higher muzzle velocity is achieved; this high velocity provides a very flat trajectory and a very short time of flight for the projectile. On the other hand, a smoothbore weapon cannot have the same accuracy as a rifled weapon over the entire range, as at slower velocities, wind becomes a factor; this means that the Soviet 115mm gun is limited in effective range but that its flat trajectory and high velocity give it an outstanding performance at shorter ranges (estimated at under 1,500 meters [1,640 yards]).

What Steuard didn't mention was that smoothbore tank main guns are less costly to build. Also muzzle velocities of the projectiles fired are higher because they do not waste energy due to the friction of rotating bands engaging the rifling grooves in a rifled barrel, and save the energy required to spin the projectile.

Vehicle Details

The T-62 had onboard stowage space for forty main gun rounds. Spent steel cartridge cases were expelled from the turret by an automatic ejection system

---

Muzzle Velocity

Higher muzzle velocities offer some advantages to increase a tank gun's lethality. Muzzle velocity itself is the speed at which a projectile exits the gun's bore. As projectiles encounter such external factors as gravity and crosswinds which degrade accuracy, higher muzzle velocity results in shorter flight time and increased probability of obtaining a hit.

Higher muzzle velocity also reduces the requirement for precise range estimation and simplifies a tank gunner's lead estimation problems when engaging moving targets. It makes possible a much flatter trajectory (flight path) for projectiles, so that there's less 'drop' as the projectile loses energy/ speed; the gun doesn't need to account for a significant drop. A post-war US Army report stated: 'Experience has shown that the ability to get a hit with the first round is often the decisive factor and that flat trajectory is necessary if this is to be accomplished.'

through a port in the turret rear. An electrically-powered servomotor opened the port when actuated by the gun's recoil, and automatically closed it when the turret's steel cartridge case had been ejected.

A declassified Defense Intelligence Agency report titled 'Soviet Tank Company', dated May 1976, identified some issues with the T-62 tank, which also applied to the T-54/T-55 series:

> The layout of the T-62 also has some basic disadvantages. Due to the extremely compact nature of the tank, interior space is limited. The fuel tanks, engine and ammunition are in close proximity. Auxiliary fuel tanks are on the tank's decks and have no armor protection. Although the flashpoint of diesel fuel is high, it cannot withstand a direct hit. Fuel tank positions increase the possibility of an ammunition fire.

As the T-62 cost more than a T-55 tank, it supplemented but did not replace them. The T-62's price also seemed to discourage any Warsaw Pact armies from adopting it. They probably decided to await the next generation of more modern Soviet Army tanks rather than invest their industrial resources in an interim tank.

As Soviet Army leadership believed that a Third World War in Western Europe would include tactical nuclear weapons, the T-62 had many features for functioning in a contaminated environment. These are called out in a passage of Captain John K. Boles III's June 1978 thesis titled 'Soviet Armored Doctrine':

> This Soviet tank [T-62] has been developed specifically to operate on the nuclear battlefield, with minimum cross-section, radiation protection furnished by lead and plastic liners, special ventilation systems, automatic control systems to seal the tank from blast effects and also monitors to activate the ventilation systems. One of these systems, the radiological alarm system, automatically shuts off the engine upon encountering a radiologically contaminated area. This action serves as an immediate warning to the crew to put on their individual CBR protective equipment before proceeding.

As with most Soviet Army Cold War tanks, the T-62 went through a series of progressive upgrades during its career, including eventual fitting of a laser rangefinder (LRF). The vehicle's weight in its final configuration rose to about 45 tons. Maximum speed on level roads topped out at about 30mph.

T-62 production ended in 1978, with approximately 19,000 examples having come down the assembly lines. Many went to countries falling within the Soviet Union's political orbit, with the largest number going to the Egyptian and Syrian armies.

In the September 1987 issue of *National Defense Magazine* there appeared an article titled 'Soviet Tanks: An Israeli View' by an Israeli Army officer, in which he cited his army's ordnance experts' impressions of captured T-62 tanks:

> Human engineering of the T-62 proved even worse than in the T-55. The fighting compartment was even more cramped due to the lower deck, and

the egg-shaped turret, flattened by some centimeters than the T-55's, leaving less headroom for the crew ... The gun's exhaust fumes are overwhelming, and the fighting compartment soon fills with carbon monoxide, despite the bore evacuator designed to remove fumes.

Retired US Army officer Ted Dannemiller recalls the appearance of the T-62:

The arrival of the 115mm gun and the T-62 in the early '60s might have started an arms race, but by the mid-70s it was passé. We'd overcome our night-fighting deficiencies with searchlights and then passive thermal imaging. Upgrades to 105mm ammunition for the M68 and L7 (US and British respectively) rifled guns restored parity to the battlefield relatively early. The size of the T-62 made it hard to see or hit if the crew wasn't disciplined, but our defensive postures and use of terrain gave us an advantage.

State-of-the-Art Tank

The Soviet Army replaced the IS-3 and T-10 heavy tanks with the evolutionary T-62. To supplement but not replace the T-62, Soviet industry came up with a revolutionary new tank, the T-64. It was designed from the ground up to incorporate the latest in-tank technology. It was on paper better-armed, better-protected, lighter and faster than some of its front-line NATO counterparts.

A 1980 declassified CIA report, 'US Intelligence and Soviet Armor' by US Army Major General Paul F. Gorman, is an interesting look at how the Soviet Army managed to come up with such innovative tanks as the T-64:

It is not that Soviet armor designers have access to technologies beyond the reach of their US counterparts. The United States could have fielded superior, or at least comparable, armored vehicles. To the degree that the Soviets today enjoy a technological advantage in their deployed, high-quality armor systems, that edge proceeds from compressed development cycles in close sequence, plus their willingness to put a partially developed vehicle into production and into operational units, allowing the vehicle to mature in use via product improvements. Thus, the gap between US and Soviet armor forces is less a function of advanced Soviet technology than a resolute, relentless matériel-acquisition process.

Not surprisingly, as a result of pushing the technology envelope, there were glitches with almost every aspect of the T-64's design. Experimental examples of the original T-64 armed with a 115mm main gun appeared for testing in the early 1960s. It took until late 1967 before production examples entered Soviet Army service.

During its service career, the T-64 was progressively improved. This resulted in different model designations, including the T-64A and T-64B and their sub-variants. The T-64A had a new 125mm main gun, as did the subsequent T-64B, based on the design of the previous 115mm main gun.

The T-64A first appeared in Soviet Army units based in East Germany in 1976. The T-64B began entering service in 1976 and appeared in East Germany in 1981. Eventually, most early-production T-64s and T-64As went through a reworking process to bring them up to the T-64B standard.

T-64 series production concluded in 1987, and estimates place the number built at approximately 12,000 examples. These included 600 of the original T-64, 5,000 of the T-64A and the remainder consisting of the T-64B. None ever served with any Warsaw Pact armies or were exported. Whereas the T-62 was usually in the modified table of organization and equipment (MTO&E) for motorized rifle divisions (MRD), the T-64 was for the organic tank divisions.

T-64 Details

The T-64's crew consisted of only three men due to the introduction of an automatic loader. The T-64 and the T-64A had a coincidence rangefinder, replaced with an LRF in the T-64B. The original T-64 weighed 40 tons. Reflecting the armour upgrades of the T-64B, its weight was 43 tons.

From a December 1984 declassified CIA report titled 'Soviet Tank Programs' is the following description of the T-64A's fire-control system:

> The gun is aimed using a partially automated, coincidence rangefinder gunsight that enables accurate range determination out to 4,000 meters [2.5 miles] – an improvement of several hundred meters [700m/765 yards] over the T-62's aiming provisions. The fire-control system is partially automated in that the rangefinder feeds data directly into a ballistic computer, which in turn shifts an aiming mark in the eyepiece to show the gunner the

---

Autoloader Advantages

In the November–December 1984 issue of *Armor* magazine, there is an article titled 'The Automatic Loader Gap' in which appears this passage:

> The advantages of an automatic loader versus the human loader begin with the physical and mental vulnerabilities of men in combat. Sustained 24-hour operations under extremes of temperature and climate have less of an effect on a machine than a human. This becomes even more significant when one considers the movement to large-caliber weapons and the probability of multiple engagements. The human loader is now in a situation where he has to move a heavier shell in a more confined space in less time than before. It is doubtful that under NBC conditions and in MOPP gear, that these tasks can be performed for any sustained period at all. Substitution of powered mechanisms for human strength and speed will maintain, if not increase, the rate of fire for the system, with the rate of fire factor often equating to an improvement in lethality. It becomes clear that the automatic loader is imperative for future battlefield conditions where friendly systems may well be outnumbered 4-to-1.

correct elevation of the gun for accurate fire. (Editor's note: as opposed to previous stadiametric rangefinders.) The gunner uses hand-operated power controls to move the gun to the firing position. As the tank approaches a fixed target, the computer can continually adjust the aiming mark to remind the gunner to compensate for the decreasing range.

The T-64 series had an NBC suite, radiation liners and a two-axis electro-hydraulic turret stabilization system. It also included an IR night-fighting system, as did the T-62 series.

It was at a disadvantage compared to the superior passive night-fighting sights on some of its then in-service NATO counterparts. Passive night-sights were far more capable than the existing IR night-sights. A significant advantage was that they required only ambient light from the moon and stars to function. Therefore, they did not reveal their location, in sharp contrast to IR night-sights, which needed an active IR illumination source to operate. The Soviet Army did not adopt passive night-sights for its tanks during the Cold War due to their cost and the fact that their electronics industry lacked the technical expertise to build large numbers.

Rather than the standard V-12 diesel engines that had powered previous generations of Soviet Army tanks, the T-64 series had a radical new multi-fuel engine design: a flat, five-cylinder, horizontally opposed 700hp engine. In 1983, an enlarged six-cylinder version of the original engine appeared.

Top speed on level roads for the original T-64 came in at 40mph, dropping to 37mph for the heavier T-64B. In comparison, the Centurion's final version, the Mk 13, had a maximum speed on level roads of 22mph and the M60A1 30mph.

Ammunition

Stowage in the T-64 and T-64A accommodated thirty-seven main gun rounds, dropping down to thirty-six with the T-64B. The ammunition was separately loaded, with the projectile going into the breech first, followed by the semi-combustible cartridge case. Upon firing, there remained only the metal stub base. The maximum effective range of its APFSDS round was around 1.5 miles.

The T-64B could fire a radio-frequency (RF) guided anti-tank missile for longer-ranged targets. A booster motor propelled the anti-tank missile down the barrel of a tank's main gun. Once the anti-tank missile exits the barrel, a single-stage short-burn sustainer motor ignites and takes it to the chosen target with the aid of an onboard guidance system. All the gunner did was maintain a sight picture of the target until impact. The reported range of the anti-tank missile was 2.5 miles.

Due to the small diameter of the T-64 missile's shaped-charge warhead, its effectiveness against more heavily-armoured NATO tanks was minimal. Instead, its main task was to destroy lightly-armoured NATO Anti-Tank Guided Missile (ATGM) platforms, ground and supposedly aerial.

Eventually, the Soviet Army developed a laser-guided ATGM for some of its T-55 series fleet. Czech, East German and Polish factories also upgraded some of their T-55 inventory to fire ATGMs. The biggest drawback was the high cost of ATGMs and the inability of Soviet industry to produce large numbers.

A New Form of Protection

In addition to the 125mm main gun, the automatic loader and the advanced engine of the T-64 series, it was the first production tank to sport a three-layer composite armour. It consisted of inner and outer layers of conventional steel armour, with a centre layer of nonmetallic substances such as ceramics and glass-reinforced plastic.

A description of composite armour appears in this passage from a 1979 thesis by Major James M. Warford titled 'The Threat of the Premium Tank: The Product and Process of the Soviet Experience':

> Composite armor is basically a type of armor plate incorporating different materials in its design. The theory was that by combining both metallic and nonmetallic materials, the armor presented multiple and varying materials for an incoming round to penetrate. The intent of this new armor was to maximize the protection provided against HEAT warheads while at least maintaining the same level of protection provided by conventional steel armor against other types of weapons.
>
> Tank turrets were cast incorporating an internal 'cavity' on both sides of the main gun at the turret front. These cavities could then be filled with a ceramic material to create the desired metallic/nonmetallic combination. When production of the turret was completed, the sealed cavities in the frontal armor were not visible to any external examination. From a distance, the T-64's composite armored turret appeared basically the same as the standard all-steel cast turrets used on earlier MBTs.

The Soviet Army began exploring the possibility of composite armour in the 1940s. The US Army had done the same between 1958 and 1960, with no conclusive results. Soviet research must have been more promising, hence its incorporation into the T-64.

The reason for the composite armor array on the T-64 series appears in a declassified CIA report dated December 1964 and titled 'Soviet Tank Programs':

> The [NATO] development of ATGMs [Anti-Tank Guided Missiles] and more effective shaped-charge warheads meant that it was no longer practical to protect a tank with solid steel armor because it would have to be so thick to be effective that the tank would be virtually too heavy to move. The T-64 designers solved this problem by incorporating nonmetallic substances into the tank's armor array. When compared with an equal weight of steel, these substances give a much higher level of protection against shaped-charge warheads.

Soviet Opinion of the T-64, by Oleg Sapunkov

The T-64 was the first MBT designed in the Soviet Union, developed and built at the Malyshev tank plant in Kharkov. It was arguably the most innovative Soviet tank design approved for mass production, since it introduced a novel engine, autoloader, armour, transmission and suspension, all of which differed significantly from those used on earlier tanks. Thus, on paper, the T-64 was superior to any earlier Soviet tanks, and the Kharkov engineering team proposed to begin its mass production on all major Soviet tank factories.

Unfortunately, the T-64 was approved for production somewhat prematurely, with many of its novel systems insufficiently tested, and its crews insufficiently trained for proper operation and maintenance. Thus, the T-64 gained a reputation for low reliability in Soviet service, while its high cost prevented its anticipated widespread adoption across the Soviet Army. The strong competition among Soviet tank factories also led to a somewhat exaggerated focus on the T-64's problems in Soviet literature, as Ural Vagon Zavod sought to promote its T-72 as a superior alternative and justify its decision to continue developing the T-72 instead of producing the T-64.

The T-64 was the culmination of a considerable effort among Soviet tank designers to produce a compact, lightweight tank with powerful armament: the reduction of height was given particular attention, since Soviet tank doctrine envisioned large-scale frontal assaults across the flat plains of Eastern Europe, where a low silhouette would help protect the tank against enemy gunfire. The same doctrine led to the T-64's thick homogeneous armour layout; while frontal turret armour was reinforced with ultrahard ceramics, against HEAT, for the first time composite armour was used in the Soviet Union. The small, lightweight aluminium roadwheels did not add much protection to the hull side, unlike the large steel wheels used on both earlier and later tanks, like the T-55/T-62 family and the T-72 family. This low level of side protection drew significant criticism from Soviet tank crews, especially since it was intended to protect the tank's vulnerable autoloaded ammunition rack from enemy fire.

The autoloader was another innovation designed to help reduce the overall size of the tank, and it also was criticized for being unreliable and excessively complex. The mechanism was prone to jamming in cold temperatures, required complicated maintenance procedures, and effectively isolated the tank driver from the gunner and commander of the tank. This led to several fatal training incidents, where the driver could not escape through his hatch due to external blockage, and could not clear out the three cartridge cases required to open an egress window in time. The design of the autoloader only allowed for rotation of the magazine in one direction, which reduced the advertised rate of fire, while the magazine indexed to the desired type of round.

One of the most innovative aspects of the T-64 design was its drivetrain. The tank was powered by the 5TDF engine, which was powerful yet compact thanks to its horizontal opposed-piston two-stroke design and used compact planetary gearboxes to reduce the overall volume dedicated to the transmission. In principle, the 5TDF was designed for reliable high-temperature operation, so that with proper maintenance, it could function at ambient temperatures up to 55°C.

Unfortunately, the T-64 engine proved to be the largest source of operational problems. Early T-64s suffered from high engine vibration, which reduced the engine lifetime to just 300 hours between major overhauls, though this was improved to 500 hours by 1976.

The T-64 engine was also highly susceptible to dust intrusion and had a low-performance air filter prone to clogging, especially if dust was mixed with soot and oily aerosols from the engine exhaust of other tanks on large-scale manoeuvres. The operational manual required tank crews to thoroughly clean their air filters at the end of each long-distance run, but the poorly-trained crews rarely followed through with the procedure, leading to frequent engine overhauls.

Clogging also affected the T-64's engine cooling system, which likewise required regular and thorough maintenance. If crews used unfiltered water instead of the dedicated coolant to refill their cooling systems, the build-up of chemical deposits in the pipes significantly reduced the coolant flow rate within the system, which led to engines overheating in ambient temperatures above 25°C.

The suspension of the T-64 likewise received significant criticism. Unlike most other torsion-bar suspensions used on tanks, where the torsion bars run the entire width of the tank, the T-64 used half-length torsion bars, fixed to central support blocks running down the middle of the vehicle. While this geometry allowed for a slight reduction in overall weight of the suspension, it led to long-term problems. The belly armour plate that served as the mounting surface for the torsion bar supports was just 20mm thick and was not structurally reinforced, so it was susceptible to fatigue cracks generated around the support blocks after a few years of operation. During aggressive driving on rough terrain, the material fatigue could also lead to individual blocks breaking free from the belly plate, which at best killed the mobility of the tank until it could be repaired and at worst could damage the engine or autoloader or maim the crew.

In summary, while the T-64 was certainly an innovative tank, which offered significantly superior firepower and protection to its predecessors, its service record was very disappointing, and it was disliked by Soviet tank crews and their commanding officers. Its extensive maintenance requirements, low operational reliability and low crew preparedness precluded its widespread

> adoption across the Soviet Army and were the main reasons that the T-72 took its place as the primary Soviet MBT. Nevertheless, the T-64 was the first Soviet attempt at developing an MBT, and the experience gained through its deployment helped inform designers of newer tanks.
>
> Sources: http://btvt.info/1inservice/432.htm
> http://btvt.info/1inservice/t-64a/t-64a.htm
> http://btvt.info/1inservice/t-64b.htm
> http://btvt.narod.ru/istoria_t64/2_1.htm
> https://www.yaplakal.com/forum7/topic1238613.html
> https://diana-mihailova.livejournal.com/2337129.html

A declassified 1984 CIA report states that the US Army concluded the composite armour array on the front of the T-64A had a thickness equivalent to between 500mm (20in) and 575mm (23in) of steel armour when stopping a HEAT round, and 370mm (14.6in) to 440mm (17in) of steel armour when defeating an APFSDS round.

A post-Cold War source states that the actual armour thickness on the T-64A and T-64B turret front, including the internal composite material sandwiched between the outer and inner steel armour, came to 340mm (13.4in). That translated to 500mm (20in) of equivalent steel armour protection against HEAT rounds and 410mm (16in) against APFSDS rounds.

One source claims that glacis thickness on the T-64 came to 305mm (12in), which provided an equivalent steel armour protection level against HEAT rounds of 450mm (18in) and 410mm (16in) against APFSDS rounds. Another source lists the glacis thickness on the T-64 as 8.7in (220mm) and that on the T-64A as 8in (205mm).

Appliqué armour arrangements, on the upper front hull and turret roof, also appeared on the T-64 series during its time in service with the Soviet Army. The former was because the Soviet Army had acquired captured examples of a new Israeli-designed ADFSDS round (from the Syrians) labelled the M111 *Hetz* (Arrow) in 1982. The latter was in response to NATO's latest generation of top attack ATGMs and smart munitions.

Beginning in 1977 through to 1981, those T-64 series tanks remaining in service went through the standard Soviet Army rebuilding process. Starting in 1985, the T-64 series began appearing with first-generation explosive reactive armour (ERA), referred to by its code-name of 'Kontakt-1'. Tanks so fitted had the suffix 'V' (standing for explosive) added at the end of their vehicle designation. Hence, there appeared the T-64AV and T-64BV.

Explosive Reactive Armour

Serious Soviet industry research into the subject of explosive reactive armour (ERA) started in the 1960s. It took the Israeli Army's use of ERA on its tanks, first seen during the invasion of Lebanon in 1982, to renew Soviet Army interest.

In a letter to the Center for Strategic and International Studies dated 6 October 1988, US Army General Donn A. Starry explained the Soviet Army's advantage posed by their widespread adoption of ERA:

> While the technology involved is not all that exotic, reactive armor in this form is a very attractive solution to what, for the Soviets since the early 1970s, has been a most vexing problem: how to quickly get through the deepening belts of anti-tank guided missile systems deployed forward in NATO without suffering inordinate losses in Soviet tanks. Here, then, is a relatively uncomplicated, fairly inexpensive solution, and one that can be achieved without building a new or rebuilding an older tank fleet. Further, it is a fairly rapid way to complete development of their conventional capability to break through quickly, strike deep to disrupt the integrity of NATO's defenses, and do so quickly enough to pre-empt a nuclear decision in the West.

NATO

The American M47 tanks the West Germany Army acquired in the 1950s and the follow-on M48 series tanks were a quick, cost-effective stopgap solution to the armour needs of the Bundeswehr, but they were not the types of tanks they felt they needed. Therefore, a decision came about in 1956 for German industry to design and build a new tank suited to their specific requirements.

The first wooden mock-up of what would eventually become the four-man Leopard 1 tank appeared in 1958, and the first four prototypes were delivered by 1962. These initially sported 90mm main guns, later replaced by the British-designed 105mm L7 gun. West German industry would build fifty pre-series production examples of the Leopard 1 for testing purposes, initially delivered in 1963.

Numbers

Testing of the fifty Leopard 1 pre-production examples continued until October 1965, with positive results. Therefore, the West German government granted approval for full-scale production, with the first examples coming off factory floors in September 1965 and the last in 1977. Production of the tank for export continued into the 1980s.

Leopard 1 Details

With the West German Army's early emphasis on firepower and mobility ahead of protection, the Leopard 1 featured thin armour, with a maximum thickness of 70mm (2.8in) on its glacis plate. Along with the French Army, the West German Army believed that the effectiveness of then-current and anticipated anti-tank weapons had outstripped the defensive properties of conventional steel armour, making firepower and mobility the more critical design features.

The 44-ton Leopard 1 received power from a multi-fuel engine (typically running on diesel fuel) and rode on a torsion bar suspension system. It boasted the highest power-to-weight ratio of any contemporary NATO tank when it entered service, providing a degree of mobility unmatched by any other NATO tank of the period. Top speed on level roads came to 40mph.

In the July–August 1970 issue of *Armor* magazine, the US Army liaison officer to the West German Army armour school describes some aspects of the Leopard 1 fire-control system and the reasoning behind its arrangement:

> The fire-control system in the Leopard was designed with the idea that the tank commander should concern himself only with target acquisition, controlling the movements of the tank and issuing the order to engage a target. He was not to get involved with ranging. For this reason, the rangefinder is mounted forward in the turret and is operated by the gunner. It has 16-power magnification and serves as the gunner's main sighting device when he is firing APDS or HEAT. The gunner can select whether he wants to operate the rangefinder in the coincidence or the stereoscopic mode. The rangefinder has both capabilities.

In 1970, the West German Army undertook a series of modernization programmes to maintain its Leopard 1 fleet's combat effectiveness. The initial process resulted in the reworked tanks of the first four batches receiving the designation Leopard 1A1. These boasted the ability to fire on the move, a significant improvement provided by a new American-designed and built two-axis stabilization system.

Up-Armouring

West German industry built 232 brand-new Leopard 1 tanks of the fifth production batch between 1972 and 1974, which received the designation Leopard 1A2. Reflecting a West German Army rethink about the value of armour protection, their cast-steel-armour turrets featured thicker armour than those of the previous four batches.

The remaining 110 examples of the fifth batch appeared with a new welded-armour turret that incorporated spaced armour and became the Leopard 1A3. The Leopard 1 tank series' sixth batch retained the welded-armour turret of the Leopard 1A3, but had a new fire-control system fitted. That version received the designation Leopard 1A4, with 250 of them built.

Spaced Armour
Spaced armour works by causing a change in the direction of an impacting AP projectile. The outer plate creates yaw and changes a projectile's impact obliquity when it strikes the inner plate, thereby reducing its armour penetration ability. With HEAT, it triggers the shaped-charge warhead at greater than the warhead's optimum distance, lessening the jet's and fragments' penetrating power when they encounter the inner plate.

Endless Designation Changes

The new emphasis on armour protection for the Leopard 1 series led to a second modernization programme involving all the vehicles in the first four batches going through a process of adding armour to their turrets between 1975 and 1977. The additional turret armour led to the designation Leopard 1A1A1.

In 1980 a passive night-fighting system was added to the Leopard 1A1A1 inventory, leading to the new designation Leopard 1A1A2. With the cast-armour turret, the fifth batch became the Leopard 1A2A1, and those fitted with the welded-armour turret the Leopard 1A3A1. The sixth batch of Leopard tanks did not receive a passive night-fighting system.

A final improvement to the first four batches of the Leopard 1A1A1 involved incorporating a new fire-control system based on that fitted to the Leopard II tank, which included a thermal imaging system. Delivery of these vehicles to the West German Army began in 1986 and concluded in 1992, with 1,300 completed.

> **Leopard 1 Memories**
> Retired Tank Commander of the Canadian Armoured Corps, Sergeant Anthony Sewards, CD, describes the Leopard C2 tank:
>
>> The first time I was close to a Leopard 1 was during my Canadian Armoured Corps' trades training in 1987. We were doing some classroom work when the Leopards rolled past our classroom, and the sound of the German MTU engine had me sold. It only took sixteen years later in my career to finally make it to the tanks; most of my career was with my regiment's reconnaissance squadron as part of the Lord Strathcona's Horse (Royal Canadians).
>>
>> Once I finally made it to the Leopards, I was tossed right into the gunner's course, and being a new tank commander, had to learn all of the turret crew stations: gunner, loader and my position as commander. I mastered all the crew drills for each position and looked forward to going to the tank gunnery simulators to put these new learned skills to use.
>>
>> Once the garrison part was complete and all our tests and crew drills complete, we headed off to conduct the course live-fire range practice. We started our gateway training for the gunner's course; first we fired on static targets with the main gun and coax. After firing that first round, I was hooked. Next came the live-fire battle runs; there is nothing better than firing a tank on the move, with STAB [stabilization] on achieving first-round hit. TARGET, TARGET STOP!
>>
>> After the course, I was posted to a tank squadron as a tank troop sergeant. In the Canadian tank squadron, the tank troop sergeant leads the troop for navigation and operations. I was always learning about the tank, helping with regular crew maintenance from changing track to helping pull the power pack out of the hull.

Those modified became the Leopard 1A5. The Leopard 1 tank series remained in German Army service until 2003.

Export Success

The Leopard 1 series became the most popular Cold War tank among various NATO armies, including Canada (127), Belgium (334), Denmark (120), Italy (720), Greece (106), Holland (468), Turkey (227) and Norway (172). While some were former West German Army tanks, most were new-built vehicles.

These exported new-built Leopard 1 tanks typically featured minor external differences due to the location of storage boxes, smoke grenade-launchers, turret-mounted machine guns, etc. Those in the Italian Army included both German-built examples as well as 200 built in Italy under licence. Leopard 1 tanks also went to some non-NATO armies.

France

When the French government decided to drop out of an agreement with Germany and Italy to develop a standard tank for their use, it authorized development of the 105mm main gun-armed AMX-30B. The first example left the factory floor in 1966 and bore the designation AMX-30A.

Like the Leopard 1, the initial iteration of the 40-ton AMX-30 put firepower and mobility ahead of protection. The tank's thickest armour, the gun shield, was 81mm (3.2in) thick.

The small size of the AMX-30 series, with a height of only 7ft 6in, made it the lowest-profile Cold War NATO tank. The Leopard 1 series came in at around 9ft. The AMX-30 series' 105mm main gun was not the British-designed rifled 105mm L7, but a French-designed smoothbore 105mm gun designated the CN-105-F1.

During a 1970 conference held at the US Army Armor School, the French Army liaison officer had the following to say about the AMX-30B:

> It was conceived on the basis of having a main weapon capable of destroying all known armored vehicles at ranges up to 2,500 meters [2,734 yards]. As actually designed and produced, its 105mm gun can be employed up to 3,000 meters [3,281 yards] with a 50 per cent hit probability on a 2 × 2 meter [6.5ft by 6.5ft] target. The gun is stabilized and fires non-rotating, shaped-charge ammunition at a high – eight rounds per minute – rate of fire. In addition, there is HE ammunition. The fire-control system makes possible great accuracy in both day and night combat. On the same models, a 20mm automatic gun serves as secondary armament for anti-personnel, anti-aircraft and light anti-mechanized employment.

An upgraded model of the four-man AMX-30B, fitted with a new fire-control system that included an LRF, appeared in French Army service in 1982. Its assigned designation was the AMX-30B2. The B and B2 models received power from liquid-cooled multi-fuel engines which provided a maximum speed on level roads of 40mph.

When production of the AMX-30 series ended in 1993, a total of 1,355 examples of the AMX-30B had entered French Army service, including 166 new-production examples of the AMX-30B2. Some 493 of the earlier AMX-30B went back to the factory to bring them up to the AMX-30B2 standard.

The French Army retired the last of the AMX-30 series tanks in 2011. The only NATO country to adopt the AMX-30 series was Greece, which took into service 190 examples in the 1970s.

AMX-13 Firepower Upgrades

In 1956, the French Army took into service the man-portable first-generation, wire-guided SS-10 ATGM. French industry soon came up with a larger version labelled the SS-11 for use by helicopters. French tankers saw the SS-11 as a cost-effective way to upgrade some of their AMX-13 tanks' combat-effectiveness. Four SS-11 missiles were fitted onto the turret front in metal trays. Tanks so armed became the AMX-13 SS-11.

Initially, the gunner on the AMX-13 SS-11 had to manually guide the missile to its target, referred to as a Manual Command to Line of Sight (MCLOS) guidance system. A subsequent version of the SS-11 used a Semi-Automatic Command to Line of Sight (SACLOS) guidance system. This required the missile operator only to keep his sight's crosshairs on the chosen target with the missile slaved to his line of sight. As larger numbers of new AMX-30 tanks entered service, the missile-firing AMX-13 tanks went off to retirement.

Both the US Army and Soviet Army experimented with externally-mounted ATGMs on tank turrets at different times. Both armies quickly decided that large ATGMs were too vulnerable to survive on the battlefield in such an arrangement and halted any further development.

As the AMX-13's 75mm main gun became obsolete by the late 1950s, the French Army began looking at upgrading to either a 90mm or 105mm main gun. The latter went into production as the AMX-13 Mle 58, but only for export, with the Dutch Army acquiring 131 examples.

French industry would up-gun 875 examples of the 75mm gun-armed AMX-13s with a 90mm main gun between 1966 and the early 1970s. These received several designations. The most often used unofficial designation was the AMX-13 C90.

United Kingdom

The British Army replaced the Centurion medium tank series and the Conqueror heavy tank with the 120mm gun-armed 'Chieftain' tank, beginning in 1966. Its frontal armour was designed to be immune to the 100mm tank-killing rounds fired by T-54/T-55 series tanks. The highly-sloped turret's front came in at 195mm (7.7in) thick, and the 47-degree sloped glacis at 120mm (4.7in).

Instead of the liquid-cooled gasoline-powered engines of previous British Army tanks, the Chieftain received its power from a multi-fuel engine, chosen to meet a NATO Standardization Agreement (STANAG). Sadly, the tank's multi-fuel engine never achieved the reliability desired by the British Army and proved to be the most significant shortcoming throughout most of its service career, despite endless design fixes.

The seriousness of the Chieftain's endless engine problems reached the highest levels of the British government, which resulted in an investigation, the findings of which were published in 1978. A passage reads:

> The performance of the Chieftain's gun and range-finding equipment is first-class. It is, therefore, all the more unsatisfactory that the tank should have been let down by its engine in the past. It is difficult to feel confident about the future performance of the engine in the light of the subsequently un-fulfilled assurances given by the Ministry of Defence ... We wish to assure the House that the present programme of engine modifications, as it has been explained and demonstrated to us, appears to be meeting with success so far.

The 8ft 3in tall Chieftains went through a succession of progressively improved iterations during their service career with the British Army. The Mk 1 up through to the Mk 5 models consisted of new-built vehicles, while the Mk 6 through to Mk 11 models were upgraded examples of earlier production versions. As the Mk 1 saw use only as a training vehicle, the initial fielding of combat-ready Chieftains proved to be the Mk 2.

In the July–August 1970 issue of *Armor* magazine is a passage by a British Army officer who had explained in a briefing at the US Army Armor School some of the features of the four-man Chieftain tank:

> Chieftain has the heaviest armour of modern tanks and the biggest gun. It weighs about 55 tons. The 120mm fires an APDS round with a muzzle velocity of about 5,000 feet per second, giving a considerably greater penetration at greater range than the 105mm. The ammunition is separate. The projectile is loaded first and then the propellant bag charge. This has the same advantage of leaving no brass cartridge as your 152mm caseless ammunition. In addition, the bag charge is light and has a minimal fire risk because the charges are stored in water-jacketed racks.

Chieftain Details

Like the Centurion and Conqueror, the Chieftain rode on a Horstmann suspension system. The Chieftain's early production versions employed a .50 calibre (12.7mm) ranging gun, as had the Centurion. An LRF first appeared on the Chieftain Mk 3/3 in 1970, replacing the ranging gun.

The Chieftain proved to be the first NATO Cold War tank to feature a Muzzle Reference Sensor (MRS), which provided the gunner with a means of correcting fire-control solutions by compensating for gun tube droop. Unlike the Centurion and Conqueror, the Chieftain had an NBC system.

In the January–February 1970 issue of *Armor* magazine, a young US Army sergeant recounted his impressions of the Chieftain tank after a ten-day visit with a British Army armour unit stationed in West Germany:

> Another point brought out in my visit with the British was their use of asbestos covers called 'thermo-shield' to keep the gun tubes at a uniform temperature in order to eliminate droop. Many Americans [tankers], especially when they are on the range, complain that the sun, early in the morning, will heat up one side of the gun tube causing rounds to drift, even ever so slightly. The same happens in the evening. To solve this problem for the Chieftain, covers are put over the tube so that it has equal heat 360 degrees around. The cover also breaks up the gun's outline for better camouflage.

Updates

Beginning in 1980, some Chieftains had their white light/IR searchlight replaced with the Thermal Observation Gunnery Sight (TOGS). Another 1980s addition to the Chieftain series was the fitting of NERA (non-explosive reactive armour) on the tank's front hull and turret. The British Army referred to it as the Stillbrew Crew Protection Package (SCPP).

Stillbrew appeared for a couple of different reasons. First was the continued development of and improvements to man-portable shaped-charge rockets and missiles, demonstrated during the Yom Kippur War of 1973. Second, work on a solution did not begin in earnest until the mid-1980s when evidence showed that Iraqi T-62 tanks were punching holes with their APFSDS rounds in Iranian Chieftain tanks' frontal armour during the Iran-Iraq War.

The Chieftain remained in British Army service until 1995, with approximately 900 examples taken into the inventory. No other NATO army acquired the Chieftain. However, the tank did achieve a great deal of sales success with non-NATO armies in the Middle East.

Chieftain Road Report

Former British Army senior non-commissioned officer Rob Griffin describes the Chieftain as used during his time with the 4th/7th Royal Dragoon Guards:

> My first dealing with the Chieftain tank came when the regiment converted from the armoured car role and moved back to tanks, along with the move back to BAOR (British Army of the Rhine). Chieftain at the time was new, and many armoured regiments still were using the venerable Centurion tank. Coupled with the move to a new country, the chance to use what at first seemed to be an exciting new piece of equipment was what most had joined up to do. At first glance, Chieftain seemed to confirm the old adage that if it looks right, it is right; however, sadly, that did not prove to be the case. However, I think most who served on it would agree they came to love the beast despite its foibles.

A quick look at why Chieftain was considered revolutionary and probably the best MBT around at the time, which it was, might make it easier to understand the issues that befell it. Chieftain introduced many novel features for the time; most drastic probably was the use of a reclining driver's position. Normally the driver would be sat vertically whether he was sat opened up or closed down; this of course raised the height of the tank to accommodate him. Chieftain used a reclining position for the driver when fully closed down, thus allowing a reduction in vehicle height; this, in turn, allowed a long sloping glacis plate.

The other controversial change to the Chieftain was the use of split three-part ammunition comprising projectile, bagged charge and a .625 vent tube to ignite the lot. Part of the reasoning was that with the switch to 120mm, a fixed round would be too large to handle using the technology available at the time. It did allow the charges to be stowed below the turret ring in charge bins.

The final change was the adoption of the L60 power pack, and this was the nail that killed the export success that could have been for Chieftain. The L60 was the wrong pack for the tank and suffered from liner leaks, oil leaks and other multitudes of faults, but many of these could be overcome with crew ingenuity, unlike efficient hi-tech engines today.

Life on Chieftain with the L60 power pack had two distinct phases when in use: either running or broken down, which in the early days and up to about half of its life was quite the normal.

Using Chieftain in the field and on the ranges, your success depended on the experience of the crew. It took around two or three training seasons to produce a top-rate crew. Ranges were probably the least problematical of the training. The often-derided three-part ammunition caused very few problems. A good loader could load very fast with no issues. Originally ranging was provided by a modified .5" Browning machine gun firing a three-round burst to establish the range; this was replaced by laser rangefinders in various marks.

Night-fighting was carried out using the 2kw searchlight and crude IR sights. Later on, these were replaced by the TI system in the later years. Armour protection at the introduction was probably the best in the world, but by the time it left service, it had lagged behind, although it was given the Stillbrew upgrade.

Towards the later years of Chieftain, its reliability improved tremendously, and I had one power pack fitted that lasted me for three training seasons; the armour was uprated, and at the end, it was still a formidable combat vehicle and at the time, the best in NATO.

Finally, one foreign user said of Chieftain: 'It is the best tank I have if I could only get it to the battlefield.' For myself, if I had to fight during the Cold War, I would have been more than happy to do so in Chieftain.

In response to the US Army's fielding of the M60 series armed with a modified version of the British-designed 105mm L7 tank gun in 1960, the Soviet Army fielded the T-62 Medium Tank armed with a 115mm main gun in 1961. Based on the lengthened chassis of the T-54/T-55 series of medium tanks, the T-62 sported a new turret design that incorporated an automatic spent cartridge case ejection system. No Warsaw Pact Army would take the T-62 into service. (*Chris Hughes*)

Two distinct external spotting features of the T-62A, besides its flatter turret design, were the bore evacuator's location compared to those on the T-54/T-55 series, and the spacing of the roadwheels, which differed from its predecessors. The 12.7mm machine gun fitted to the loader's rotating hatch of the T-62A was a late-production feature, first introduced in 1972. This was in response to NATO's fielding of specialized helicopter gunships. (*Pierre-Olivier Buan*)

The Iraqi T-62 pictured has suffered an internal explosion during Operation Iraqi Freedom in 2003. The crew's fate cannot have been pleasant. The tank is 31 feet in length with the 115mm main gun pointed forward and has a width of 11 feet. It can cross a trench 9 feet wide and climb over a 32-inch vertical obstruction. Without its fording equipment fitted, the tank can cross a water obstacle 55-inches deep. The tank can snorkel across a water obstacle 14 feet deep with the fording equipment fitted. (*Department of Defense*)

Posing for a picture during a training exercise is a trio of Soviet Army T-62s. The turret-mounted 12.7mm machine gun on the tank in the foreground identifies it as a T-62A. The four-man crew reflects that the T-62 was the last Soviet production tank to feature a human loader. Vehicle length with its main gun pointed forward was 31ft. Its width came in at 11ft and height at 8ft. Maximum speed on level roads was approximately 30mph. (*Author's collection*)

(**Above**) T-62A tanks on the move. By the early 1970s, most Soviet Army tanks with the Group of Soviet Forces, Germany (GSFG, organized in 1954), were T-62s. Like the late-production T-55 series tanks, the T-62 came with a basic nuclear warfare protection system for its crew. The vehicle commander of the T-62 had a turret traverse override, but could not take over the main gun elevation and depression from the gunner. (*Dreamstime*)

(**Opposite, above**) Soviet Army T-62s taking part in a training exercise with simulated artillery explosions going off. The smoothbore 115mm main gun on the T-62 fired various rounds, including a potent Armor-Piercing, Fin-Stabilized, Discarding Sabot (APFSDS) round, and two types of High-Explosive Fragmentation (HE-FRAG) rounds. The gun also came with a High-Explosive Anti-Tank (HEAT) round. The T-62 had stowage for forty main gun rounds. (*Author's* collection)

(**Opposite, below**) An illustration of the height difference between an American M60A1 and a Soviet T-62. The T-62 turret had a two-axis stabilization system, which the M60A1 did not acquire until 1972. The turret traverse system on the T-62 was electrically-operated. In contrast, gun elevation and depression depended on an electro-hydraulic system. Like the T-55 series, the T-62 had an infrared driving and night-fighting system, as did the M60A1. (*US Army*)

US USSR

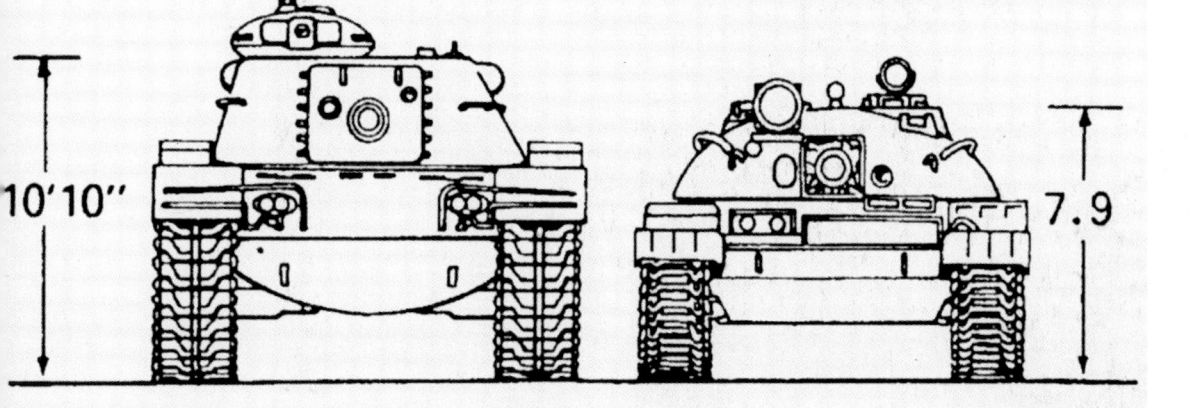

10'10" 7.9

This overhead illustration of a T-62 shows the hatch behind the vehicle turret hatches through which spent cartridge cases automatically ejected upon the firing of the main gun. Left of the spent cartridge case ejection port is a smaller circular object, which is the uppermost armoured covering for the electrically-powered turret ventilator. On the right-side fender are the three externally-mounted armoured fuel tanks with an embossed X-pattern. (*US Army*)

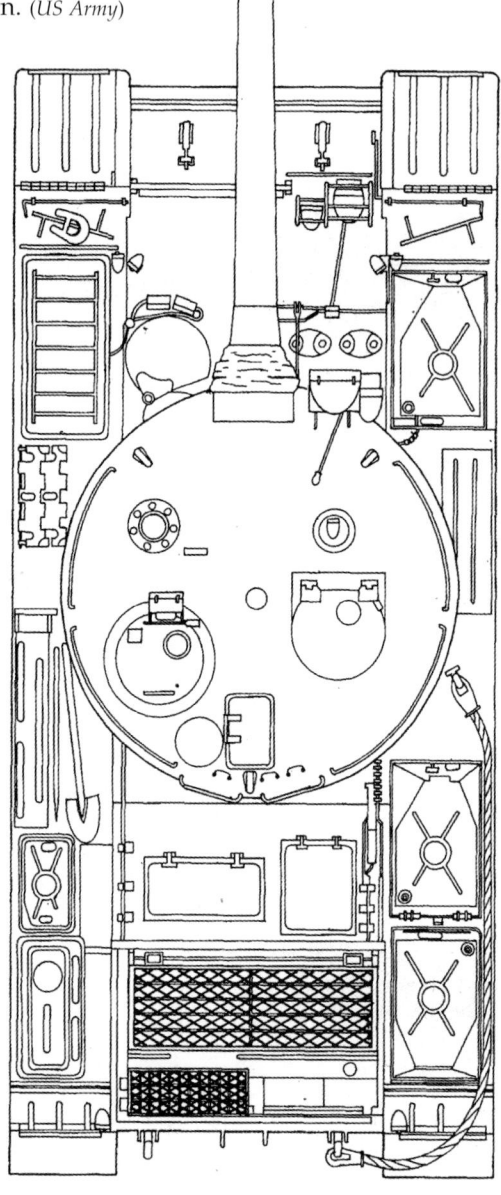

A T-62A at an outdoor museum display. Three-quarters of the way back on the vehicle's left fender is the long narrow rectangular covering for the tank engine exhaust vent. Spraying diesel fuel into the engine exhaust manifold generated white smoke from the tank's engine exhaust port that could last from two to four minutes. *(Dreamstime)*

The T-62 series tank pictured here had various optical sighting devices for both the vehicle commander and gunner. The gunner's daylight telescope featured a rotating reticle for applying superelevation to the multiple types of main gun rounds fired. The gunner's sight also had a dual magnification feature, as did the vehicle commander's sight, with a lens filter capacity and an integral lens wiper. Very late-production T-62 series tanks came with a laser rangefinder (LRF). *(Dreamstime)*

Some T-62s appeared with the BDD brow armour arrangement as pictured here starting in 1983, alongside other upgrades. Besides providing enhanced protection from NATO main gun anti-tank rounds, BDD brow armour also proved to be effective against the RPG-7s employed by the Afghan guerrillas during the Soviet Army's time fighting in Afghanistan, which ran from 1979 until 1989. (*Dreamstime*)

Looking to supplement its older-generation medium tanks and to keep ahead of NATO tank development, Soviet industry eventually came up with the T-64 series. The initial version, the T-64, had a 115mm main gun and entered service in 1967. The second version, the T-64A, is pictured here and came with a 125mm main gun. The third and fourth versions, the T-64B and T-64BV, retained the 125mm main gun and respectively entered service in 1976 and 1985. (*Dreamstime*)

To keep the weight of the T-64 series down, with a T-64A pictured here, Soviet industry abandoned its long tradition of evolutionary development and took a more radical approach. One aspect involved rejecting the V-12 series diesel engines that had long powered Soviet tanks. Instead, the T-64 would receive power from a new, lightweight, compact yet more powerful two-stroke, five-cylinder, opposed-piston diesel engine. Despite high hopes for the new engine, its reliability and durability never lived up to expectations. *(Dreamstime)*

Another weight-saving design feature of the T-64 was lightweight ceramic armour in conjunction with conventional steel armour. To reduce turret dimensions (and by default, weight), the T-64's designers replaced the human loader with an autoloader. The suspension system on the T-64 series, an example of which is pictured here, consisted of small, lightweight steel roadwheels with internal rubber buffers. Unfortunately, they lacked durability and proved unreliable. *(Dreamstime)*

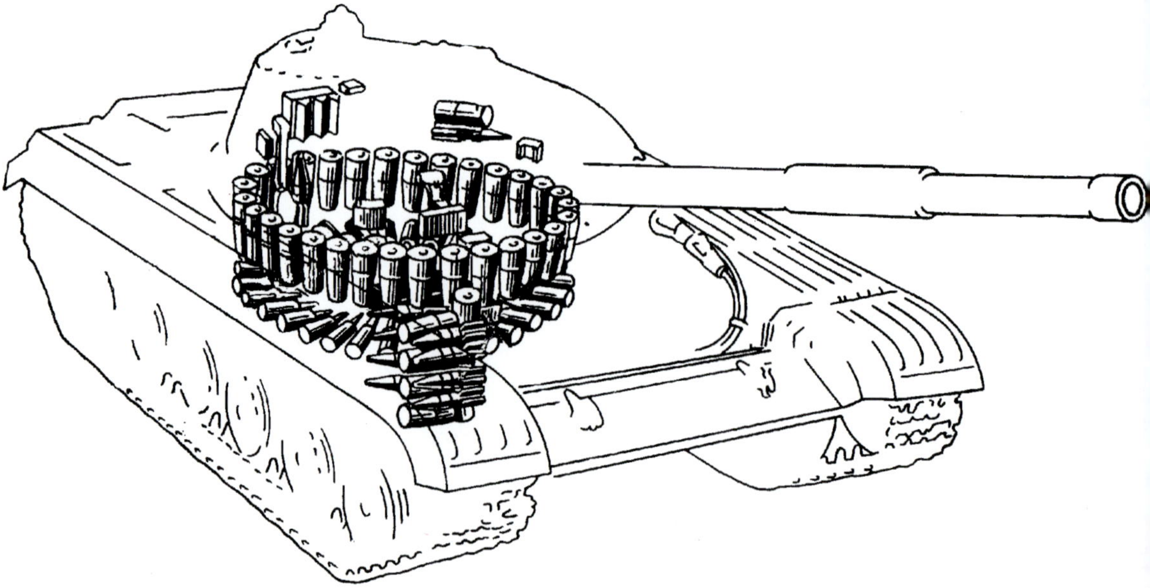

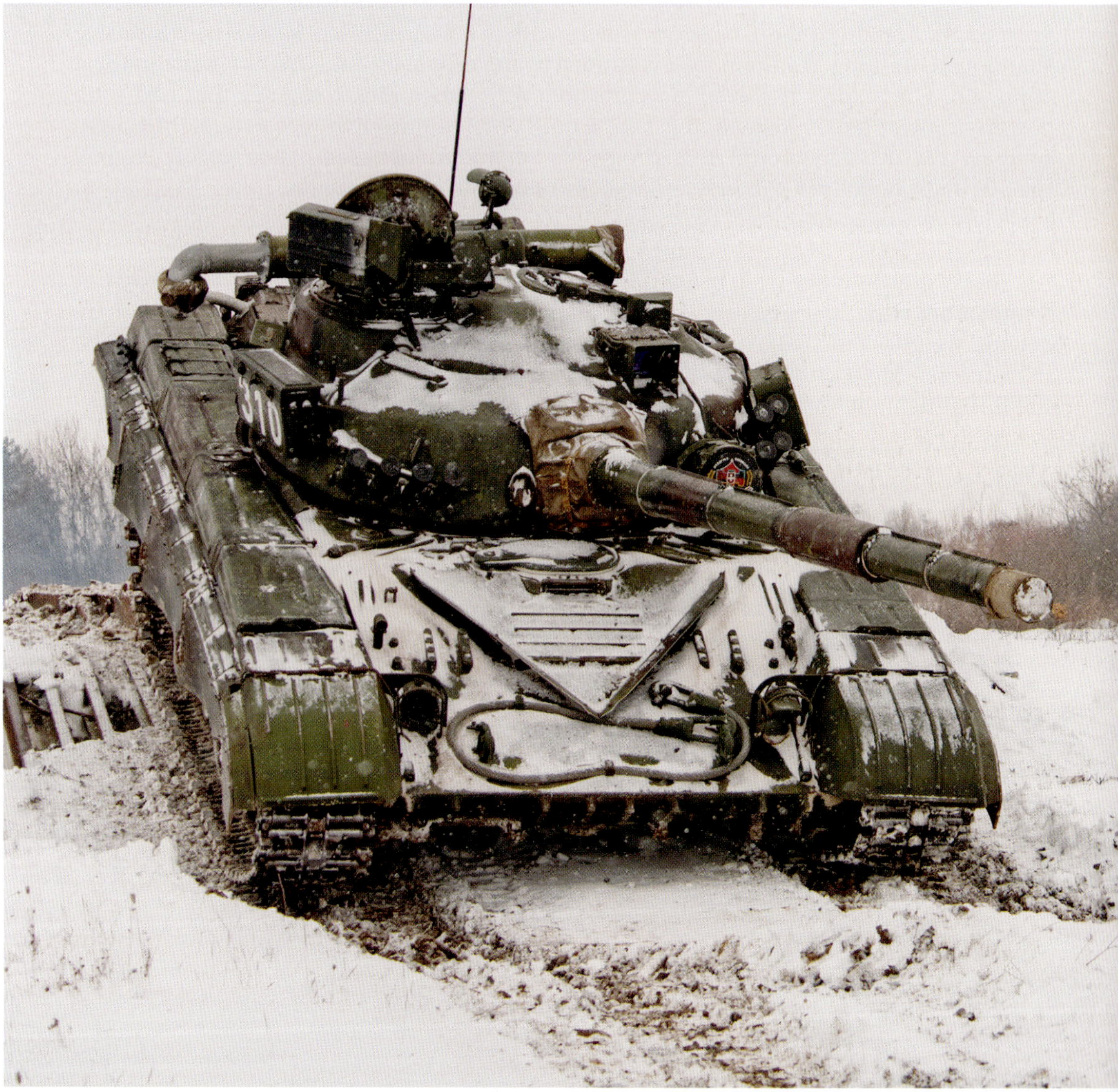
310

(**Opposite, above**) The T-64 series proved to be the first Soviet Army tank with an autoloader as seen here in an illustration from a Soviet Army manual. In operation, the autoloader carried both the separate-loading projectile and propellant charge up to and level with the gun's breech. It loaded both with a single action of the power rammer. This complicated design required a unique ammunition arrangement, with the projectiles placed horizontally (pointing towards the centre of the circular carousel) and the propellant charges positioned vertically. (*Author's collection*)

(**Opposite, below**) The T-64B could fire a two-part radio-command-guided missile from its 125mm main gun. The missile was much smaller than the one-piece American 152mm Shillelagh anti-tank missile to fit the tank's main gun's bore and the confines of the vehicle's autoloader. Hence, the T-64B missile warhead lacked the punch of its American tank-fired counterpart. Those T-64Bs without the fire-control system to launch a radio command-guided missile had the designation T64B1, as shown here. (*Dreamstime*)

(**Above**) The appearance of Israeli Army M60A1 tanks fitted with explosive reactive armour (ERA) during the June 1982 invasion of Lebanon sparked a renewed Soviet Army interest in the subject. The relatively cheap ERA kits seemed like the answer to overcoming NATO's significant investment in Anti-Tank Guided Missiles (ATGMs). T-64As fitted with ERA became the T-64AV, and the T-64B became the T-64BV. The 12.7mm NVST turret-mounted machine gun identifies this tank as probably a T-64BV. (*Dreamstime*)

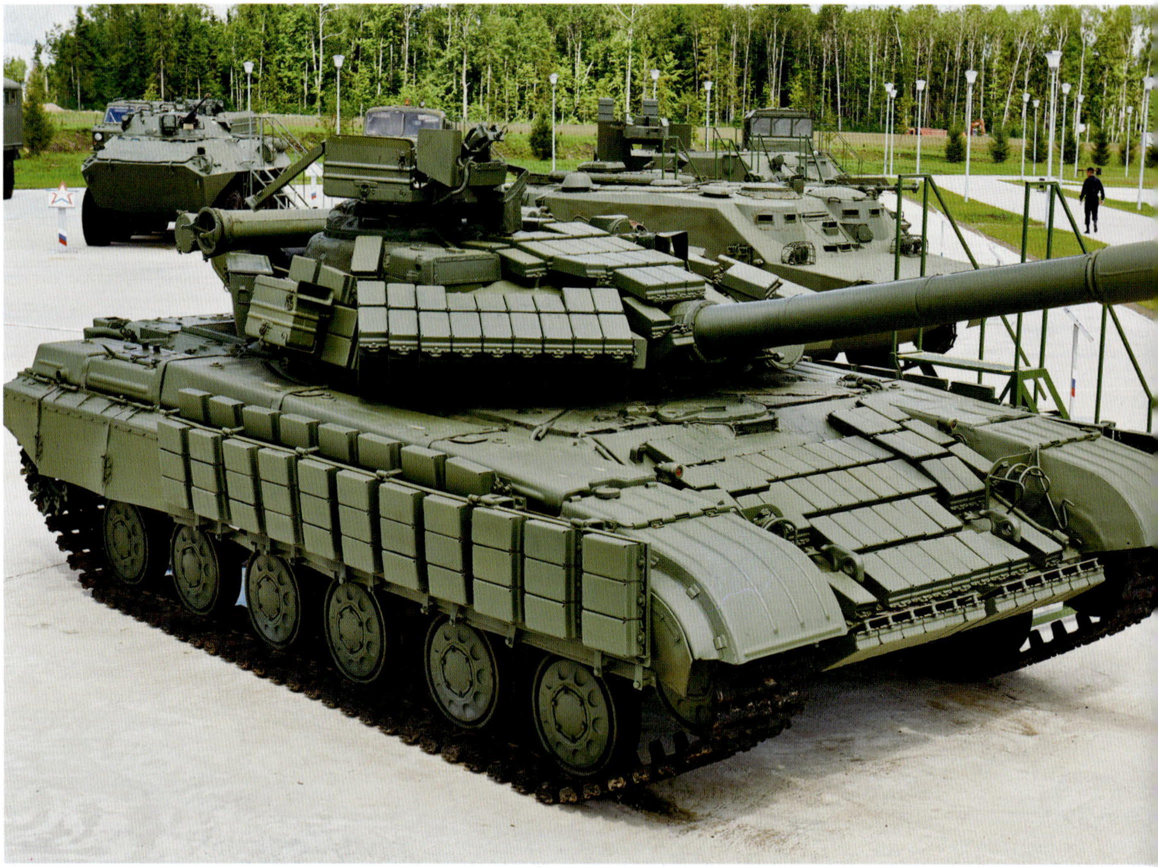

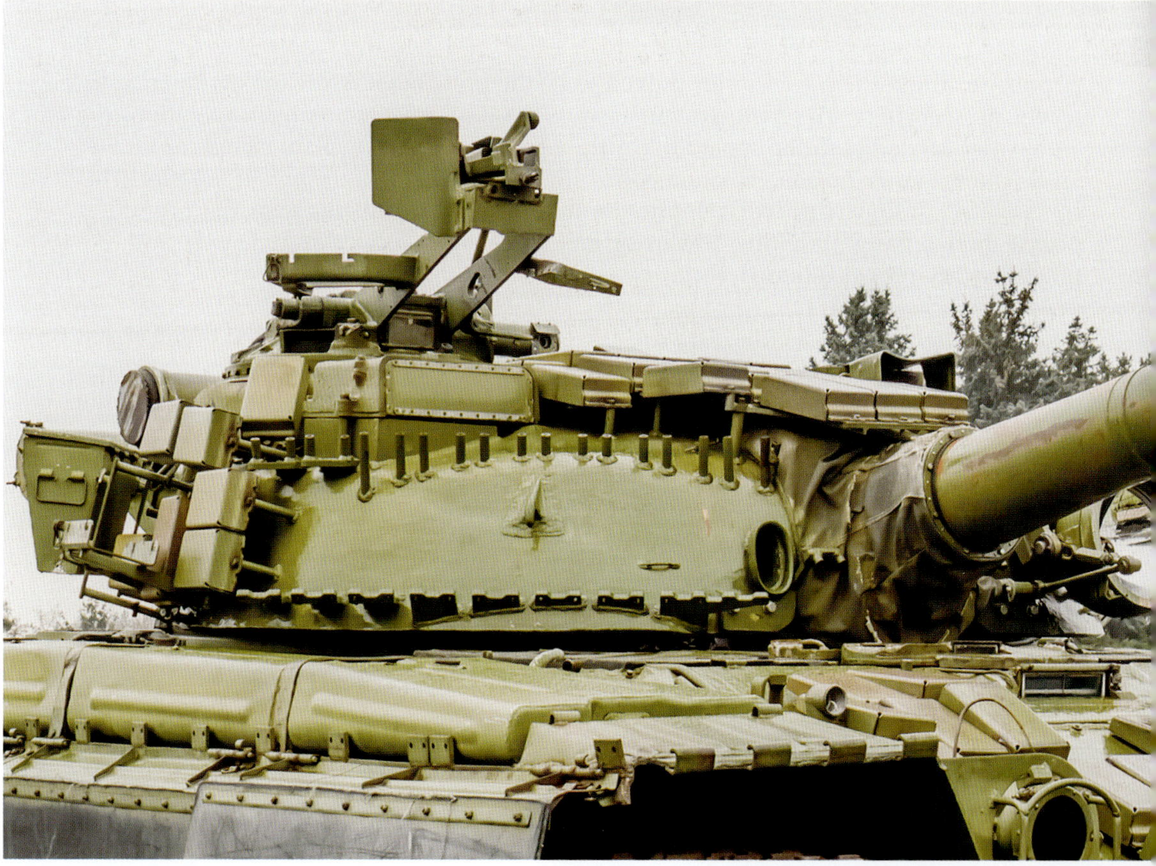

(**Opposite, above**) A T-64BV on display here shows an extensive arrangement of explosive reactive armour (ERA) tiles. The original Soviet industry version of ERA bore the label Kontakt EDZ. The suffix letters translate to dynamic protection element armour. Like the Israeli Blazer ERA, the original version of Soviet ERA only offered protection from shaped-charged rounds. A later version of the Soviet ERA, introduced in 1985, gave protection from kinetic energy rounds and is known as Kontakt-5 Heavy ERA. (*Dreamstime*)

(**Opposite, below**) A close-up image of a T-64BV turret, identified by both the presence of ERA tiles and the mounting brackets for the tiles. Another external spotting feature of the T-64BV is the supporting frame of a remote-control NVST 12.7mm machine gun. Below the machine gun's supporting structure and directly to the front of the loader's cupola is the box containing the antenna that guides the radio-command missiles, referred to as the 9M112 Kobra by the Soviets and the AT-8 Songster by NATO. (*Dreamstime*)

(**Above**) A NATO agreement came about allowing for the establishment of a West Germany Army in 1955. By the next year, the leadership of that same army had already formulated a new tank's requirements for building in-country. A wooden mock-up appeared in 1959, followed by prototypes in 1961. Following the prototypes, there were fifty pilots with examples seen here intended for troop trials. The new tank received the name Leopard in 1963. (*BMV/g*)

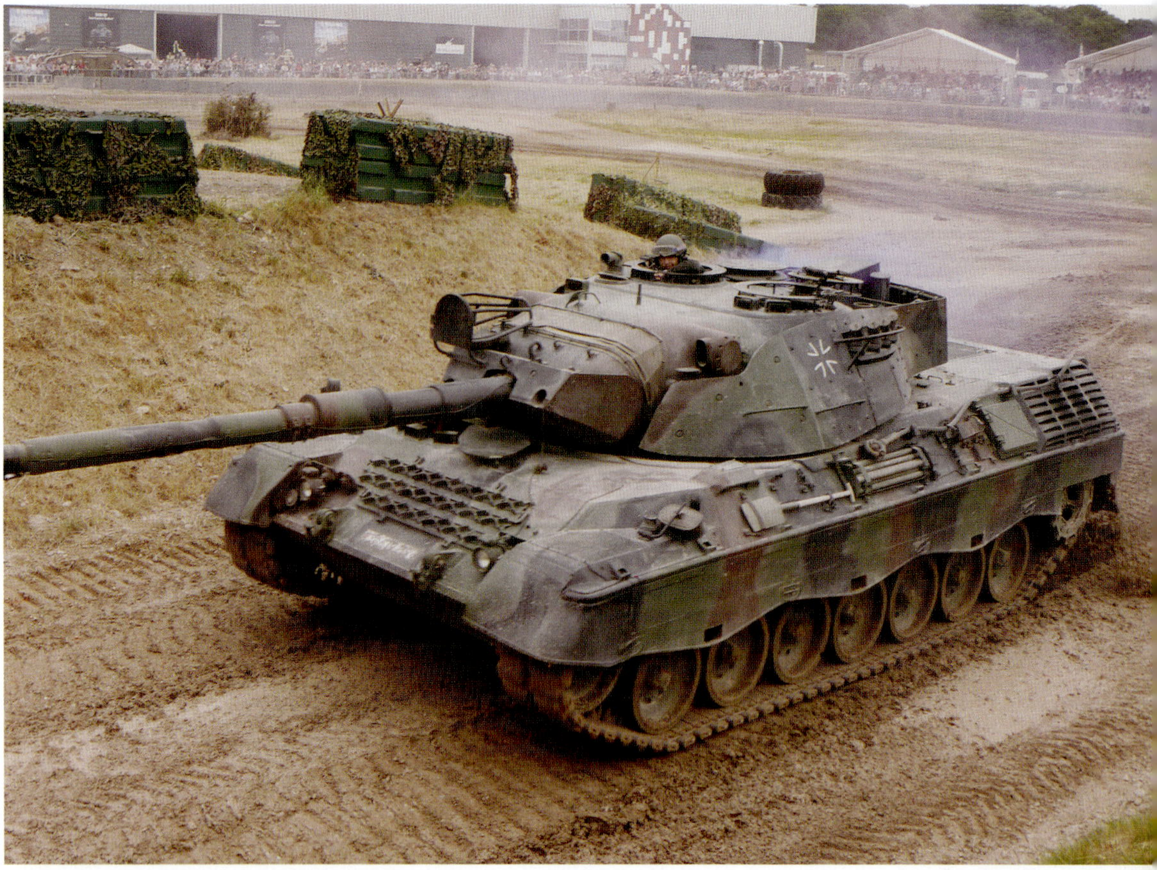

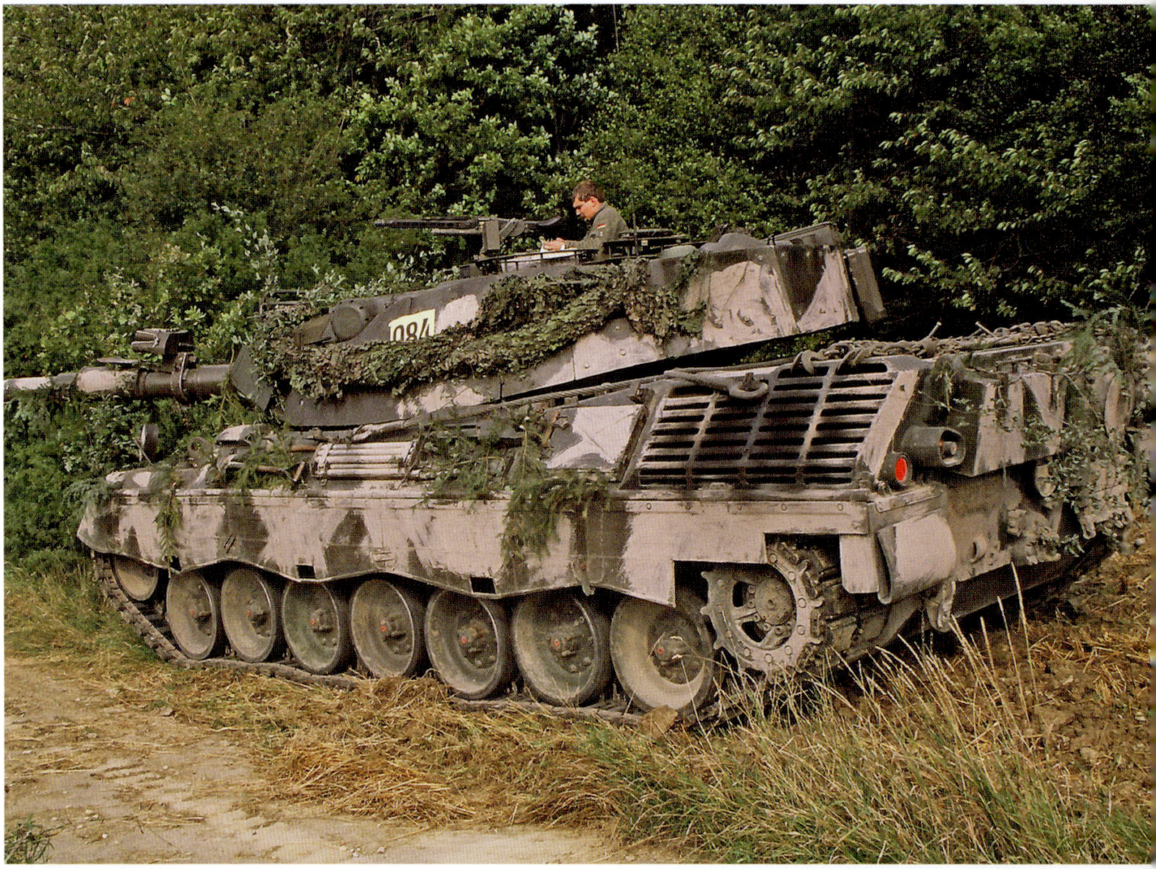
084

(**Opposite, above**) When originally envisioned, the Leopard would have had a 90mm main gun. However, that soon changed and the Leopard tank found itself armed with a slightly modified version of the British-designed and built 105mm L7 gun. In German service, it received the designation L7A3. Pictured here is what appears to be an example of the Leopard 1A1 that featured an up-armoured arrangement for both its turret and gun shield. Modernized Leopard 1A1s became the Leopard 1A1A1. (*Ian Wilcox*)

(**Opposite, below**) A West German Leopard 1A1 or 1A1A1 and its four-man crew taking part in a training exercise. The tank is camouflaged with a pattern of mud bands. The West German Army constituted the largest NATO ground force in Western Europe from the 1960s through the Cold War. At one point in time, it had approximately 2,500 Leopard 1 series tanks in front-line service. Older-generation American-supplied M48 series tanks had gone off to secondary units. (*DOD*)

(**Above**) The Leopard 1 series enjoyed sales success with many NATO armies during the Cold War. These included Belgium, Canada, Denmark, Greece, Turkey, Italy, Holland and Norway. Pictured here is a Norwegian Army Leopard 1 during a training exercise. On the gun shield of the tank pictured is the box-like infrared and white light searchlight. Visible on the barrel is a gunfire simulation device. (*Dreamstime*)

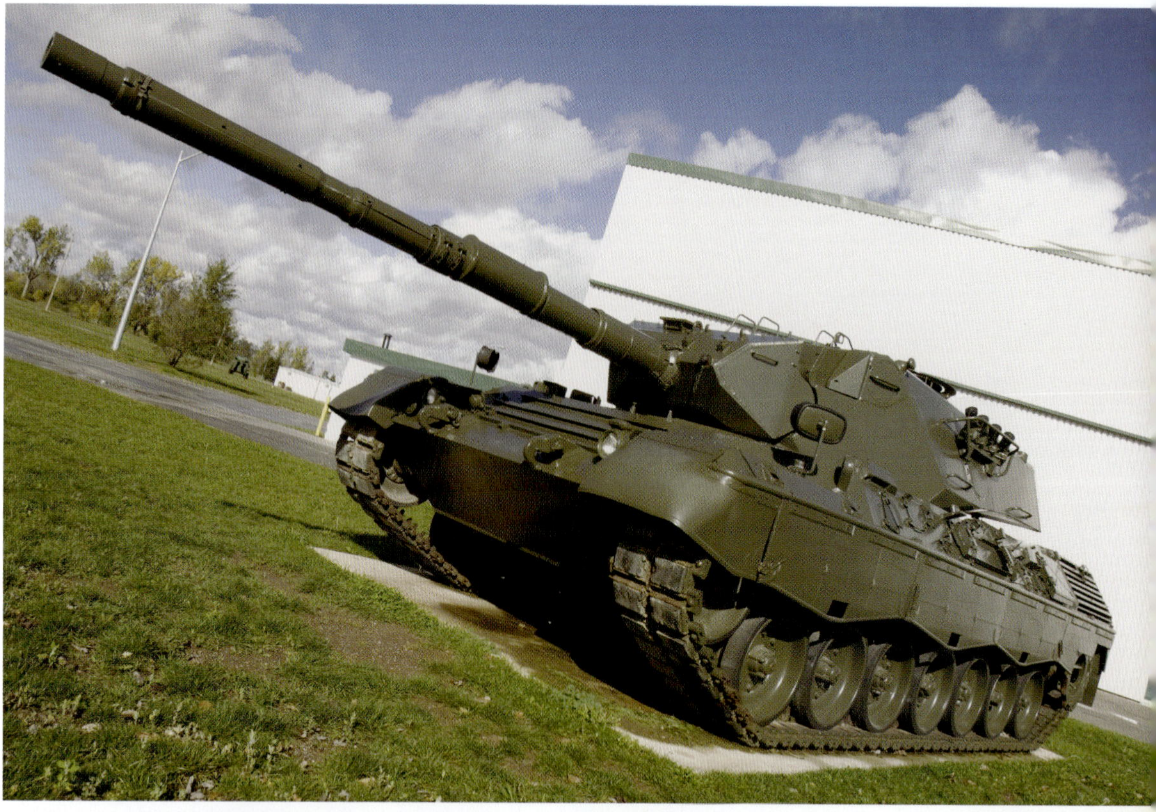

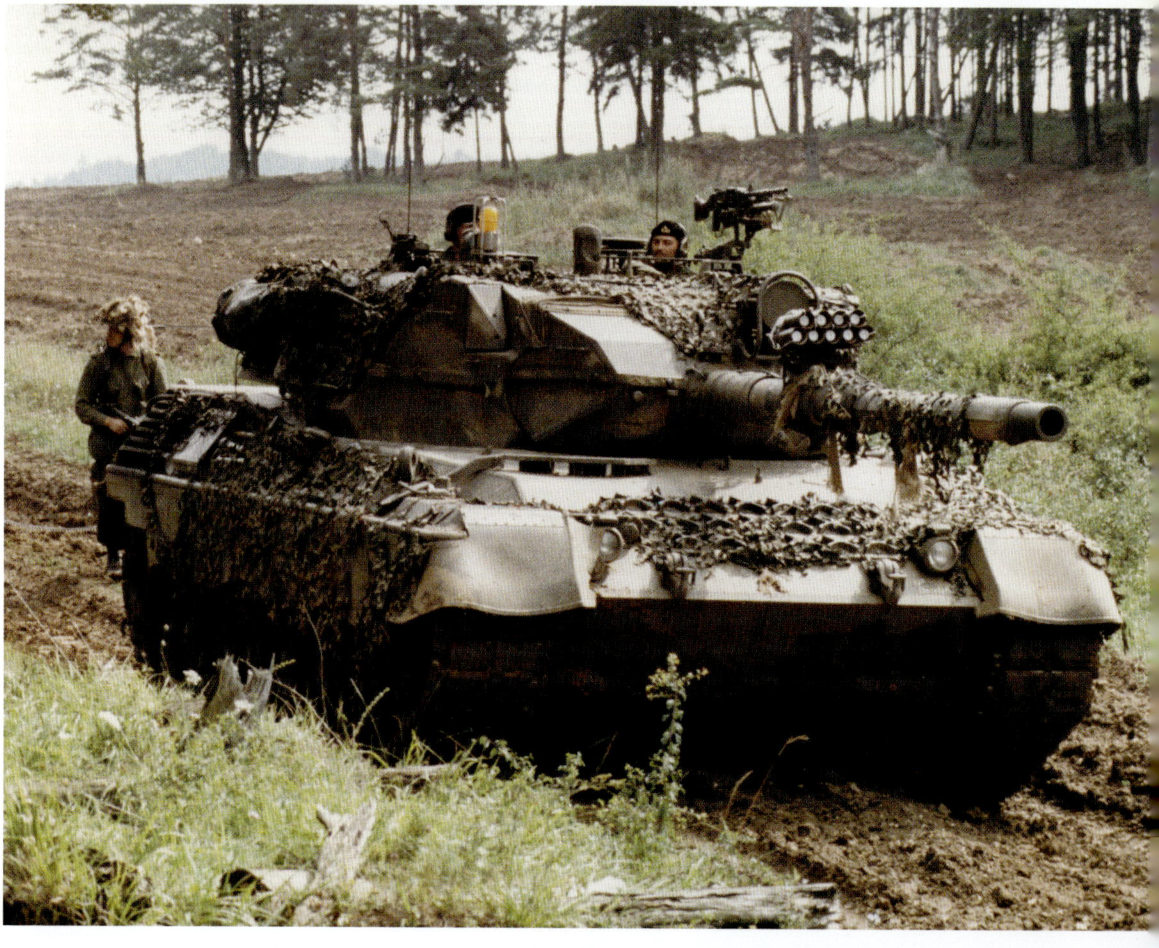

(**Opposite, above**) When originally conceived, the West German Army believed that modern anti-tank weaponry made thick conventional steel armour obsolete. Hence, the Leopard 1 design would stress firepower and mobility, with protection coming in as a distant third. The West German Army eventually began to rethink those attributes and made armour protection more critical. The development of a Leopard 1 fitted with a welded armour turret that incorporated spaced armour rather than the cast armour of earlier production models proved to be a partial answer. (*Dreamstime*)

(**Opposite, below**) Pictured here during a NATO training exercise is a Canadian Army Leopard 1 tank with a welded armoured turret. In Canadian Army service it received the designation Leopard C1. The barrel has a gunfire simulation device with an attached strobe light on the turret roof that flashes when a laser gun illuminates the vehicle. Visible behind the gunfire simulator device, mounted on the gun shield, is a circular low-light television camera surrounded by a protective steel framework. (*Canadian Army*)

(**Above**) Before the Leopard 1 entered service with the West German Army in 1965, French, Italian and West German governments tried to co-operate in coming up with a new tank that would meet all three armies' requirements. When that plan foundered, each country went its own way. The French Army began fielding the AMX-30 seen here in 1966, armed with a French-designed and built 105mm main gun. (*Pierre-Olivier Buan*)

The 105mm main gun on the AMX-30 pictured here fires a variety of French-designed and built ammunition. It can also fire all the various types of main gun rounds developed for the British-designed 105mm gun L7. The tank has stowage for forty-seven main gun rounds, nineteen stored in the turret and twenty-eight in the hull. The French tank came with a coaxial 20mm automatic cannon in place of the more common small-calibre coaxial machine gun fitted in most tanks. (*Pierre-Olivier Buan*)

As the replacement for the Conqueror heavy tank and the Centurion tank series, the British Army would field the four-man Chieftain beginning in 1967. Armed with a fully-stabilized 120mm main gun (not the same gun as in the Conqueror), the tank had a sharply-sloped glacis and front turret. The sizeable armoured box seen attached to the tank's turret housed an infrared/white light searchlight. (*Dreamstime*)

Rather than the torsion bar suspension system on which most NATO and Warsaw Pact tanks rode during the long-running Cold War, the Chieftain came with a hydro-pneumatic suspension system consisting of three independent suspension assemblies on either side of the tank's hull, which did not protrude into the hull. These made it much easier to replace them if destroyed by mine damage. Note the thermal shroud on the barrel of the tank pictured here. (*Tank Museum*)

An unexpected design problem with the entire Chieftain tank series proved to be its multi-fuel opposed-piston engine. Multi-fuel was a NATO recommendation at the time. In theory, it meant that a tank could tap into a wide variety of fuel sources, be it diesel, gasoline or kerosene. Unfortunately, the engine proved to be unreliable in service despite endless attempts by the firm that had designed and built it to fix the problem. (*Dreamstime*)

Pictured here is a Chieftain Mk 11. The last model proved to be the Mk 12. The original infrared/white light searchlight and the large armoured housing of earlier-production models disappeared. The Mk 11 came with a much smaller armoured housing fitted to the tank's turret and equipped with a thermal imaging system. The tank pictured here has Stillbrew passive armour applied to the front of the turret and around the driver's position. (*Dreamstime*)

Chapter Six

Height of the Cold War

In the late 1950s, the tank design and production arm of the Soviet military-industrial complex was no longer a single entity but several competing factions. Each was interested only in preserving its bureaucratic power by acquiring tank-building contracts. In this endeavour, the competing factions used their respective connections with high-ranking Soviet Army officers and civilians to win favour for their tank designs.

This convoluted system led to the Soviet Army having overlapping production of three MBTs during the Cold War. These included the T-64 (1967–85), T-72 (1974–91) and T-80 (1976–91). These shared many design features, such as size, main guns and autoloaders. They differed significantly in other areas, such as their engines, numbers built and design problems. All three were referred to as 'standard', comparable to the American and NATO use of the term MBT.

The Rationale Behind the T-72

The revolutionary design of the T-64 series had a downside: its cost and complexity, which limited the numbers built. Therefore, it would serve as a specialized breakthrough tank with Soviet armoured divisions assigned to lead an invasion of Western Europe from bases in East Germany at the beginning of a Third World War.

A declassified CIA report titled 'Soviet Tank Programs' dated December 1984 contains this passage: 'We expect the Soviets to continue to adhere to their deployment strategy of the past 35 years: they will equip tank units opposite NATO forces in Central Europe with the latest, most capable tanks before they begin to send large numbers to units in other theaters of military operations.'

The intended role of the T-72 was to provide a cheaper and less complicated counterpart to the T-64. They would replace T-62 and T-54/T-55 series tanks in the Soviet Army's motor rifle divisions. The earlier-generation medium tanks desperately needed replacement since they could not keep up with the BMP-1, the Soviet Army's new infantry fighting vehicle introduced in 1966.

To bring down the three-man T-72's cost, it used an upgraded version of the same diesel engine that had propelled the Soviet T-34 tank during the Second World War. Another cost-cutting measure was not equipping it with the T-64's ATGM guidance system.

Like the T-64, the 45-ton T-72 initially depended on simple infrared sights and driving lights, a significant deficiency by NATO tank design standards. Eventually, some received passive night sights for the gunner.

More traditionally-minded Soviet Army generals did not embrace the concept of fielding a high-end T-64 and low-end T-72 tank at the same time. They remained steadfast in their belief that one tank design should be selected and built in large numbers. They lost that argument to more powerful high-level civilians at top levels of the Communist Party.

Soviet Army Version

Development of the T-72 series began in 1968, with production for the Soviet Army beginning in 1973. In a declassified CIA report titled 'The Soviet T-72 Tank Performance' dated August 1982 is the following:

> The Soviets seem to have carefully integrated a variety of armored vehicle technologies into the T-72. Their design philosophy seems to have been to use proven components whenever possible, modify proven components as necessary, and when this was not possible, design new components ... As is evident, for underwater fording; radiation protection; nuclear; biological and chemical warning/protection; night vision; and gun stabilization probably originating from designs dating back to the T-55, which was fielded around 1958. All other requirements were filled using T-64 or newly-designed components.

Construction of an improved 48-ton T-72A began in 1979. Unlike the original version of the T-72 that had a conventional steel armour turret and a front hull array incorporating composite armour, the 'A' model of the T-72 had both a composite upper front hull and turret.

Unlike the slightly sloping turret front of the original T-72, composite armour on the turret front of the T-72A led to a very noticeable increase in thickness, with a near-vertical appearance. That design feature led to the tank acquiring the unofficial nickname of 'Dolly Parton' within the American defence establishment, referencing the well-endowed American country music star.

Other improvements to the T-72A included its suspension system and new turret-mounted smoke grenade-launchers. It also came with the latest version of the 125mm main gun that had initially appeared on the T-64A. Like the T-64 series, the T-72 series had an autoloader.

In the July–August 2001 issue of *Armor* magazine is an article titled 'Some Russian Tankers' Experiences in the Second Chechen War' by Adam Geibel. In the following passage from that article are comments on the T-72's autoloader:

> After five or six hours of continuous firing, the sabot ejection rack in some T-72s became unserviceable, and the magazine lifting mechanism failed. In that case, the ammunition stowage location in the tanks' fighting compartments made it difficult for crews to load the gun from the manual ammunition stowage racks. After the basic load of ammunition was expended, the tank had to leave its position in order to reload a container. Valuable time was lost.

A translated article regarding the T-72 that appeared in the May 1981 issue of a Soviet Army magazine titled *Banner Bearer* or *Standard Bearer* is a passage on the capabilities of the tank's main gun:

> Maximum sighted range of the 125mm gun is 4,000 metres [2.5 miles] in daylight and up to 800 metres [875 yards] using a night vision sight. The gun's flat trajectory range for the armour-piercing discarding sabot (APDS) round is 2,100 m[eters, approximately 1.3 miles]. High-Explosive (HE) fragmentation rounds are used from indirect or covered fire positions at ranges up to 9,400 metres [6 miles]. The rate of sighted fire is eight rounds per minute.

Like the T-64 series, the T-72 series had a two-axis stabilization system; an LRF on the T-72A replaced the coincidence rangefinder of the tank's original version.

Impressions from a Museum Curator

Despite the T-72 tank's continuous upgrading, like the previous T-64 series, it had some less than optimum design features and some good ones. Charles Lemon, the retired curator of the Patton Museum of Armor and Cavalry, mentions examples of both:

> The T-72 is the Soviet equivalent of the US M60, not the M1 Abrams, despite all the comparisons made between the two ... One problem is that the ammunition is mostly stowed in a carousel directly under the turret; all you have to do is get a round in between the road wheels and you're pretty well guaranteed to have a secondary explosion that destroys the tank and instantly kills the crew.
>
> But the fire-control system is excellent: it has a laser rangefinder that works quite well and a good fire-control computer, and that infamous auto-loader actually works pretty well. The T-72's gun stabilizer is the equivalent of the M60's – it will lock onto a target and track it; we've done it here [Fort Knox], and it works quite nicely.
>
> It [the T-72] has another odd feature, which is that the turret will wobble back and forth unless you've got the turret lock engaged or power applied to the system. Otherwise, the turret will swing back and forth a bit as the tank corners left and right, which is a bit disconcerting.
>
> The autoloader is supposed to be dangerous to the gunner, and you hear stories about gunners having their arms crushed in the thing; actually, in my experience, the gun tube – when controlled by the gun stabilization device – is more dangerous to the tank commander. With the gun depressed, the automatic loader can potentially crush the arm of the tank commander against the turret roof if he doesn't keep out of the way. And when you're distracted by searching for targets and watching what's going on outside the tank, it's easy to get in range of the automatic loader.

T-72B

Another up-armoured version of the T-72 series, the T-72B, appeared in Soviet Army service in 1985. A sub-variant became the T-72B1. The difference: the T-72B could fire a laser-guided ATGM, whereas the T-72B1 lacked that ability. Soviet export versions of the T-72B and T-72B1 appeared in 1987 and respectively became the T-72S and T-72S1.

Because of a 3-ton increase in weight due to the addition of more armour, the 50-ton T-72B and T-72B1 had an uprated diesel engine. They also received a layer of anti-radiation matting on their turrets, a feature also backdated to some T-72A tanks.

The T-72B and T-72B1 received the unofficial nickname of the 'Super Dolly Parton'. Their introduction reflected the Soviet Army's unpleasant surprise discovery in 1982 that the new NATO 105mm APFSDS round could penetrate frontal armour on the T-64, T-72 and T-80 series tanks.

By way of comparison, the initial Soviet Army version of the T-72, with steel armour turret and composite armour glacis, provided far less protection. The front turret provided the equivalent steel armour protection level of 410mm (16in) against HEAT rounds and 380mm (15in) when struck by an APFSDS round.

New Type of Armour

On acquiring a T-72B in the late 1980s, the US Army discovered that the armour array in two cavities on either side of the tank's 125mm main gun did not consist of composite armour but 'special armour'.

These cavities had removable steel armour cover plates, allowing for the special armour arrangement to be changed if required. For example, this could occur should a new type of advanced special armour become available.

An article published in the May 2002 issue of the *Journal of Military Ordnance* titled 'The First Look at Soviet Special Armor' by James. M. Warford explains the significance:

> Special armor is more advanced in design and application than the composite armor used to protect previous Soviet tanks. In fact, it was thought that special armor developments were still beyond the design constraints of Cold War-era Soviet tanks. This surprising confirmation was truly a revelation; the Soviets had perfected a type of special armor and successfully incorporated it into a tank turret, without making the leap to a large box-shaped design characteristic of US and NATO special armored MBTs [the American M1 Abrams and the British Challenger 1 tanks].

The special armour on the front of the T-72B/T-72B1 received the classification of NERA (non-explosive reactive armour). It consisted of some three-layer plate arrangements glued together. In the middle of each spaced three-layer plate, a layer of rubber is compressed between steel layers by an attacking HEAT 'jet'.

> **Composite Armour for Older-Generation Soviet Tanks**
> One of the most noticeable early 1980s improvements to the T-62 series and the preceding T-55 series proved to be the addition of non-explosive reactive armour (NERA) to the tanks' glacis and turret fronts. The Soviet Army labelled the add-on protection arrangement 'BDD'. It received the nickname 'Brow' armour due to its resemblance to Communist Party founder Vladimir Ilyich Lenin's thick eyebrows. The BDD consisted of steel armour boxes containing thin steel plates encased in solid polyurethane, which made them almost immune to early-generation 105mm L7 APFSDS rounds.

The compressed rubber then expands (or rebounds) and moves the steel layers of each arrayed plate, which causes multiple-layered reactions, disrupting the attacking jet and causing it to lose all or most of its energy (penetrating power). The arrayed three-layered plates are backed up by a heavy steel plate (the innermost layer in each frontal armour cavity) to ensure the jet's remaining energy dissipates within the cavity.

A post-Cold War source states that the frontal turret armour on the T-72B and T-72B1 boasted the equivalent steel armour protection of 950mm (37in) against HEAT and 520mm (20in) of steel armour against APFSDS rounds. The tank's glacis had the equivalent steel armour protection level of 900mm (35in) when confronted by HEAT rounds and the equivalent steel armour protection level of 520mm (20in) against APFSDS rounds.

Export T-72 Tanks

Besides seeing the T-72 as a replacement for its T-54/T-55/T-62 series tank inventory, the Soviet Army also saw the T-72 doing the same for its Warsaw Pact allies. Following three-way negotiations among the Soviet Union, Poland and Czechoslovakia, a deal came about in 1978. The Warsaw Pact countries could build their version of the T-72 under licence, labelled the T-72M.

As the Soviet Army began introducing progressively improved models of the T-72, some design features were adopted by the Polish and Czech factories and received the designation T-72M1.

The T-72M retained the same armour protection levels of the Soviet Army's initial model of the T-72. The T-72M1 rose to the equivalent of 490mm (19in) of steel armour on the turret front and the equivalent of 380mm (15in) of steel armour against APFSDS rounds.

The glacis plate of the T-72M1 boasted the equivalent of 490mm (19in) of steel armour when struck with a HEAT round, and the equivalent of 400mm (16in) of steel armour when hit by an APFSDS round.

Besides the Polish and Czech armies, the East German, Hungarian and Bulgarian armies also adopted the 49-ton T-72M and T-72M1. Polish and Czech factories also sold the T-72M and T-72M1 to non-Warsaw Pact armies. The largest number of these went to Iraq, which took into service about 1,000 examples of the

> **T-72 Road Report**
> Marc Sehring, the curator of the Virginia Museum of Military Vehicles, shares his impressions of a Czech-built T-72M1 tank in their collection:
>
>> The T-72 is another awesome Soviet invention. It uses the same engine as the T-55, but turbocharged, with lots of guts. I like the driver's compartment very much; it is like a cockpit. You sit nice and low, in a comfortable seat. Visibility is pretty good: one large periscope forward and two smaller ones for the side. You have lots of armor around you.
>>
>> You've got lots of controls: preheater, air system, smoke generator, heating, good instrumentation for the engine, good communication systems. When you are flying down the field in something like that (and it accelerates well), you don't have to worry about hitting anything because you can go through or over almost anything in your way.
>>
>> The silhouette is even lower than the T-55, one of the lowest of its era. The 125mm cannon is a hell of a gun – just keep your arms tucked in, away from the automatic loader, and you'll be okay. I think it was able to take out anything in its time – and that was the 1970s when we only had the M60. If the crews were equally well-trained (and that's a key ingredient), the T-72 would probably have been the winner.

Polish-built T-72M1. Main gun ammunition supplied for the non-Warsaw Pact export tanks proved to be older-generation examples.

T-80 Tank

In 1971, Soviet tank designers started developing the T-80, the intended replacement for both the T-64 and the T-72. Production of the initial model began in 1976.

Unlike the liquid-cooled diesel engine of the T-64 series, the new T-80 chassis received power from a gas turbine engine. Despite high expectations, the T-80's gas turbine engine initially proved unreliable in service. The fuel-thirsty engine also severely limited the vehicle's operational range.

Newer Models

The initial version of the T-80 proved less capable than the T-64B and only a couple of hundred rolled out of the factory doors between 1976 and 1978. A second model, the T-80B, appeared in 1978, with a new turret design. It matched the T-64B in many areas, such as its fire-control system and its ability to fire ATGMs.

As a newer tank, the armour protection levels of the T-80B were superior to those of the T-64B. The first examples of the T-80B began showing up with Soviet Army armoured divisions in East Germany in 1983. Subsequent versions of the T-80 series included the 47-ton T-80BV that appeared in 1985.

The same year that the T-80BV emerged, another version of the T-80 series labelled the T-80U came down the production lines. It had an LRF and TIS. The T-80U also had an auxiliary power unit (APU), allowing the tank's subsystems, such as the radios, to operate without running the gas turbine engine.

A post-Cold War source stated that the front of the composite armour turret on the T-80U, supplemented with second-generation exterior ERA (Kontak-5), provided the equivalent steel armour protection from HEAT rounds of 1,320mm (52in) and APFSDS rounds of 780mm (31in).

In its final guise, the 50-ton T-80UD appeared in 1988, with a liquid-cooled diesel engine replacing the gas-turbine engine. The T-80 series production ran to approximately 5,000 vehicles, with most assigned to Soviet Army armoured divisions based in East Germany and Poland until the end of the Cold War.

Soviet View of the T-80, by Oleg Sapunkov

The T-80 was much better received in the Soviet Army than its predecessor, the T-64, and Soviet literature does not carry as much harsh criticism against the turbine tank. The criticism that is voiced primarily addresses the cost of the engine and the resultant overall cost of the tank.

When first introduced, the cost of the T-80's GTD-1000 gas turbine engine was comparable to the cost of an entire early-model T-64 MBT; thus early T-80s were around three times more expensive than a contemporary T-72 MBT.

In addition to the increased production cost, the T-80 was much more expensive to operate due to the turbine engine's high fuel consumption: almost twice as much as a diesel engine of comparable power output, on average. The high fuel consumption also reduced the T-80's effective driving range, even though it was equipped with larger fuel tanks than the T-64 or the T-72. Finally, early T-80s proved to be susceptible to turbine blade damage from dust intrusion, especially when continuously operating in a large dust cloud raised by a tank column on a long run.

Overall, however, the Soviet Army appeared to be pleased with the capabilities, performance and reliability of the T-80, especially when compared to the T-64. The gas turbine engine allowed the tank to achieve a slightly higher top speed and much better acceleration, and it remained reliable at low temperatures encountered in rough winter weather. Additionally, the turbine engine was quieter than a comparable diesel engine, as it produced less noise at low frequencies that most easily propagate at long range.

The T-80 introduced rubberized roadwheels and rubberized tracks, which helped reduce vibrations generated during travel, and also helped reduce the tank's acoustic signature. Following the issues encountered with the T-64's half-width torsion bars, the T-80 was built with conventional, full-width torsion bars, which were more reliable over the tank's lifetime.

Due to the high expenses associated with the gas turbine engine, the T-80's drivetrain was engineered for reliability, to reduce the wear on the turbine and extend the engine's lifetime between overhauls. Most importantly, the main turbine itself was not mechanically linked to the drivetrain, but instead sent air to two independent turbo-compressors, which were linked to the tank's planetary gearboxes. This avoided directly stressing the turbine during sudden speed changes, gear shifts, braking or obstacle collisions. Furthermore, the turbine inlet was fitted with a gas cyclone air separator, which filtered out the majority of dust from the air intake without the need for a physical filter, which would quickly clog up and cut off the flow of air to the turbine. The fine dust particles that were able to pass through the air separator and settle on the turbine blades were cleaned off when the engine ran through a vibration cycle, advised to happen every three or four hours of operation, and latent dust was cleaned with a full engine air blow through before and after each drive.

Finally, as the T-80 was expected to operate with limited logistical support, the gas turbine engine was designed to be able to run not only using aviation-grade jet fuel, but also diesel fuel and even low-octane automotive gasoline, though the latter would allow for lower power output.

The T-80 also received improved optics, including vision blocks that allowed the driver a much wider field of view, and an improved gunsight and range-finder, which allowed more accurate gunfire at ranges over 2 km [1.2 miles]. The crew compartment was fitted with an internal heating system for use in cold weather operation, which also helped keep the electronics within the tank warm. The armour protection increased significantly along the frontal arc.

The T-80 was generally regarded as being a much more reliable tank than the T-64, and it is interesting to note that while there is considerable criticism regarding the reliability of the T-64's autoloader mechanism, there does not appear to be as much criticism against the T-80's autoloader, even though it was practically the same design. This could be due to the improvements made to the autoloader or to the somewhat reduced amount of critical commentary offered by late Soviet tank factories about each other's designs since there was less perceived or anticipated pressure from the Soviet government to unify the nation's tank production to a single model.

Sources: https://topwar.ru/5513-t-80-35-let-na-sluzhbe.html
http://btvt.info/1inservice/t-80.htm
http://btvt.info/1inservice/t-80u.htm
https://thesovietarmourblog.blogspot.com/2016/02/t-80-gambol.html

M48A5 Tank

As the 1973 Yom Kippur War raged, it resulted in heavy losses to the Israeli Army tank fleet. Fearing an Israeli defeat, the American government decided to aid the country's military by supplying many M60A1 tanks from the US Army's pre-positioned stockpiles in Europe.

As American industry could not replace all of the M60A1s supplied to Israel, a decision was made to make up for the US Army's tank shortfall by upgrading some of its existing inventory of 90mm gun-armed M48 series tanks with the 105mm M68 tank gun. The up-gunned M48s received the designation M48A5. The process took place at a US Army depot.

Around 2,000 M48A5s came out of the US Army depot between 1975 and 1979, divided into three different batches. The initial batch consisted of 501 re-worked examples of the M48A3 version. Approximately 400 of these were former Marine Corps' M48A3s, as the Marines had switched to the M60A1.

The second batch of 708 M48 series tanks and the third batch of 960 vehicles consisted of unmodified M48A1 tanks. Bringing the M48A3 up to the M48A5 standard involved only eleven new major sub-assemblies, as the tank already featured some M60 components. To bring the M48A1 up to the M48A5 standard involved a bit more work and took sixty-seven new major sub-assemblies.

From an article in the September–October 1980 issue of *Armor* magazine titled 'A New Tank on the Block' comes the following extract:

> The M48A5 rebuild process began with destruction. Each old tank [M48A1] was taken apart in the disassembly area of Building 400, the Depot's five-acre building used for tracked vehicle maintenance. Here the turret and chassis were separated, with the turret going off to an adjacent building for further disassembly ... while the chassis was being refitted, the turret had also been undergoing its own rebuild procedure ... Every lens, mirror and optical window in the periscopes and range-finding system had been checked for scratches and irregularities in surface flatness. If necessary, they were reground and polished to a surface flatness tolerance of a millionth of an inch ... Once a tank was completed, it was turned over to the Depot's Directorate of Quality where it was driven 25 miles on a test track, and 60 and 40 percent inclines to check for all possible defects.

Israeli Army Tank Influence

Before the first M48A5 entered US Army service, a decision was made to modify them with some design improvements based on Israeli Army combat experience. These included increased main gun ammunition storage and an Israeli-designed low-profile vehicle commander's cupola with three periscopes and a two-position scissors-type mount for a 7.62mm machine gun.

A novel feature of the Israeli-designed low-profile vehicle commander's cupola was its overhead hatch, which provided a couple of different options. If the TC (tank commander) feared overhead threats (such as artillery air bursts or small-arms fire), he could move his overhead hatch to a horizontal orientation that lay just a few inches above the rim of the cupola. By doing so, he could maintain his direct vision of the battlefield and maintain a higher level of situational awareness than if he depended only on the cupola's periscopes.

The bulk of the M48A5s went off to US Army Reserve and National Guard tank units, where they remained until they passed from service in the early 1990s.

Many of these tanks then went off to non-NATO armies under military aid programmes.

The Turkish Army had its existing inventory of American-supplied early-model M48 series tanks upgraded to the M48A5 standard between 1983 and 1993 with American-supplied industrial equipment installed in two Turkish depots.

M60A3 Tank

In 1979, the upgraded 57-ton M60A3 appeared, reflecting the US Army's effort to keep the M60 tank series viable on future battlefields. It came with an LRF and an add-on stabilization system. A TTS (tank thermal sight) appeared in 1980, replacing the gunner's original passive night sight.

In the July–August 1979 issue of *Armor* magazine is an article titled 'M60A3 Update' that mentions the advantages brought to the tank from its TTS:

> The tank thermal sight provides a marked improvement over image intensification sights. It employs thermal technology so that its detection range is not dependent on moon or starlight. It sees as well in total darkness as it does in daylight and can detect targets through smoke, fog and dust. It can also penetrate camouflage because it senses the heat of objects hidden by natural and man-made materials. It is equipped to provide the tank commander with the same thermal image display as seen by the gunner. In a force-on-force operation against image intensification devices, the thermal sight demonstrated an average 7-to-1 loss exchange rate during attack and defense scenarios.

Range data for the 105mm main gun of the M60A3 went into a solid-state ballistic computer that produced aiming information for the gunner. Simultaneously, the computer also compensated for a wide range of interior and external factors that could influence the gun's accuracy, such as crosswinds, cant and barrel wear.

External identification features of the M60A3 included a thermal sleeve on the main gun barrel and British-designed M239 smoke grenade-launchers, one on either side of the turret. The M60A3 also received a new coaxial machine gun, the Belgian-designed 7.62mm M240.

To help create a large smokescreen, the M60A3 came with the Vehicle Engine Exhaust Smoke System (VEESS) copied from Soviet Army tanks. The system worked by spraying fuel into the tank's hot exhaust duct, where it evaporated. When the hot fuel vapour reached the cooler outside air, it formed a dense smoke cloud.

Production of the M60A3 took place between 1979 and 1987, with a total of 5,400 vehicles constructed. Newly-built vehicles totalled 1,700 examples, with the remainder being re-worked M60A1s, modified at two US Army depots.

As more M1 Abrams series tanks entered US Army service, the M60A3s went to National Guard tank units, with the last examples remaining in service until 1997. Both Greece and Turkey received M60A3 tanks before the Cold War ended.

> **The Soviet Army View on Smoke-Generating Systems**
> The Soviet Army had long seen smoke as a cost-effective solution to decreasing its tanks' vulnerability on the modern battlefield. An example of that train of thought appeared in the following passage from an article titled 'Under Smoke Conditions' in the October 1975 issue of a Soviet military magazine titled the *Military Herald*:
>
>> Now, when the effectiveness of all types of weapons is significantly growing, screening with smoke plays an even more important role in safeguarding the combat operations of troops. It makes observation, aimed fire and control [of tactical units) difficult and does not permit the use of infrared, television, laser and other (viewing) equipment.

The Need

Even before the first M60 series tank rolled off the production line in 1959, the US Army began thinking about its replacement. In January 1972, the army established a task force to conceive a superior MBT that offered a much higher degree of performance and capabilities than the existing M60 tank.

A Defense Systems Management College report titled 'Lessons Learned: M1 Abrams Tank System' dated July 1983 listed M60 shortcomings and why it needed replacement as soon as possible:

> The M60 tank was deemed tactically and technically incapable of defeating a numerically superior threat under day, night, adverse weather, Nuclear, Biological and Chemical (NBC) and normal battlefield obscurant conditions. The following M60 tank operational deficiencies existed:
> - Large silhouette in both height and width; larger than any other tank in the world.
> - Inadequate acceleration and cross-country speed.
> - Unacceptable reliability of mobility and firepower systems.
> - Lack of adequate firepower on the move.
> - Insufficient ballistic protection against hypervelocity kinetic energy munitions.

However, the path to a new tank proved a long and frustrating one for the army. The M60's replacement, the initial iteration of the M1 tank, officially nicknamed the 'Abrams', did not come off the assembly lines until 1980. Between the M60 and M1 lay the costly failures of the MBT-70 (Main Battle Tank 1970) and its cheaper cousin, the XM803.

Painful lessons from the MBT-70 and XM803 debacles led the US Army to do away with some of those programmes' more complex and costly design features. Those included the 152mm Gun/Missile-Launcher, an autoloader, the driver's placement in the turret and a hydro-pneumatic suspension system.

Working Towards a Common Goal

In a vaguely-written memorandum signed in 1974, the US Army and West German Army agreed to work together to develop and field an MBT that could fulfil both countries' requirements. Eventually, this would involve competition between the American-designed and developed XM-1 and an early version of what eventually became the West German Army's Leopard 2 tank. The contest ended when the West German tank was pulled from consideration in January 1977, with no reason given.

In a passage from a May 1974 report by the Defense Management School titled 'An Examination of the XM-1 Tank System Acquisition Program in a Peacetime Environment' is a listing of reasons why co-production agreements involving equipment such as tanks typically do not work:

1. National pride and capabilities to produce the item.
2. Differences in employment philosophy of the item.
3. Differences in required capabilities of subsystems.
4. Management chain of approval.
5. Differences in national development philosophy.
6. Differences in contracting methods.
7. Lack of common international standards, i.e. metric vs. English measurement systems.

M1 Description

The initial version of the four-man M1 (later referred to as the basic M1) had a 105mm M68 series main gun, with onboard stowage for fifty-five rounds. Early plans had called for the M1 tank to mount an American version of a West German-designed 120mm smoothbore main gun. However, its development was not yet complete when the M1 entered service. Provisions existed to mount the 120mm main gun later.

The M1 turret had a two-axis stabilization system, a laser rangefinder, a digital fire-control system and a TIS. US Army Lieutenant General Louis C. Wagner testified before Congress in 1985:

> [The M1's] stabilized sighting system ensures that speed is combined with accurate firepower. Tankers are able to routinely hit 5-foot targets over a mile away while moving rapidly cross-country. This kind of shoot-on-the-move capability is made possible by design features of the fire control and improved suspension systems ... the gunner need only squeeze the trigger to hit the target.

A well-trained gunner or vehicle commander on the M1 could identify distant objects such as tanks or trucks with his TIS using engine and exhaust cues to discern if they were taking evasive action. In response, the Soviet Army fielded a smoke-screening grenade system that generated an aerosol cloud of heated particles capable of blocking thermal energy transmission.

The M1 weighed about 61 tons and rode on a torsion bar suspension system. Since the springing action of torsion bars alone would cause the tank to pitch wildly, even on level surfaces, the tank featured six rotary hydraulic shock absorbers that prevented the tank's heavy hull from oscillating on the torsion bar suspension system, a process known as dampening.

The M1 received power from a gas turbine engine, with its preferred propellant being kerosene-based aviation fuel. It could also work with diesel and gasoline. The gas turbine engine provided a top speed on level roads of 45mph and off-road 30mph. Its predecessor, the M60A3, could barely muster 15mph off-road.

General Donn A. Starry mentioned in a 15 May 1981 letter to another general a problem with the mobility imparted to the M1 by its gas turbine engine:

> I followed them [the M1 tanks] through a night road march in which they made about 80 kilometers [50 miles] in an hour and a half with no problem at all. All the infantry carriers, command and control and support vehicles were hours behind, struggling along, and the tank battalion had swung into the attack! It is quite like the time 20 years ago when we first fielded the M60 tank and had the M59 armored personnel carrier to go along with it – a vehicle with scarcely half the capabilities. We had a devil of a time until we got the M113, which could keep up at least most of the time.

The M1's cruising range came in at about 275 miles on level paved roads, and the M60A3 about the same. Cross-country range for both tanks proved dramatically lower, as it is with all tanks.

Driving the Abrams

Dan Shepetis, a retired Marine Corps master sergeant, recalls his impressions when given the chance to drive a pilot XM1 tank:

> I twisted the throttle, and off we went. 'Damn,' I said to myself, 'this thing is a hot rod.' I mean, it has power up the ass, no lugging at the start, just enough power! As we moved down a road, I backed off the power and discovered no engine braking. That was something new for me. I was soon moving a little too fast, and I let the instructor know some bumps were coming. The instructor was waiting for that and told me to pour on the speed. 'She can take it,' he shouted into the intercom. As we hit the series of bumps, the damn tank floated over them. If it had been an M48 or M60, we would have gone airborne as we hurled off the first bump and crashed into the ground with enough force to snap everybody's neck back and forth and maybe a few teeth loose. The crew would have been bloodied and mad as hell. It was then I thought to myself that this was the tank tankers have been dreaming about for the last twenty years.

From a November 1982 US Army report titled 'Lessons Learned: M1 Abrams Tank System' is this passage on some of the perceived advantages offered by powering the M1 with a gas turbine engine:

> The turbine engine is nearly 1 ton lighter than a comparable diesel engine. At maturity, the turbine is expected to operate up to 12,000 miles without requiring overhaul, nearly 2½ times greater than the diesel engine used in the M60. Furthermore, the turbine never requires an oil change and has the capability of operating on a wide range of fuels, including diesel, jet fuel and gasoline. Approximately 70 percent of the engine accessories and components can be removed without removing the powerpack from the tank.

Fuel-Hog

The fuel economy of a tank is stated in gallons per mile rather than miles per gallon. During Operation DESERT STORM in 1991, Abrams tanks consumed about 7 gallons of fuel per mile of cross-country travel. Unlike most tanks' diesel engines, gas turbine engines consume almost as much fuel while idling as they do at full power.

The difference between tested fuel consumption figures and actual operational consumption is because tanks in a combat situation seldom move in continuous marches. Instead, tank units tend to move in bounds, with one part of the unit moving while another part covers by fire from protected positions. Tank units' movement by bounds can often involve significant stationary periods for individual tanks. Thus, a given element of a tank unit spends over half its time stationary.

Some US Army Abrams tank units ran out of fuel during DESERT STORM before their fuel supply trucks could reach them. The US Army lacked enough fuel trucks with the necessary cross-country mobility to keep up with the tanks.

In a February 1991 GAO titled 'Abrams Tank: Operating Cost More Than Expected' is this passage:

> Fuel consumption has been a continuing concern since the M1 tank was fielded. The Army expected the Abrams tank to use more fuel than the M60A3 tank ... According to Army officials, the Army originally estimated the M1 turbine engine would use about 100 percent more fuel than the M60 diesel engine. However, current Army data shows that the M1 tank uses 251 percent more fuel [than the M60].

M1 Protection

Unlike the M60A3's cast-armour turret, the M1's turret was afforded protection by an American version of a British-designed special armour code-named 'Burlington' (but more commonly referred to as 'Chobham' armour). A US Army Center for Military History publication on Operation DESERT STORM described the special armour on the M1 tanks as 'ceramic blocks set in resin between layers of conventional armor'.

Soviet military sources, quoted by one author, stated that the initial version of the M1 had the equivalent of 650mm (25in) of steel armour against HEAT rounds and the equivalent of 470mm (18in) of steel armour against APFSDS rounds.

Some defence-related websites and unclassified publications have described how the special armour worked on the M1 tank. When penetrated by a shaped-charge warhead, the ceramic blocks at the point of impact shattered and formed a thick cloud of small ceramic particles. When the high-speed molten jet of the shaped-charge warhead reached the ceramic cloud a fraction of a second after impact, it is effectively defeated. These same ceramic particles can also whittle down the mass of a KE projectile as it travels through a special armour array on the M1, a process referred to as erosion.

Of the conventional steel armour box that contains the ceramic blocks on an M1, it is the rear plate, referred to as the 'backing plate', that is key to defeating KE projectiles. The reason is that it determines the strength and resistance of the ceramic blocks contained within. The front plate only contains the ceramic blocks and confines the ceramic particles when struck. The ceramic blocks on the M1 were removable when damaged by taking off the overhead covering armour plate or installing a newly-available special armour arrangement.

From a December 2005 unclassified report by the Center for Technology and National Security Policy titled 'Critical Technology Events in the Development of the Abrams Tank' is the following extract on the Abrams' tank special armour:

> Details of the Abrams' armor design and composition are classified, but this much can be said: instead of using a single material – steel – the Chobham concept uses steel over one or more layers of different materials, each layer designed to perform a different function against incoming munitions. The armor is, therefore, a layered composite. The result is that one can either have protection equivalent to using only steel at a much-reduced weight, or one can have much more protection at the same weight as a steel-only configuration. A great deal of research was performed to perfect the design.

An important survivability feature of the M1 is that most main gun rounds reside in the rear of the vehicle's turret behind two 1in-thick blast-proof steel doors. The door of the ready rack only opens when the loader withdraws a main gun round. Thus, should the main gun round stowage space suffer a penetration that detonates the main gun rounds stowed within, lightly-attached blow-off panels on the rear turret roof allow the resulting gases to vent up and out, saving both the crew and their tank.

The M1 also featured an advanced fire-suppression system consisting of seven dual-spectrum infrared detectors. These activate when sensing a hydrocarbon fire's radiation characteristics. The system proved sufficiently sensitive to tell the difference between a flashlight beam, matches and sunlight. The detectors can detect an 18in-diameter fire at a distance of 1.6 yards (1.5m) within 6 milliseconds; this is fast enough to extinguish a fire and prevent the build-up of an explosion.

Adding to the M1 tank and follow-on models' survivability were two six-round smoke grenade-launchers, designated the M250, one affixed on either side of the tank's turret. The vehicle commander or loader activates the system from inside the turret. Typically, it only takes six smoke grenades to hide a vehicle. However, heavy rain, windy conditions and very low humidity can reduce the smoke grenades' effectiveness.

A Round-Up

A total of 2,374 examples of the basic M1 version came off the production lines between 1980 and 1985. After that, the contractor upgraded 894 M1s, labelled the Improved Product M1 (IPM1), between 1984 and 1986. This programme ran concurrently with the phasing-out of the basic M1.

The 105mm gun-armed IPM1 featured several improvements incorporated into the next version of the M1 armed with a 120mm main gun. The upgrades included thicker frontal turret armour and a bustle rack at the turret's rear, a feature absent on the basic M1. The basic M1 lasted in US Army service until 1986, with some surviving in National Guard use until 2007. All the basic M1s and IMP1s went into storage to rebuild into newer versions if the need arose.

Change is Inevitable, Misery is Optional: The M60 and the M1
Larry Levasseur (Sabot Member):

> During my time in the Army, I trained on the M60A3 and then crewed the M60A1, M1, M1A1 and M1A2. The tale I want to relate is about the differences I noticed when jumping from the M60A1 to the M1A1. Some may think the things I mention just a bit odd, but for me, they were real and were what we really experienced.
>
> The first issue was a stronger sense of community within our tank platoon when crewing the M60A1. It was the early '80s, and parts were few and far between. We did not have four-man crews in many cases, and our tanks really needed a lot of love. The platoon had only two heaters that worked. During field training exercises, we would pile 5, 6 or 7 guys into the vehicles that had working heaters when we were not actually maneuvering. We had space inside the M60A1! How could this not make the platoon bond stronger? Never in my time on the M1 series did we attempt to wedge so many into the vehicle; lack of space would have prevented this. One other odd thing that happened on the M60A1 was where my TC would sleep. Quite often, he would open the rear grill doors, crawl onto the heat shield and rack out. This is something that could not happen on the M1 series tank.
>
> The other issue that was evident between our M60A1s and the M1 series tank was the level of trust the old-time tankers had with the vehicles. Yes, our 60s were old and beat up, but the men crewing them knew the quirks

and all the workarounds. Degraded mode gunnery was more often the norm than the exception. Those that crewed the M60A1 had no doubt that they could roll onto the range and qualify their tank no matter the situation. We had supreme confidence in our fire-control systems, especially in the defense.

Our shiny new toys (the Abrams) looked great with all the latest advanced technology, but we took them with just a bit of skepticism. How would all those new electronic components work when they got jostled around or wet? Sure, as with most things, time and training taught us that the M1 was a machine far superior to anything we had ever seen. We learned to be very proficient at troubleshooting it. Every once in a while, when the turret would spin because the delta-p was bad, I would think to myself, 'This beast is possessed.' These things never happened to our old girl. We did not need to troubleshoot the electronics on the M60A1. We just broke out the chicken bones, loaded sabot, fired battlesight and drove on. And, of course, we never forgot to check the heat shield for our sleeping TC before cranking the old girl.

Endless problems with the T-64 series, including price, led the Soviet Army to embrace a simpler and less costly tank design, the T-72. Production of the initial version of the T-72 began in 1973. In 1975, it became the T-72 Ural. Early-production examples had the infrared searchlight on the left side of the 125mm main gun, as shown in this photograph. Following troop trials, the infrared searchlight moved to the right side of the 125mm main gun on later-production examples of the T-72 Ural. *(Dreamstime)*

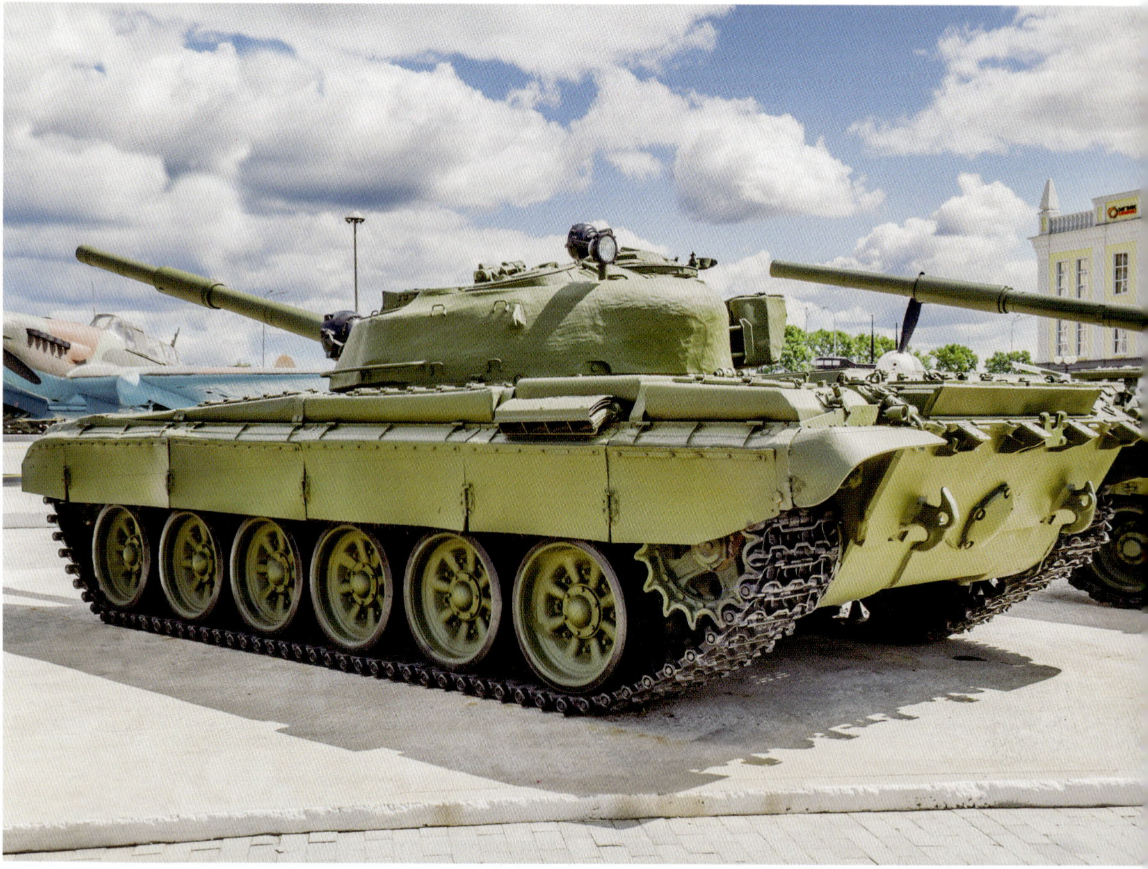

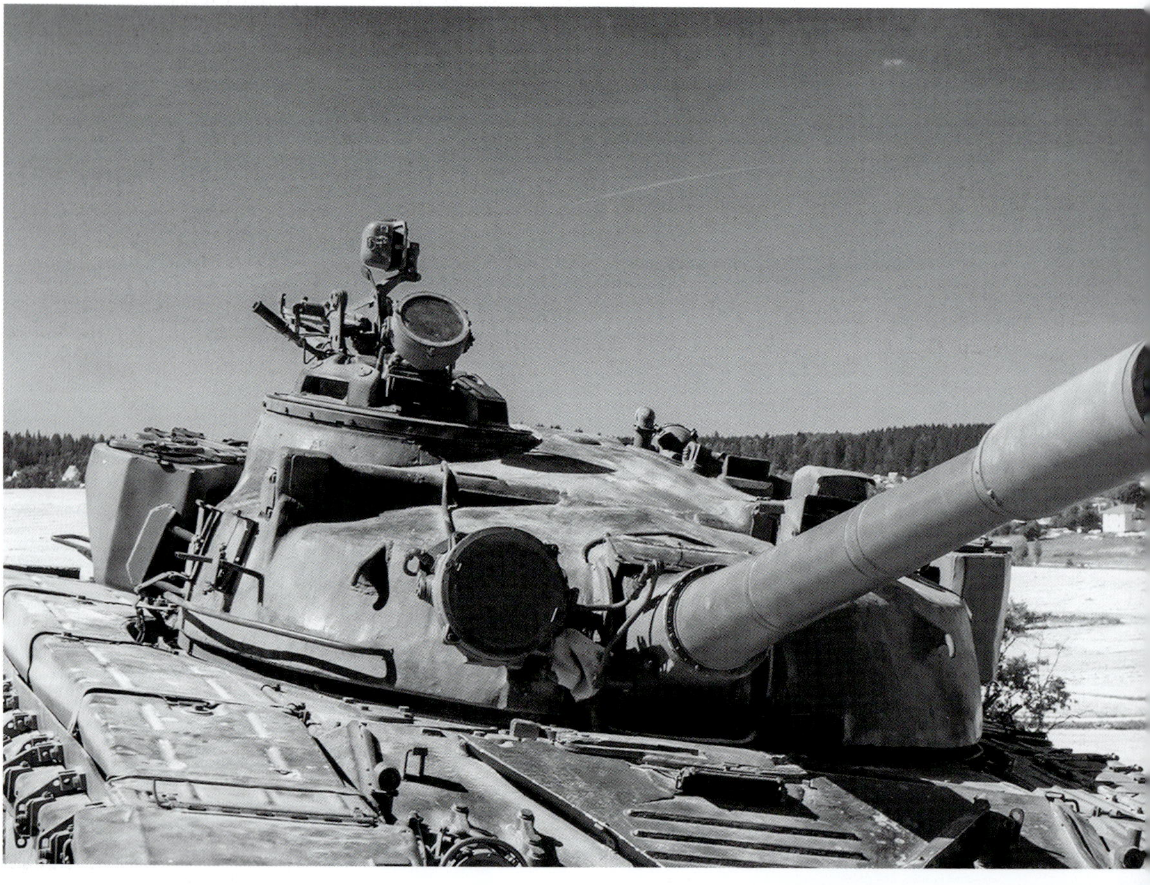

(**Opposite, above**) A preserved T-72 Ural as indicated by the infrared searchlight on the left-hand side of the 125mm main gun. It lacks one of the two external rear turret stowage containers. Later models had three. The roadwheels on the T-72 series were larger than those on the T-64 series and made of steel with rubber rims. The diesel engine of the tank is an upgraded version of that powering the T-54/T-55 series and the T-62. (*Dreamstime*)

(**Opposite, below**) The T-72 Ural featured an optical rangefinder. The turret roof protrusion for the optical rangefinder appears in front of and off to the right below the vehicle commander's cupola of the vehicle pictured here. As this rangefinder proved costly to build and difficult to use, a laser rangefinder (LRF) took its place. With the fitting of an LRF, the optical rangefinder port was sealed and the turret roof protrusion on subsequent models of the T-72 Ural disappeared. (*Dreamstime*)

(**Above**) An upgraded version of the T-72 labelled the T-72A is visible in this picture and entered into production in 1979. It featured much thicker frontal turret armour than its predecessor and received the unofficial US Army nickname of the 'Dolly Parton' after the well-endowed American country music star. On the turret roof is a layer of anti-radiation matting, a feature that also went onto earlier-generation Soviet Army tanks. (*DOD*)

202

(**Opposite, above**) Shown here is a Soviet industry-built T-72A. Czech and Polish factories did not build a direct copy of the T-72A; rather they constructed a less capable version labelled the T-72M. Generally speaking, even after some armour upgrades, it had less effective armour protection than that of the Soviet-built T-72A. Czech and Polish T-72Ms, as well as those acquired by other Warsaw Pact armies, were eventually updated with some of the design features of the Soviet-built T72A, including add-on armour and smoke grenade-launchers on the front of their turrets. (*Dreamstime*)

(**Opposite, below**) The Warsaw Pact-built T-72M pictured here has all its flip-out plastic and metal panels deployed. Unofficially nicknamed 'gill' armour, they protected the tank from smaller shaped-charge warheads. When not in use, they folded back against the sides of the tank's hull. The Soviet-built T-72As did away with the flip-out panels and went with a conventional plastic and metal arrangement affixed to either side of the tank's hull. Czech and Polish factories began building a more capable version of the T-72M labelled the T-72M1 in the mid-1980s. (*Hans Halberstadt*)

(**Above**) Looking down into the vehicle commander's position on a T-72M, one can see his periscope sight. It's a day/night binocular device that has an integral infrared feature for night observation. The black upward-pointing handles on the periscope's bottom allow the vehicle commander to turn his cupola left or right. The vehicle commander also uses the handles to steady himself from the main gun's recoil when fired. (*Hans Halberstadt*)

204

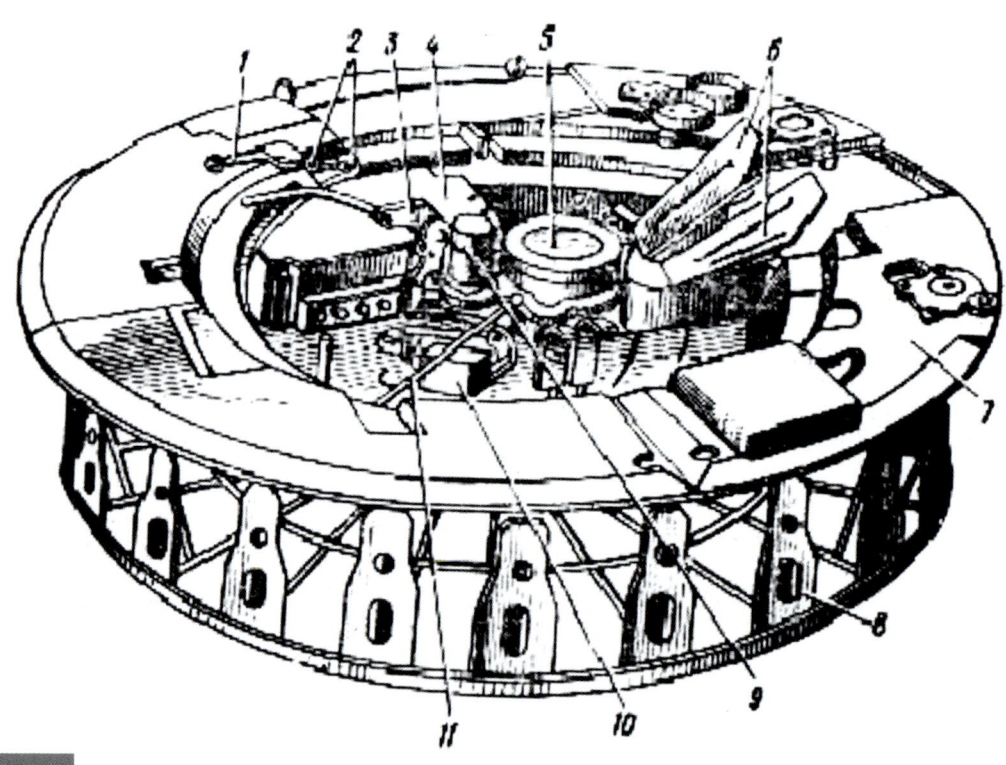

(**Opposite, above**) The gunner's optical equipment in a T-72M tank. The sight on the left of the image is the gunner's infrared sight. To the right is the gunner's primary daylight sight that includes a laser rangefinder (LRF). Unlike the fire-control equipment on the M1 Abrams tank series that automatically input information into the tank ballistic computer, most of the firing information must be manually entered into the ballistic computer of the T-72 by the gunner. (*Hans Halberstadt*)

(**Opposite, below**) From a T-72 series manual, an illustration of the tank's autoloader. In the T-72, the separate loading projectile and propellant charge are both stored horizontally, with the propellant charge attached to the projectile's top. The autoloader lifts both propellant charge and projectile level with the breech and then loads the projectile and propellant charge in two separate actions. (*Author's collection*)

(**Above**) The pronounced thickening of the frontal turret armour on the T-72B tank pictured here resulted in its unofficial nickname of the 'Super Dolly Parton' armour arrangement. The T-72B entered into Soviet Army service in 1985 and could fire a tube-launched laser-guided anti-tank missile named the 'Svir'. A later version bore the name 'Refleck'. NATO referred to the missiles as the AT-11 'Sniper'. Those T-72Bs without the ability to fire laser-guided anti-tank missiles were designated the T-72B1. (*DOD*)

(**Above**) As with all the Soviet Army tanks in service during the 1980s, they appeared with explosive reactive armour (ERA) tiles as seen here with a T-72B1 sporting the first-generation version. When fitted with ERA tiles, the T-64 tank series had the suffix 'V' (for explosive) added to their designations. However, for unknown reasons, the Soviet Army did not add that suffix letter to the designations of the T-72A and T-72B tanks fitted with ERA. (*Dreamstime*)

(**Opposite, below**) The last tank series to enter into service with the Soviet Army before the Cold War came to an end is the T-80B pictured here. The original version, the T-80 (built in small numbers), appeared in 1976 and featured the turret of the T-64. Sporting a completely new turret design, the T-80B came into service in 1978. Its fire-control system allowed its 125mm main gun to fire the radio-controlled Kobra anti-tank missile (NATO code-name 'Songster'), with later-production examples able to fire the laser-guided Svir/Refleck anti-tank missiles. (*Dreamstime*)

(**Above**) The radio antenna for the Kobra anti-tank missile on the T-80 resided in an armoured box directly below the vehicle commander's cupola, as visible on this T-80B. The tank pictured here has the supporting bracket and an ammunition box for a 12.7mm machine gun. However, the machine gun itself is missing. T-80B tanks first appeared in the Group of Soviet Forces, Germany (GSFG) in 1983. (*Dreamstime*)

There existed in smaller numbers a command version for every tank in Soviet Army service during the Cold War, starting with the T-54 series. Those configured as command tanks had additional radios and antennas, resulting in less main gun ammunition storage. To identify them, the suffix letter 'K' appeared at the end of their designations. Pictured here is a T-80BK. It lacks the armoured box in front of the commander's cupola that contained the radio antenna for the Kobra anti-tank missile system. *(Dreamstime)*

Unlike the diesel engines in the T-64 and T-72 series, the T-80 series had a gas-turbine engine. The B model of the T-80 series can be identified by the smoke grenade-launchers' location on the front of the tank's turret. With the advent of explosive reactive armour (ERA) tiles for the T-80 series, the smoke grenade-launchers moved to the turret's sides. The T-80B fitted with ERA received the designation T-80BV. *(Dreamstime)*

The gas turbine engines on the T-80 series proved very sensitive to dust. Rubber mats appeared on the bottom of the T-80 series hulls to reduce the amount of dust generated, as seen on this T-80BV. The vehicle shown here is a BV version of the T-80 series due to the smoke grenade-launchers' location and the numerous mounting brackets for explosive reactive armour (ERA) tiles. (*Dreamstime*)

As is evident from the explosive reactive armour (ERA) tiles visible (obviously inert) on this display vehicle, it is a T-80BV. The roadwheel design on the T-80 series differed from that on the T-72 series. The large cylinder attached to brackets on the rear of the tank's turret provides stowage for the vehicle's two-deep fording snorkels (one inside the other). The two roughly square-shaped boxes attached to the fording kit storage cylinder contain emergency breathing apparatus for the crew. (*Dreamstime*)

(**Above**) In this photograph, we see the exhaust grillwork on the rear of a gas-turbine-engine-powered T-80BV. The Soviet Army disliked the tank's gas turbine engine as it was neither fuel-efficient nor reliable. It also proved very expensive to procure and to maintain. In response, the Soviet Army considered replacing it with a suitable diesel engine. That finally occurred in 1988 with the introduction of the T-80UD. However, only around 500 had come off the factory floor when the Cold War ended. (*Dreamstime*)

(**Opposite, above**) To make up for many M60A1 tanks supplied to the Israeli Army during the Yom Kippur War of 1973, the US Army decided to have some of its M48 series tanks up-armed with the British-designed 105mm L7 gun and diesel engines for those still powered by air-cooled gasoline engines. The up-armed M48 series tanks received the designation M48A5, with two examples pictured here. Between 1975 and 1978, around 2,000 examples came out of a US Army depot. (*Richard and Fran Eshleman*)

(**Opposite, below**) Some 140 examples of the M48A5 were shipped to a US Army division in South Korea in 1978. This facilitated the return of their M60A1s to the United States for overhaul. The majority of M48A5s went directly off to US Army National Guard units like the example pictured here, and to US Army Reserve units. With the replacement of the M48A5s in the National Guard and Reserves by newer-generation tanks, M48A5s went to friendly armies under military aid programmes. (*Author's collection*)

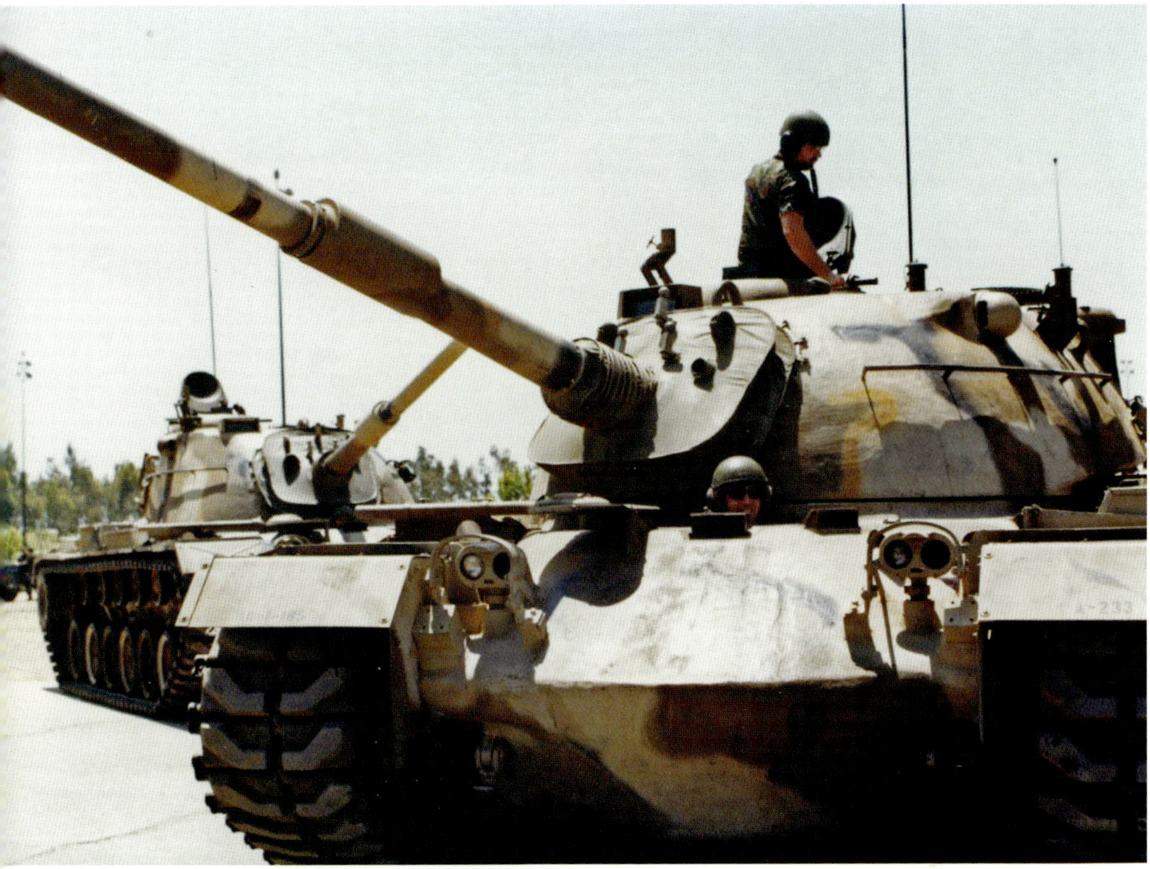

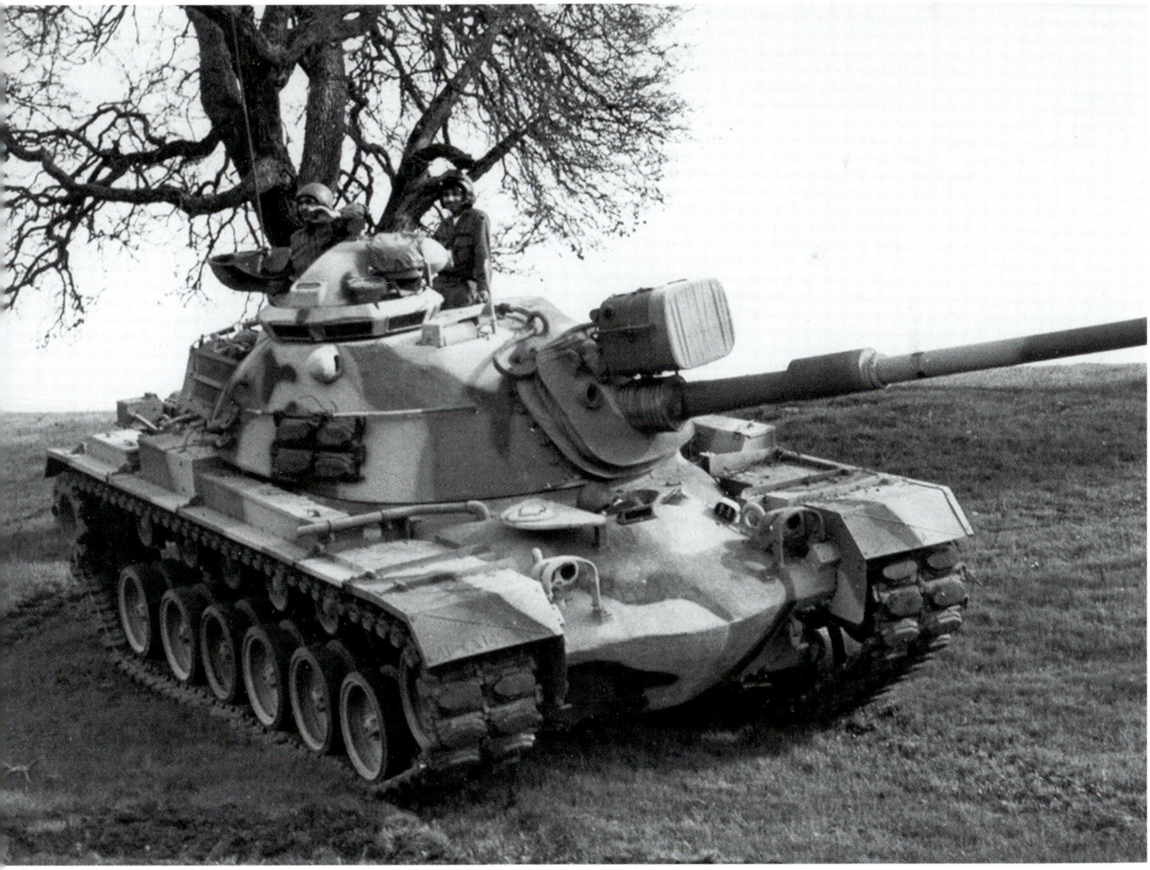

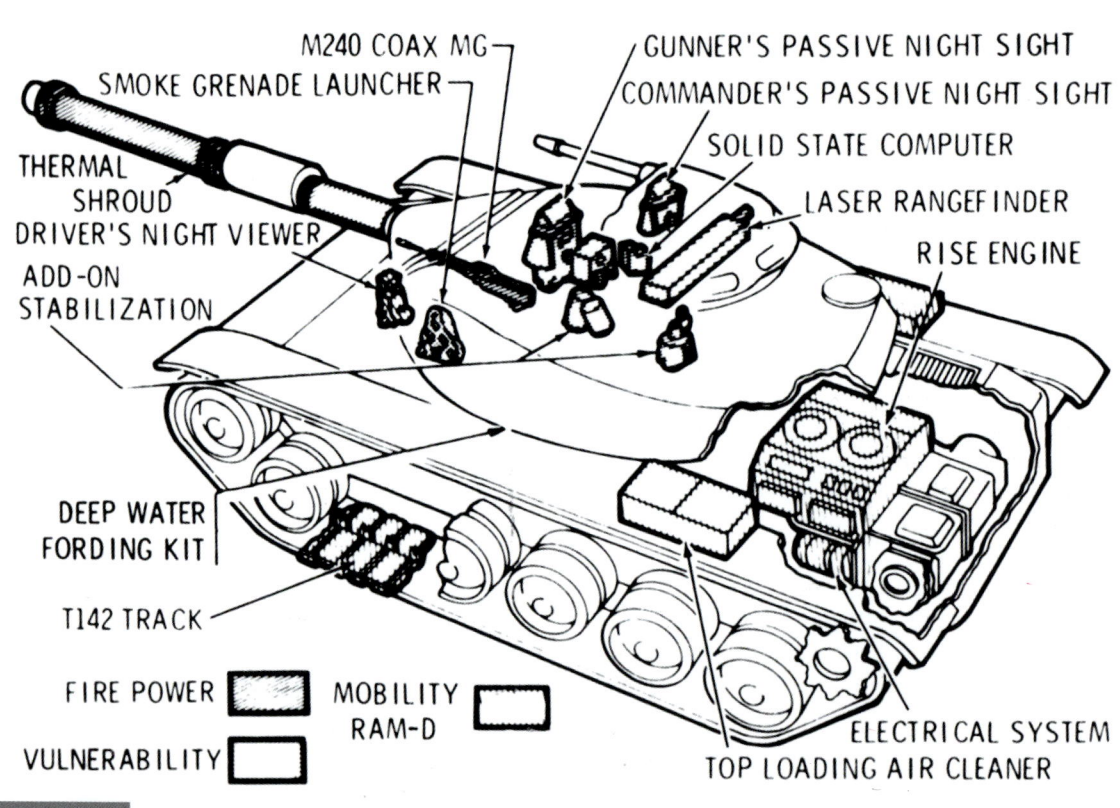

M240 COAX MG
SMOKE GRENADE LAUNCHER
GUNNER'S PASSIVE NIGHT SIGHT
COMMANDER'S PASSIVE NIGHT SIGHT
SOLID STATE COMPUTER
THERMAL SHROUD
DRIVER'S NIGHT VIEWER
LASER RANGEFINDER
RISE ENGINE
ADD-ON STABILIZATION
DEEP WATER FORDING KIT
T142 TRACK
FIRE POWER
MOBILITY RAM-D
VULNERABILITY
ELECTRICAL SYSTEM
TOP LOADING AIR CLEANER

(**Opposite, above**) The last version of the M60 series proved to be the M60A3, approved for production in 1979, with a preserved example pictured here. At one point, the US Army had considered both a hydro-pneumatic suspension system and an advanced torsion bar suspension system for the M60A3. However, in the end, the US Army retained the suspension system of the M60A1. The external thickening of the 105mm main gun barrel seen here came about due to the addition of a barrel shroud. (*Dreamstime*)

(**Opposite, below**) A US Army illustration showing the numerous upgrades that went into the M60A3. One of the improvements to the tank was replacement of the original optical rangefinder with a laser rangefinder (LRF). Other improvements included a new, more reliable 7.62mm coaxial machine gun, as well as a new British-designed smoke grenade-launcher system mounted on both sides of the tank's turret. (*US Army*)

(**Above**) The M60A3 came with a brand-new solid-state ballistic computer. Some of the information fed into the computer to provide a fire-control solution included input from a vertical wind sensor mounted at the turret roof's rear. Other information fed into the computer included horizontal target motion, altitude, gun tube wear, sight parallax and gun jump. Note the smoke grenade-launchers on the tank's turret. (*Dreamstime*)

SYSTEM CHARACTERISTICS

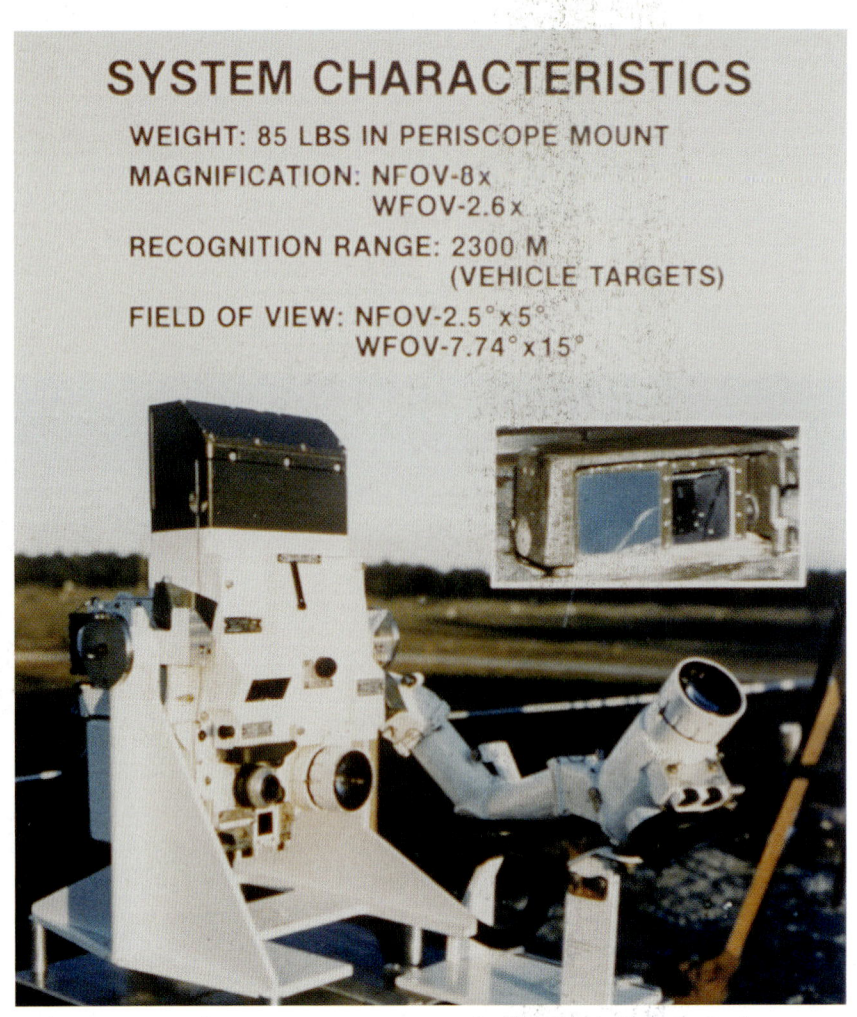

WEIGHT: 85 LBS IN PERISCOPE MOUNT
MAGNIFICATION: NFOV-8x
WFOV-2.6x
RECOGNITION RANGE: 2300 M
(VEHICLE TARGETS)
FIELD OF VIEW: NFOV-2.5°x5°
WFOV-7.74°x15°

(**Above**) The most significant improvement to the M60A3's fire-control system was the addition of the thermal tank sight (TTS) seen here, beginning in August 1979. It was the first production tank to feature such a device. The TTS allowed the crews of tanks so fitted to identify targets despite a wide variety of obscurants including smoke, rain and dust. A TTS extension was routed to the vehicle commander of the M60A3 so he could see what the gunner was looking at. (*DOD*)

(**Opposite, above**) Inside the turret of an M60A3 tank is a close-up of the Commander's Thermal Sight Display (CTSD) in the foreground. The vehicle commander has his right hand on a control handle (TC override) allowing him to take over target engagement from the gunner, including traversing the turret and the elevation and depression of the main gun. The downside of fitting tanks with a TTS is their cost. (*DOD*)

(**Opposite, below**) Shown here during a training exercise is a US Army National Guard M60A3. Upgrades to the tank would eventually include replacing the original aluminium track return rollers and roadwheels with those made of steel. They were heavier than their aluminium counterparts, but cheaper and more durable. Instead of the carbon dioxide fire-protection system on earlier M60 series tanks, the M60A3 came with a more advanced Halon fire-suppression system. (*Author's collection*)

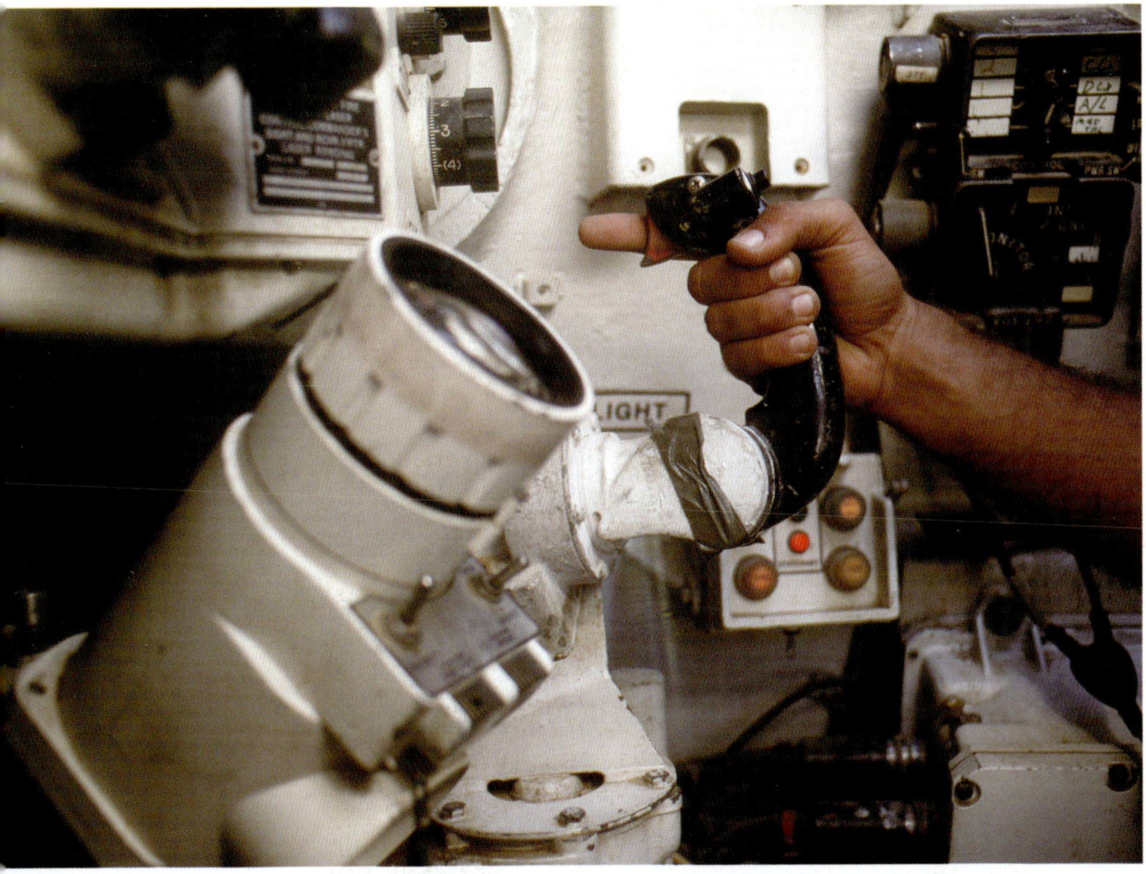
LIGHT

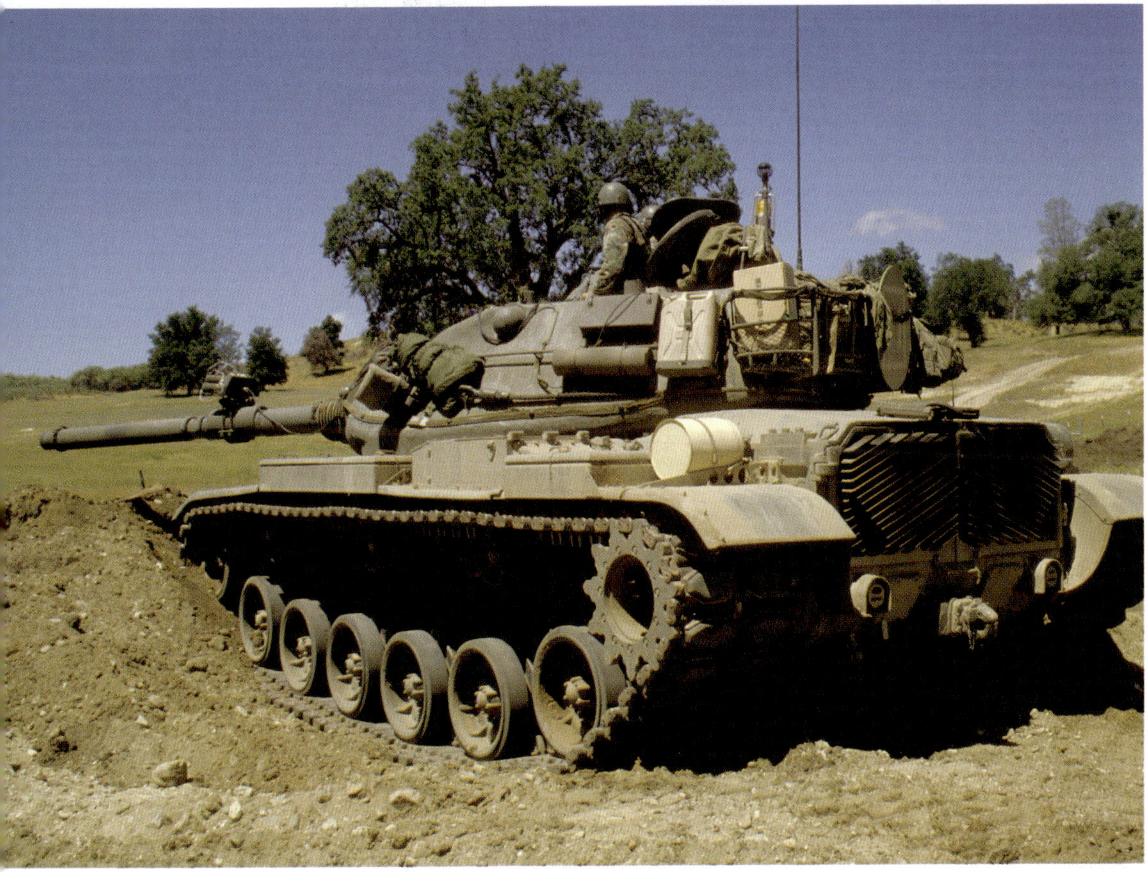

(**Above**) The US Army's eventual replacement for the long-serving M60 series proved to be the M1 tank armed with the American licence-built 105mm main gun designated the M68. Unlike the conventional cast-armour turrets of previous American tanks, the M1 appeared, as seen here, with a slab-sided turret composed of welded-armour construction which incorporated what the US Army referred to as 'special armour'. This dramatically improved its protection from shaped-charge warheads. (*Hans Halberstadt*)

(**Opposite, above**) Instead of the air-cooled diesel engines of the M60 series tanks, the US Army took a bold step and decided to go with an air-cooled gas turbine engine for the M1 tank series. That decision came about as the army saw the gas turbine engine as less complicated than comparable air-cooled diesel engines. That meant fewer parts, resulting in a higher level of reliability and reduced long-term maintenance costs. Pictured here is an M1 during a NATO training exercise. (*DOD*)

(**Opposite, below**) From the loader's position on a 105mm gun-armed M1 tank, the vehicle commander's position and the gunner appear in this photograph. The vehicle commander has several posts from which to manage his tank. He could stand waist-high on his seat, look out over his cupola (best view, worst protection) or, as pictured here, sit under his closed hatch and look outside the tank with various optical devices such as a periscope (best protection, but worst view). (*Hans Halberstadt*)

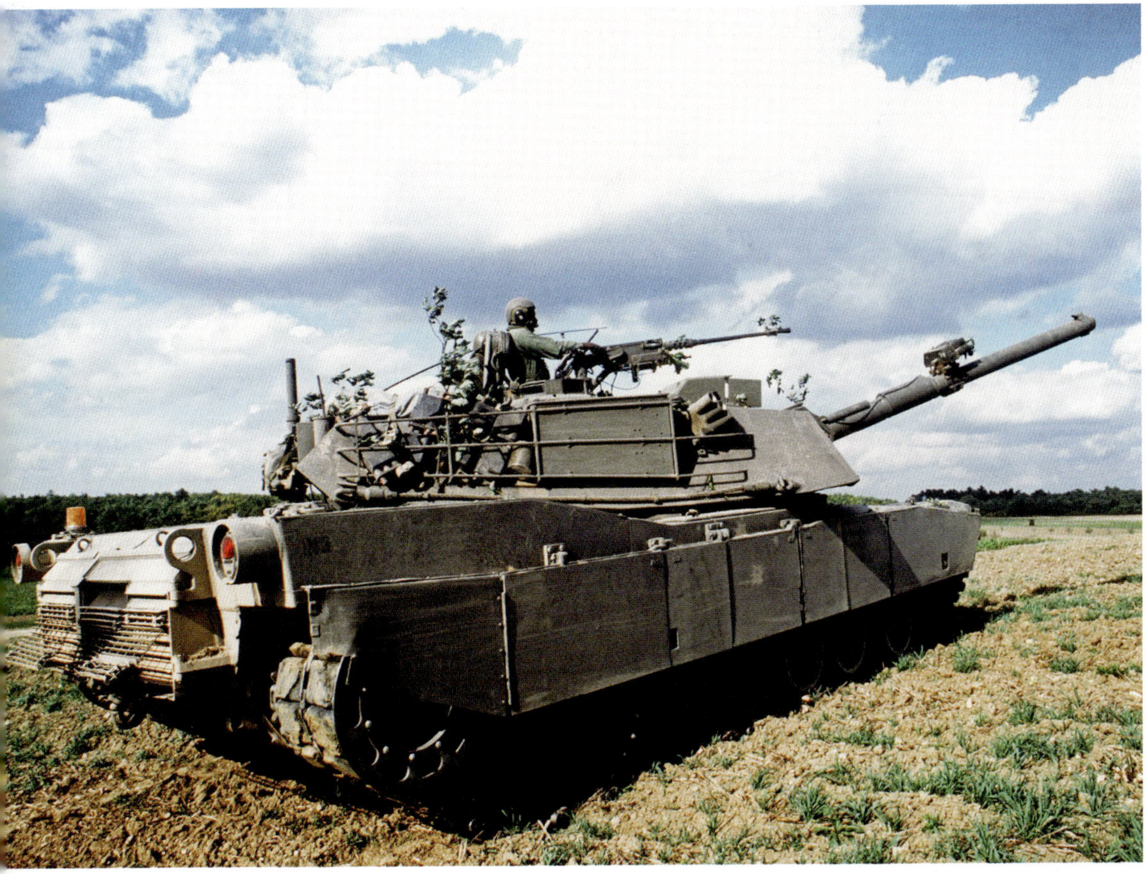

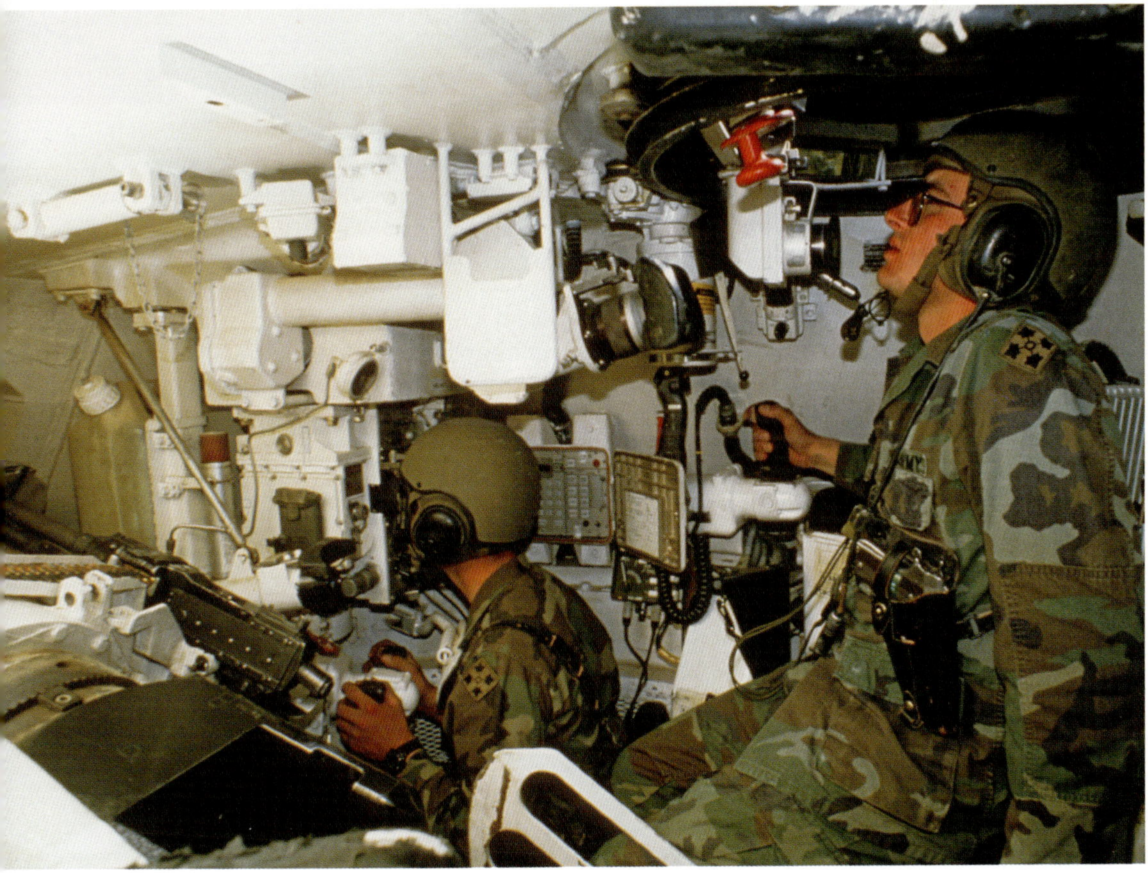

(**Above**) The loader on a 105mm main gun-armed M1 tank is seen here removing a training round from the ready rack. The loader will have marked the bottom of each aluminium cartridge case with the letter 'S' for anti-tank sabot rounds or 'H' for high-explosive rounds. As the loader reaches for a round, a small clip at the base of the individual ammunition racks is swept aside by his hand as he selects a round for his reload. (Hans Halberstadt)

(**Opposite, above**) The firing of the 105mm main gun on the M1 Abrams. The type of round fired by the tank is typically the vehicle commander's choice. He must evaluate a target's vulnerability to determine the type of round to use in an engagement. When multiple targets appear on a battlefield, the vehicle commander decides what to shoot based on the significance of the threat they represent. The US Army classifies enemy targets as most dangerous, dangerous and least dangerous. (Hans Halberstadt)

(**Opposite, below**) The driver's position on a 105mm main gun-armed M1 tank. With his front hatch closed, the driver lies supine in the seat. A feature first seen on the British Army Chieftain tank, it was intended to lower the vehicle's profile by a few inches. With his front hatch open, the M1 driver raises his seat to look out over the glacis. He steers the tank with a small pair of motorbike-type handlebars. There are armoured compartments holding fuel tanks on either side of the driver's position. (Hans Halberstadt)

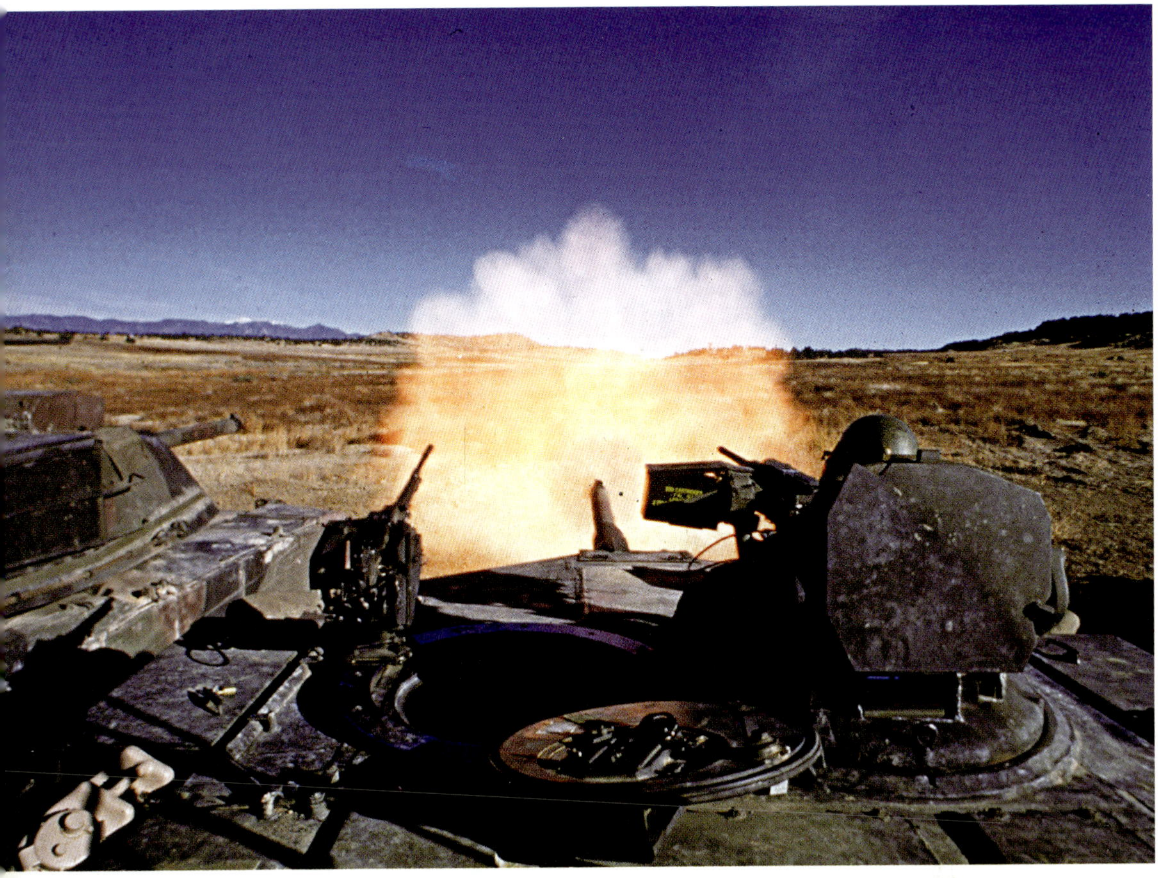

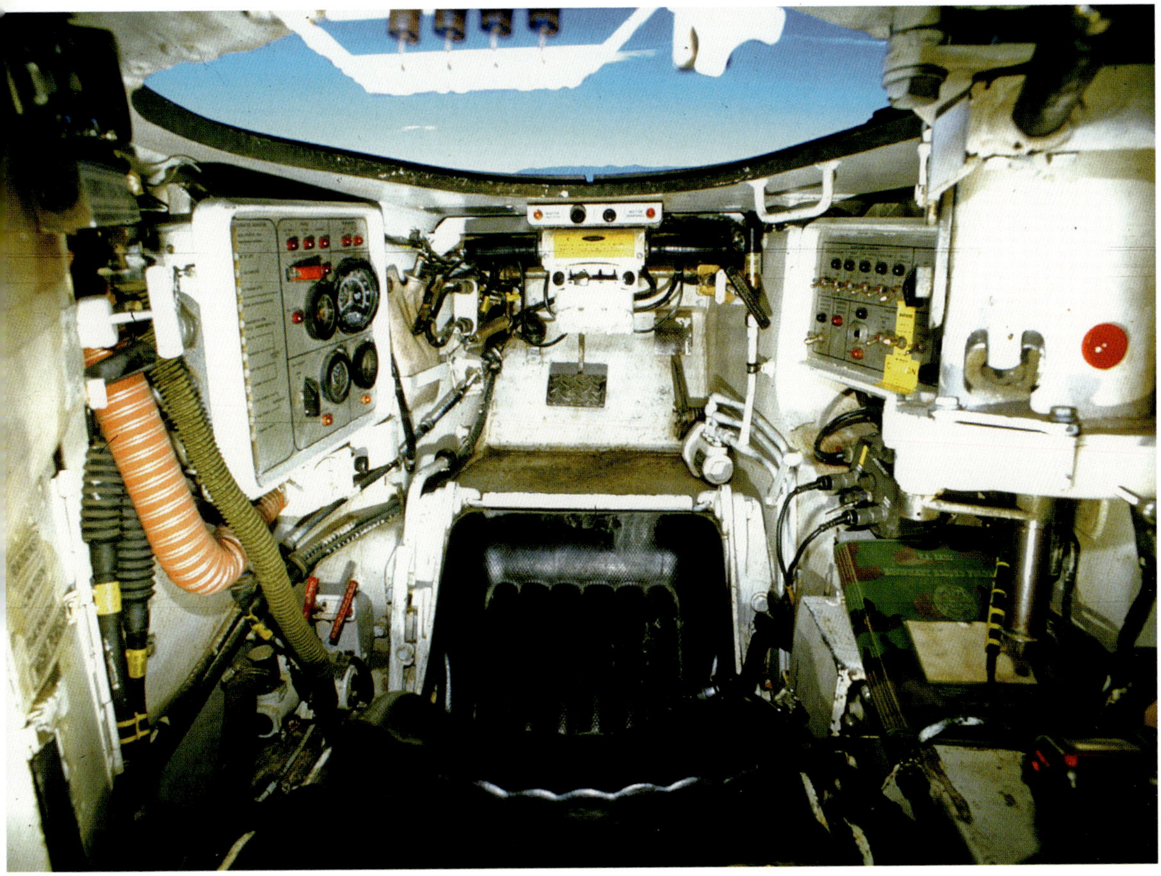

Chapter Seven

NATO Catches Up

The prototype of what would eventually become the Leopard 2 appeared in 1972, initially armed with a smoothbore 105mm gun. After analyzing 1973 Yom Kippur War results, German industry came up with an up-armoured and up-gunned model using a 120mm smoothbore gun. The West German Army received its first production examples of the Leopard 2 in 1979.

The four-man Leopard 2 carried forty-two main gun rounds. Rather than using aluminium cartridge cases, it used semi-combustible cartridge cases, with only a 10lb aluminium and rubber stub base ejected from the gun's breech upon recoil into an attached bag. The tank gun fires an APFSDS round with a tungsten penetrator and a HEAT-MP (Multi-Purpose) round. The West German government banned the use of DU in its 120mm APFSDS round over safety concerns and environmental damage.

The Leopard 2 has fifteen main gun rounds in the rear of the turret behind an electrically-operated blast door and twenty-seven rounds in the left front hull. If the tank's turret ammunition racks suffered a penetration, the gaseous energy created by the detonation of the main gun rounds present would vent through a lightly-attached armoured blow-off panel on the turret roof.

A 2011 US Army TRADOC report listed the Leopard 2 as having an armour array equivalent to 1,000mm (39in) of steel armour when confronted by a HEAT round and the equivalent of 700mm (27in) of steel armour against APFSDS rounds.

The Leopard 2 originally had a two-axis electro-hydraulic stabilization system. The tank also came with a laser rangefinder, NBC protection system and a passive night-fighting system (for the first 200 built). All subsequent examples featured a TIS, which was retrofitted to the initial 200 tanks.

The Leopard 2 series tanks did not use Chobham armour. German engineers developed a spaced composite armour array; one that they felt equalled the protection provided by Chobham armour without the weight penalty.

The Leopard 2 rides on a torsion bar suspension system and receives power from a liquid-cooled diesel engine, providing it with a maximum speed on roads of 45mph and an operational range of 342 miles.

Models and Numbers

The West German Army took into service more than 2,000 examples of the Leopard 2, divided into eight progressively modified batches. The first batch comprised 380 examples, with the first delivered in 1979 and the last in 1982.

The second batch, designated Leopard 2A1, began coming off the factory floors in 1982, with 450 examples completed by the following year. The third batch of Leopard 2s, comprising 300 vehicles, drove off the assembly lines between 1983 and 1984 and retained the Leopard 2A1 designation.

Between 1984 and 1987, the first batch of 380 Leopard 2s was reworked and brought up to the latest standards. They received the designation of Leopard 2A2. The fourth batch of 300 tanks built between 1984 and 1985 became the Leopard 2A3.

The fifth through to the eighth sets of Leopard 2 tanks rolled out of the factory between 1985 and 1992, totalling 728 vehicles, all assigned as Leopard 2A4s.

With the upgrading of the first through to the fourth groups of Leopard 2 tanks to the latest standards, all received the suffix designation 'A4'. Envisioned upgrades to 699 Leopard 2A4s did not occur following the end of the Cold War in 1991.

The only NATO army to take the Leopard 2 in service before the Cold War concluded proved to be the Dutch. They bought 445 slightly modified German-built examples, delivered between 1982 and 1986.

Challenger 1

The British Army replacement for the Chieftain tank proved to be the Challenger, the first example entering service in 1983. The British government's original order called for 243 of the four-man Challengers, eventually increased to 420 examples, with the last delivered in 1990.

The Challenger main gun was the same rifled 120mm weapon that had armed the Chieftain. As with the last production example of the Chieftain tank, the Challenger had a laser rangefinder and a TIS, which the British Army referred to as TOGS (Thermal Observation and Gunnery Sight).

The 70-ton Challenger incorporated Chobham armour in both its turret and hull. Sources suggested that the Challenger's frontal armour provided the tank with an equivalent of 1,000mm (39in) of steel armour protection from HEAT rounds.

The Challenger employed separately-loaded main gun rounds. Rather than the semi-combustible cartridge cases used with the 120mm main gun on the Leopard 2, the British depended on a combustible bag charge that went into the gun's breech following the projectile's insertion. This was the same system employed with the Chieftain tank series.

All the tank's combustible charges resided in its hull, protected by pressurized water jackets. With no explosive elements, the KE projectiles lined the turret's interior, with some stored in containers attached to the turret's exterior. The British Army embraced this arrangement as it allowed for carrying more main gun rounds; the Challenger had room for sixty-four projectiles and forty-three combustible propellant bag charges.

The Challenger received power from a liquid-cooled diesel engine instead of the Chieftain's troublesome multi-fuel engine. Maximum speed on level roads was 35mph with a reported range of 280 miles and off-road around 155 miles. Instead of the Centurion and Chieftain tanks' Horstmann-type suspension, the Challenger rode on a hydro-pneumatic system.

From an article in the March–April 1982 issue of *Armor* magazine titled 'British Army Introduces the Challenger' by Richard M. Ogorkiewicz, he discusses the tank's hydro-pneumatic suspension system:

> The Challenger is fitted with a completely new hydro-pneumatic or, as the British keep calling it, 'hydro-gas' suspension system. It is, in fact, the first British battle tank to have such a suspension system ... like all other hydro-pneumatic suspensions, it is inherently superior to suspensions based on torsion bars or other metallic springs and offers a better ride over rough ground, which implies higher cross-country speeds. At the same time, the self-contained units of which it consists are mounted outside the hull and makes them easy to replace and saves critical space inside the hull.

A Major Problem

An out-of-date fire-control system that harked back to the Chieftain's 1960s design proved a serious handicap during its time in service. The serious nature of this defect manifested itself at a 1987 NATO tank competition. The British tank crews scored poorly against other NATO tank teams equipped with the US Army M1A1 Abrams or the West German Army Leopard 2, so much so that the British Army pulled out of the annual competition the following year.

In a 14 July 1987 British government transcript, Mr Ian Stewart (Minister of State for the Armed Forces) answered a question posed by a member of the House of Commons on the Challenger's poor showing during the tank competition:

> I do not believe that the performance of tanks in the artificial circumstances of a competition, such as the recent Canadian Army Trophy, is a proper indication of their capability in war. Challenger's gun gives the best penetrative performance against the tanks of a potential enemy. The tank itself is arguably the best protected in the world and has excellent mobility. It carries an advanced thermal imaging system, which is much admired by our allies and ensures that Challenger can fight effectively by night and by day. Participation in international tank gunnery competitions is one useful option in the complete spectrum of training opportunities available in preparing our tank crews for war, but it is not on its own a basis for judgement of overall capability.

The realization that there was no way to bring the fire-control system on the Challenger up to the same standards as other modern NATO tanks led the British Army to consider replacing it with another NATO tank, such as the M1A1 or the Leopard 2.

Due to national interests, the British Army decided to acquire an improved version of the Challenger labelled the Challenger 2, with the first production vehicle appearing in 1994. The last of the now-named Challenger 1 tanks were retired in 2002.

M1A1 Abrams

The US Army approved the development of a 120mm gun-armed M1 tank in September 1981. The first of fourteen prototypes, designated the M1E1, went off to the army starting in March 1981 and underwent extensive testing at various military bases. The army was satisfied with the testing process and approved the tank for production as the M1A1 in August 1984.

The first production examples of the M1A1 came off the factory floor in August 1985 and began appearing in the field with US Army armour units the following year. Armoured units in West Germany received priority on the M1A1 tanks. In turn, their 105mm gun-armed M1s were returned to the United States and issued to US Army Reserve and National Guard armour units.

As the replacement for the M60A1, the Marine Corps took into service 269 examples of the M1A1 between 1990 and 1991. Eventually, Congress provided funding for the Marine Corps to arrange the transfer of 134 examples of the M1A1 from the US Army's inventory to its own between 1994 and 1995.

Former US Army tank officer John Blumenson recalls during his time facing the Warsaw Pact as commander of a company of M1A1s in 1990:

> We were confident in our systems, our equipment and our crew training ... That said, our numbers were limited ... I'm confident that we would have inflicted a large number of casualties on enemy forces. However, that said, being up on the front lines right at the border, our chances of long-term survival were not real good. We expected to fight in a dirty environment, meaning chemical, nuclear and biological.

M1A1 Detail and Numbers

Weighing about 63 tons and armed with a modified version of the 120mm main gun mounted on the Leopard 2, the M1A1 had stowage for forty rounds, thirty-four in the turret rear with its blow-off panels and the remaining six in the hull. The cartridge cases for the 120mm main gun rounds on the M1A1 are semi-combustible, like those employed by the Leopard 2.

Having only forty main gun rounds proved to be of initial concern among some US Army tankers who wanted to retain the fifty-five main gun rounds of the 105mm gun-armed M1. On the other hand, the first-round accuracy of the M1A1 120mm main gun meant that fewer rounds were required to assure target destruction. Other sources have suggested that few front-line tanks would have lasted long enough to use all their onboard main gun rounds if a Third World War had taken place.

Unlike the basic M1, the M1A1 came with an NBC protection system and a microclimate controlled cooling system for the crew. It provided cooling air to the tank's crew by way of individual vests.

The US Army referred to the M1A1 as the third version of the series or the M1 with Block I product improvements. By the time production of the M1A1 concluded in April 1993, the contractor had built 4,550 examples.

Former US Army tank officer H.R. McMaster compared his M1A1s in Operation DESERT STORM to the Iraqi Army's T-72s encountered by his command:

> Our optics and especially our thermal sights gave us an advantage in acquiring the enemy, especially in limited visibility conditions … The T-72 proved inaccurate due to several factors. Every tank round fired at us, of which there were four, fell short. Contributing factors included worn gun tubes and wet or damp propellant in the T-72, which had an exposed ammunition compartment. Every T-72 or personnel carrier that the troop shot exploded in a fireball … Because of the slow speed of the T-72 autoloader, an M1A1 crew could fire three rounds to every one of a T-72 crew.

M1A1 Protection

From a November 1983 document prepared for the US Army by the contractor, the following passage explains the M1A1's armour arrangement. There is no mention of Chobham armour:

> Weld-fabricated rolled homogenous armor [RHA] combined with hull and turret armor assemblies provided frontal armor protection. The turret front, including the gun shield, and the turret sides are protected against the specified large-caliber threats. Large-caliber protection for the hull front is provided by an armor assembly across the entire hull width with high obliquity upper and lower glacis plates. Hull side protection consists of armored skirts and structure. The rear hull structure and the rear grill doors give protection from small-arms fire.

In May 1988, all new production examples of the M1A1 came out of the factory with a DU armour layer inserted into the frontal armour protection compartments. The layer of DU armour did not replace the ceramic armour already installed; it merely supplemented it as the DU armour provides a heightened degree of protection from KE rounds.

The addition of the denser and hence heavier armour raised the M1A1's weight by around 1 ton. Those with the DU armour bore the designation of the M1A1 Heavy Armor (HA) tank. There was no outward difference between M1A1s with and without DU armour.

According to some unclassified sources, the addition of DU armour to the front of the M1A1's HA turret provided the tank with the equivalent of 1,300mm (51in) of steel armour when confronted by a shaped-charge projectile and the equivalent of 600mm (24in) of steel armour protection against APFSDS rounds.

Armour protection on the glacis of the M1A1 HA was supposedly the equivalent of 1,050mm (41in) of steel armour against HEAT rounds and 590mm (23in) of steel armour against APFSDS rounds.

Despite the impressive armour protection on the front and sides of the M1A1, the rear hull of the tank still proved vulnerable to overmatching threats, as seen in this passage from a US Army report describing an incident during Operation DESERT STORM:

> B-23 (M1A1 Heavy Armor) was hit by an unknown round that penetrated through the rear grill doors. A fire started in the engine compartment which was automatically extinguished by the onboard Ealon system. Initially there were no injuries. The tank engine stopped and the crew attempted to traverse the turret over the right flank due to smoke still coming from the engine compartment. The decision was made to evacuate the tank, at which time a second 'unknown round' penetrated the rear of the tank, knocking the loader to the turret floor. As he fell, he struck his knee on the turret ring, bruising his knee and twisting ligaments. The loader was the only crewman injured in this engagement. The crew was picked up by the D Co Executive Officer's tank. The resulting fire caused a catastrophic fire in the hull, and a complete meltdown of the suspension system. B-23 sustained sufficient heat and fire damage to cause the ammo blowout panels to function; they worked as designed. There was no ballistic damage to the inside of B-23's turret as a result of enemy fire. The tank was recovered on or about March 7, 91.

Issues

Despite the army's acclaim for the M1 and the M1A1 tanks, there remained unresolved issues. One appeared in a February 1991 GAO report titled 'Abrams Tank: Operating Cost More Than Expected':

> The poor durability of the Abrams tank track has been a key contributor to the high cost of maintenance. The T-156 [sic] tank track, which has been in the fleet since the M1 tank was first fielded, has never met its original reliability, availability, maintainability and durability requirement of 2,000 miles without replacement. This track's average durability is 850 miles on the M1 tank and 710 miles on the M1A1 tank. Army data from its 1988 Abrams cost estimate showed that tank track costs accounted for 47 percent of the M1 tank's and 52 percent of the M1A1 tank's annual per-mile repair parts cost.

In another GAO report dated January 1992 and titled 'Operation Desert Storm: Early Performance Assessment of Bradley and Abrams', the crews of the M1 series tanks had overwhelming praise for their vehicles' performance in combat. However, the poor fuel-mileage of their tanks remained an issue, as seen in this passage:

> High fuel consumption limited the tank's range, and refueling the tank was a constant consideration in operational planning throughout the ground war. Tanks were refilled with fuel at every opportunity in order to keep the fuel tanks as full as possible. Prior to the start of the ground war, units practiced refueling procedures such as refueling on the move and in organized

columns. Once in the Persian Gulf area, Army operational plans generally called for refueling every three to five hours. Although these efforts provided optimum fuel availability, almost everyone we interviewed agreed that the tank's high fuel consumption was a concern. Typically, those we interviewed said that high fuel consumption was a trade-off for increased power and speed, but that fuel economy could be improved by the addition of an auxiliary power unit.

Another Armour Upgrade

The late-production examples of the M1A1 came out of the factory doors with an even higher protection level than the M1A1 HA tanks. These vehicles received the designation of the M1A1 HA+ (plus). The first of these reached army units in the field in 1991 and the last in 1994.

Of the 4,450 examples of the M1A1, a total of 2,388 were the initial version without DU armour. There were 1,328 examples of the M1A1 HA constructed, with 834 featuring the additional armour protection package labelled the M1A1 HA+. Before Operation DESERT STORM in 1991, some earlier-production M1A1 Has found them brought up to the M1A1 HA+ standard.

The Demons We Never Knew

Ted Dannemiller, US Army (retired), 1970–97, former Cavalry, Infantry and Armor officer:

> The T-64 was a huge leap for the Soviet Union. It arrived in the Group of Soviet Forces Germany (GSFG) in the early 80s. The initial impressions often confused it with the T-72. Furthermore, intelligence seemed to indicate that the hydraulic system was prone to fires (we'd learned that lesson from the Yom Kippur War). Stories of atrocities committed on crews by the autoloader also filled bull sessions at the clubs and GDPs (general defensive positions). The limited space did not mean Soviet crews were midgets, but it did limit emergency maintenance should the autoloader fail. Further, reports of mobile contact teams that were 'resident' due to reliability challenges also peppered the intelligence stories. The T-72 raised the bar.
>
> The T-72 arrived on the scene with a same 125mm main gun, more prominent ERA (external reactive armor) attached like bricks nearly everywhere, and ammunition that began to close the penetration gap. For example, the front of an M60A3 turret and hull (measured as Line of Sight: LOS) was approximately 10 inches. The earliest versions of the 125mm 2A46 ammunition could penetrate an equivalent of about 12 inches of rolled homogeneous armor (RHA). NATO development of better ammunition again began to overcome the gap between NATO ammunition and T-72 protection levels.
>
> Conversely, Kontakt ERA increased survivability of the T-72, leading to significant improvements in the M829 series of APFSDS ammunition.

Crews of the M60A3 and M1A1 (and later variants) considered the T-72 as a peer, with some limitations based on the three-man crew's endurance, the reliability and speed of the autoloader, and the relatively poor accuracy of the 2A46 125mm gun. It turned out that the fire-control system accuracy was only about 1 meter [1.1 yards] or more at NATO-standard ranges of 1,800 meters [1,968 yards]. NATO tank accuracy was significantly better: the typical screening bullseye for the 120mm M256 cannon is less than 7 inches at 1,500m [1,640 yards] and would be about 8 inches at 1,800m [1,968 yards]. Also, most T-72s did not have passive night sights. Nearly all the export versions (T-72M1 being common) lacked laser rangefinders. This would play a significant role later in the twentieth century during Operation DESERT STORM. Also, the Yom Kippur War provided valuable insights into ATGMs' (anti-tank guided missiles') effectiveness against the T-72.

Most US personnel thought the T-80 was revolutionary. In some ways, it mimicked the M1: it had a gas turbine engine, laser rangefinder and an excellent fire-control system. These allowed hitting targets at acceptable ranges on the move using conventional ammunition, or the still-revolutionary Kobra ATGM that could be fired from the main gun. The tank was fast, with an excellent power/weight ratio and good flotation. However, few made it to the GSFG, and most intelligence and command personnel thought it was intended as a breakthrough tank held in Soviet reserves. We thought that client states like East Germany (DDR), Poland, Czechoslovakia and the frontal Guards Tank Divisions would fight the initial assaults and still be in T-72 variants (or T-62 in the case of the DDR).

The evolution of attack helicopters, especially the US AH-64 and the new Hellfire ATGM, appeared to us as the greatest invention since sliced bread. Further, the evolution of the M1A1 and especially its DU (depleted uranium) ammunition convinced crews and leaders that we maintained an above par status compared to the Soviets. The Chechen War in 1994 also revealed some serious flaws and exceedingly high operational costs for the T-80, coupled with a low ORR (operational readiness rate), according to intelligence shared to unit Intelligence officers (the S2) and staff.

American and NATO crews respected the Soviet tank designs. They emphasized US and NATO crew skills over those of the Soviet conscript army and focused on the vulnerability of early Cold War designs to penetration and subsequent destruction. It wasn't until Operation DESERT STORM that the T-72M1 and non-export T-72 of Soviet/client states could be compared. The export variants skewed NATO perceptions of their survivability incorrectly, and evaluations late in the twentieth century drove development of the M829A3 to restore true overmatch by NATO 120mm guns against the ubiquitous Soviet 2A46 and its ammunition.

Pictured here during preparations for a public display is a Leopard 2. The first six production examples of the tank entered the West German Army inventory in 1979. By the time production concluded in 1992, a total of 2,125 examples had been supplied to that army. They were delivered in eight progressively improved batches with small external differences between them. (*Dreamstime*)

A factory shot of a brand-new Leopard 2. Although the West German Army received information on the British-developed composite armour unofficially nicknamed 'Chobham' in the 1970s, it decided not to use it for the Leopard 2. Instead, it had its own multi-layer spaced armour arrangement for both the hull and turret. As with all the then-latest NATO and Warsaw Pact tanks, the Leopard 2 had a nuclear, biological and chemical (NBC) protection system. (*Krauss-Maffei*)

(**Above**) Seen here is a Leopard 2 operating during an historical military vehicle event. It was unlike American tanks, from the M47 through to the M1 series, with the driver located in the hull's front centre, just under the main gun barrel. That on the Leopard 2, as seen in this picture, is offset to the right-hand side of the front hull. Twenty-seven main gun rounds are stored to his left. He has a sizeable single-piece hatch with two periscopes and a third to the left of his hatch. (*Ian Wilcox*)

(**Opposite, above**) The Leopard 2 features a fully-stabilized turret mounting a 120mm smoothbore gun coupled to an advanced fire-control system. This included a laser range-finder (LRF) and a thermal imaging sight (TIS) along with other sensors. Pictured here are a couple of Leopard 2 tanks at a firing range. In addition to the twenty-seven main gun rounds in the vehicle's left-front hull, another fifteen are stored in the rear turret bustle behind the loader's position. (*Public domain*)

(**Opposite, below**) Power for the Leopard 2 comes from the turbo-charged liquid-cooled V12 diesel engine pictured here. Using multi-fuel if needed, it provides the vehicle with a maximum speed on level roads of 42mph and an approximate range of 300 miles. The tank rides on a conventional torsion bar suspension system. The Leopard 2 powerpack, including the engine and transmission, can be removed and replaced in about a half-hour. (*Public domain*)

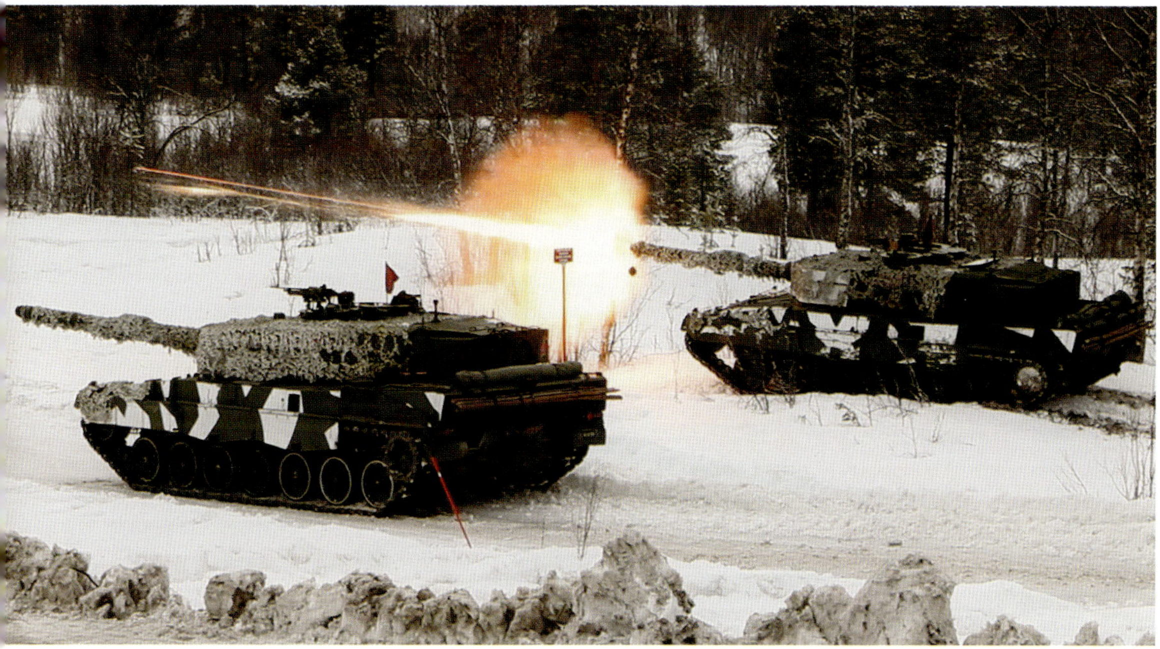

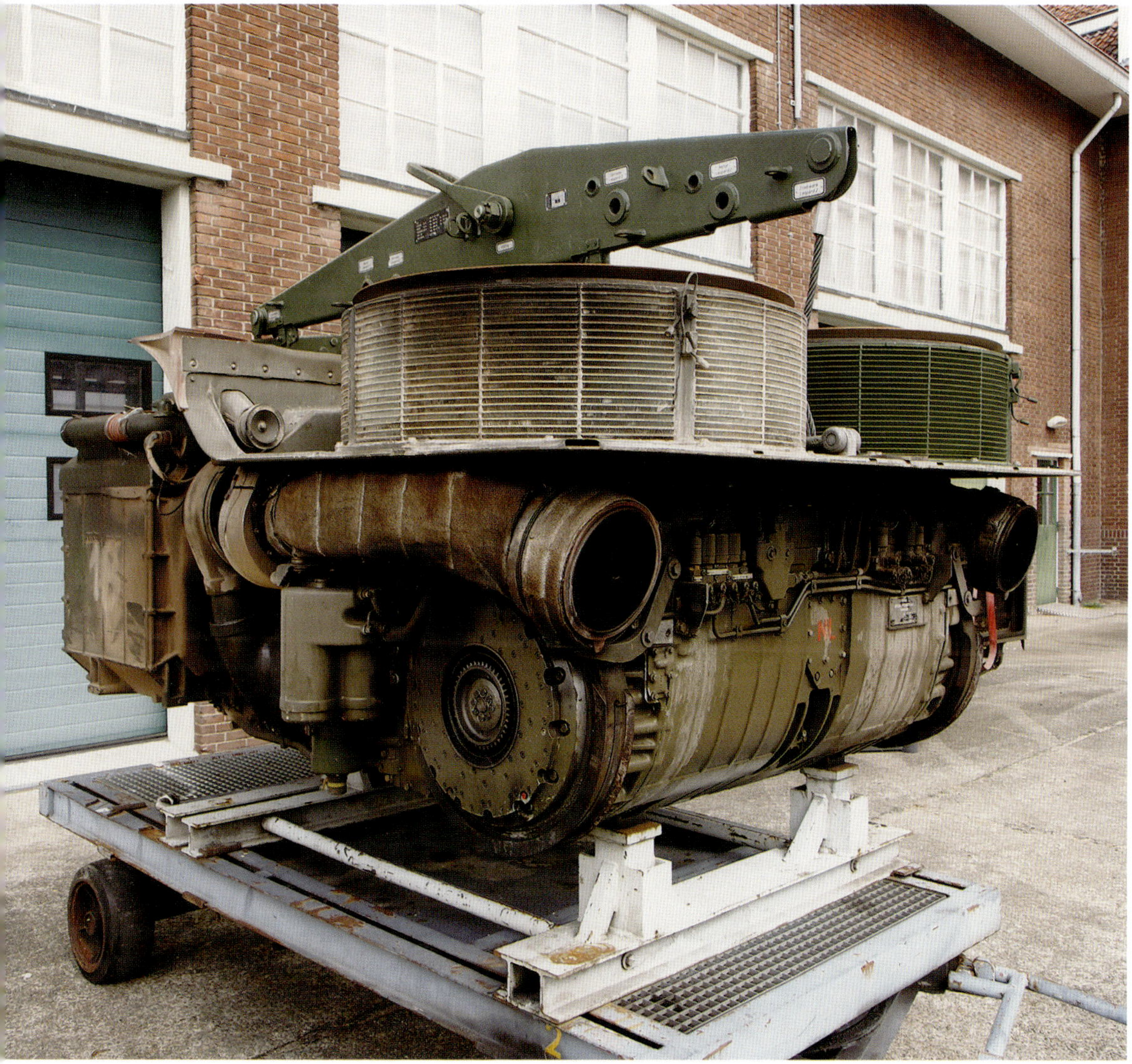

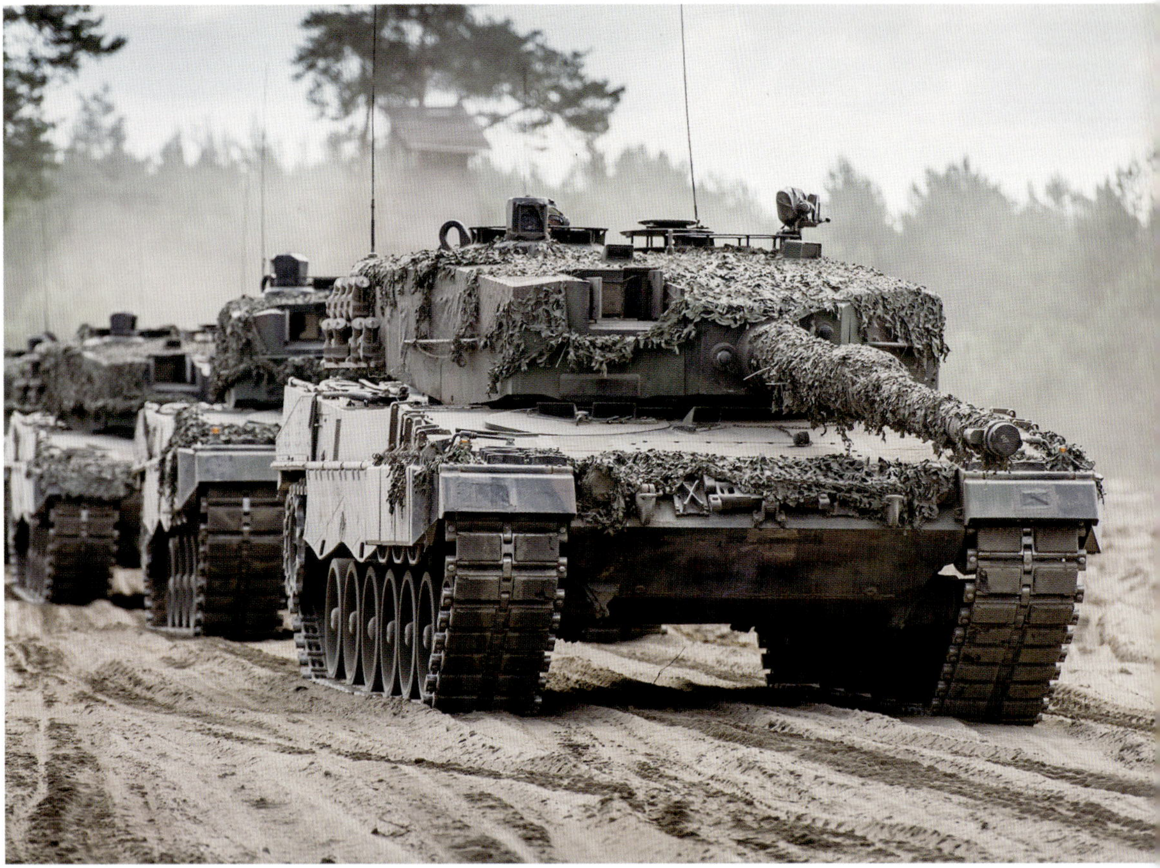

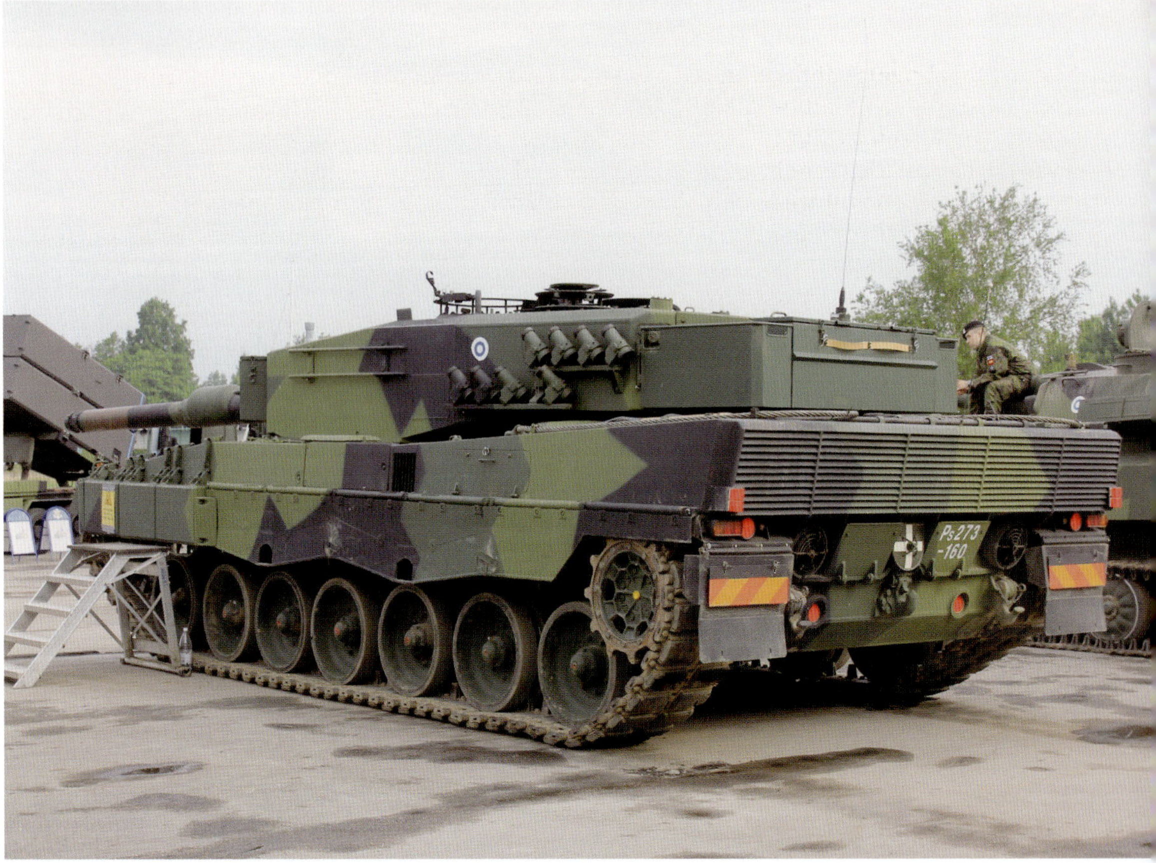
Ps 273
-160

(**Opposite, above**) A formation of Leopard 2 tanks during a training exercise. The steel track has removable rubber pads. All Leopard 2 tanks carry steel grousers as standard equipment. When dealing with ice, the crew replaces existing rubber pads with steel grousers to provide more traction for the tracks. The first three side panels on either side of the Leopard 2's hull are thickly-armoured. The remaining side hull panels are a simple rubber and metal combination. (*Dreamstime*)

(**Opposite, below**) A Finnish Army Leopard 2 on public display. Following the end of the Cold War, the German government sold many of its now redundant Leopard 2 fleet to other NATO and non-NATO armies at very reasonable prices. As with the West German Army models, this vehicle features two rows of smoke grenade-launchers found on both sides of the turret. They can fire off individually or four at a time. (*Dreamstime*)

(**Above**) In this image, a Leopard 2 is climbing aboard a floating section of military bridging equipment. The tank can ford about 4ft of water without prior preparation. The erection of snorkel equipment permits the Leopard 2 to cross a calm section of inland waterway up to 13ft deep. The loader's 7.62mm machine gun is covered by a tarp in this picture. The vehicle commander's cupola also has a provision for mounting a 7.62mm machine gun if desired. (*MOD*)

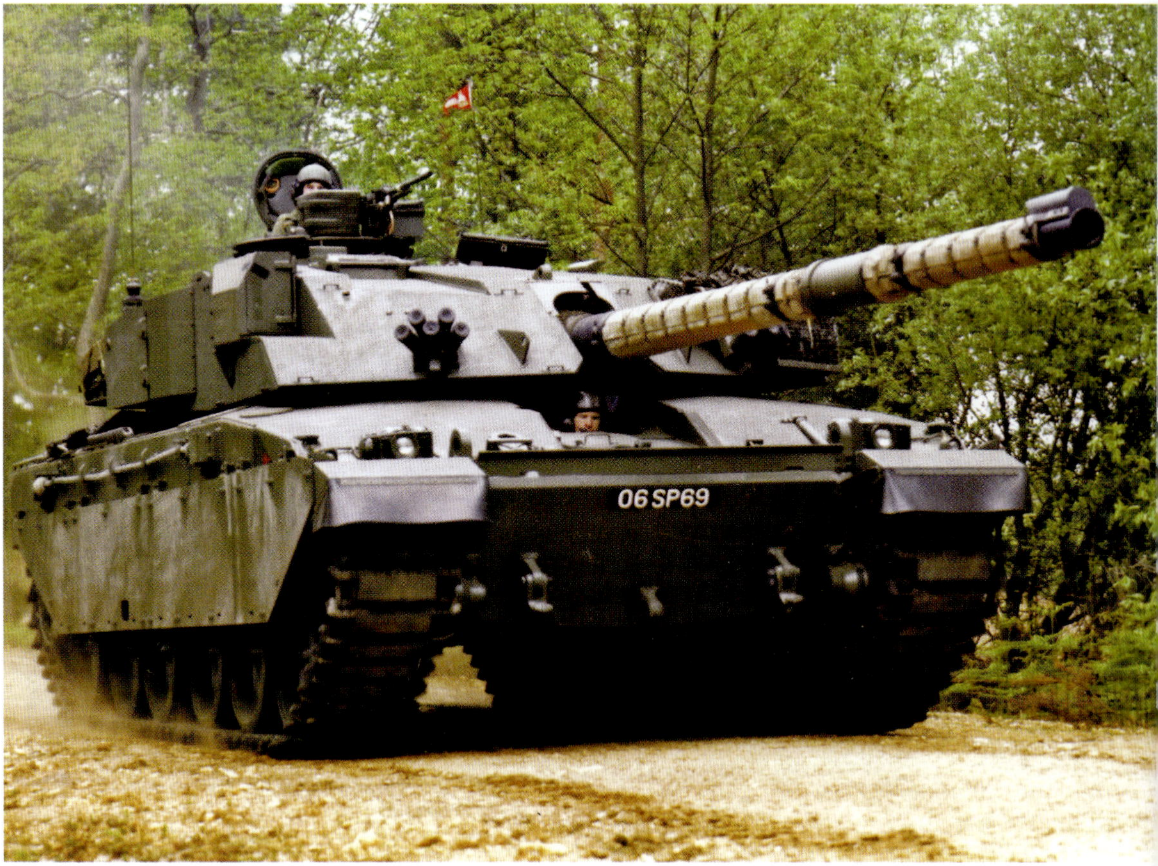
06 SP69

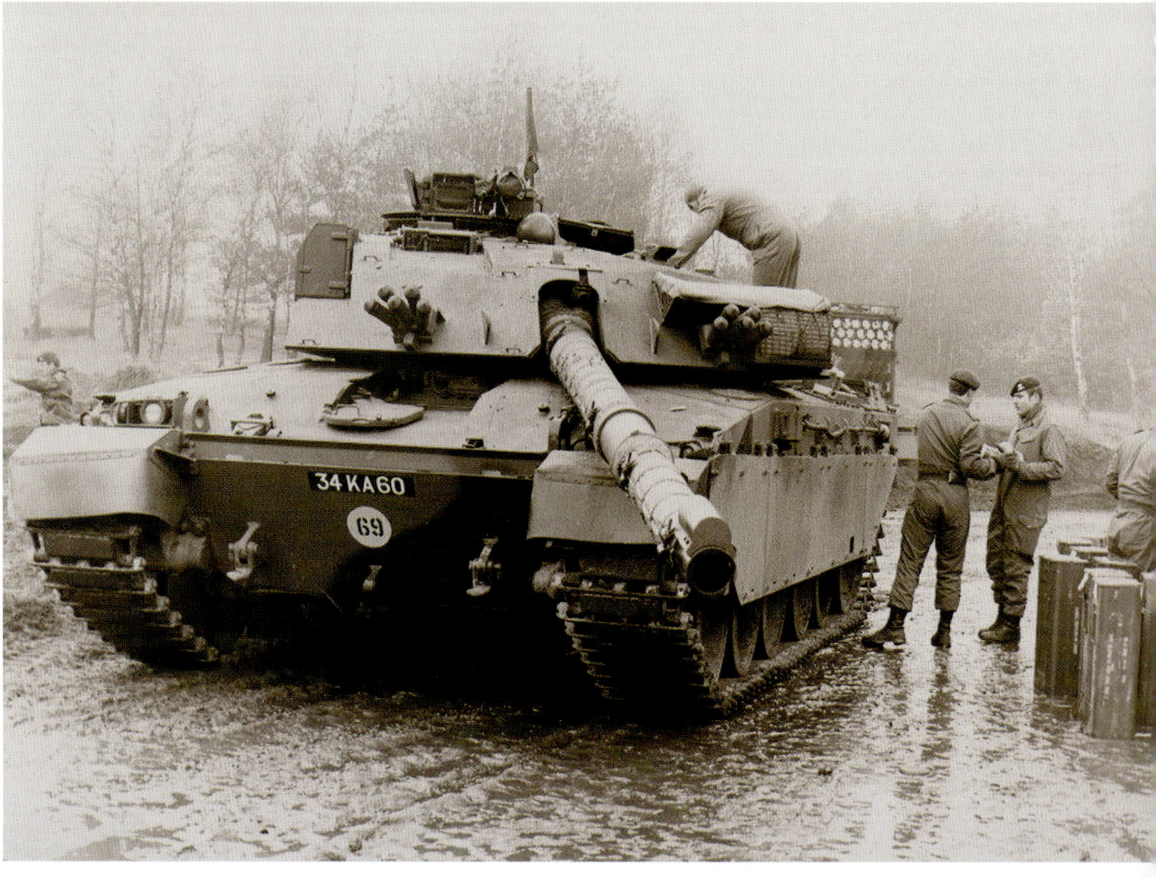
34 KA 60
69

(**Opposite, above**) The British Army replaced its Chieftain tank with the Challenger 1 pictured here. The tank was not their first choice. The original plan called for the British and West German armies to adopt a co-production tank. When that programme died in 1977, the British Army looked at acquiring a foreign tank design, an idea eventually rejected. Next up was the Main Battle Tank-1980 (MBT-80), which died in 1979. In the end, they went with adopting a modified version of a British-designed tank ordered by the Imperial Iranian Army, the Shir 2. (*Tank Museum*)

(**Opposite, below**) A Challenger 1 in the process of loading up with main gun rounds. The tank sported the same 120mm rifled main gun as the Chieftain. Similar to late-production Chieftains, the Challenger 1 came with a thermal tank sight (TTS) seen here in its armoured housing on the tank turret's right side. On the end of the barrel can be seen the Muzzle Reference System (MRS). Also, the tank featured two 7.62mm machine guns: one the coaxial and the other attached to the vehicle commander's cupola. (*Royal Hussars*)

(**Above**) The first production examples of the Challenger 1 came off the factory floor in 1993 and the last in the mid-1990s. In total, the British Army acquired 420 examples. Unlike the Chieftain adopted by several Middle Eastern armies, British industry received no export orders for Challenger 1. Its slab-sided turret and front hull indicate how the tank received protection from the British-developed composite armour. This was popularly known by its nickname 'Chobham', the first British Army tank to be so fitted. (*Tank Museum*)

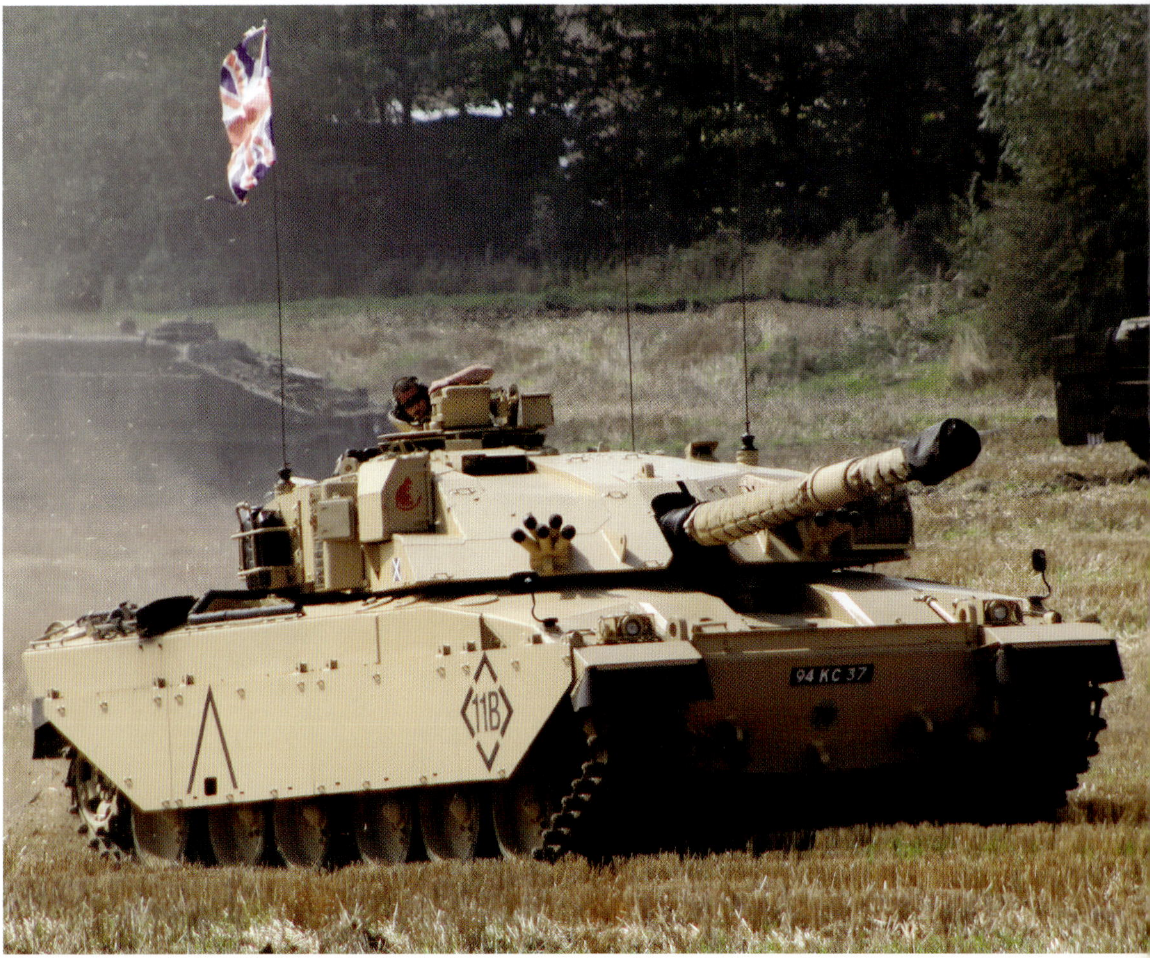
11B
94 KC 37

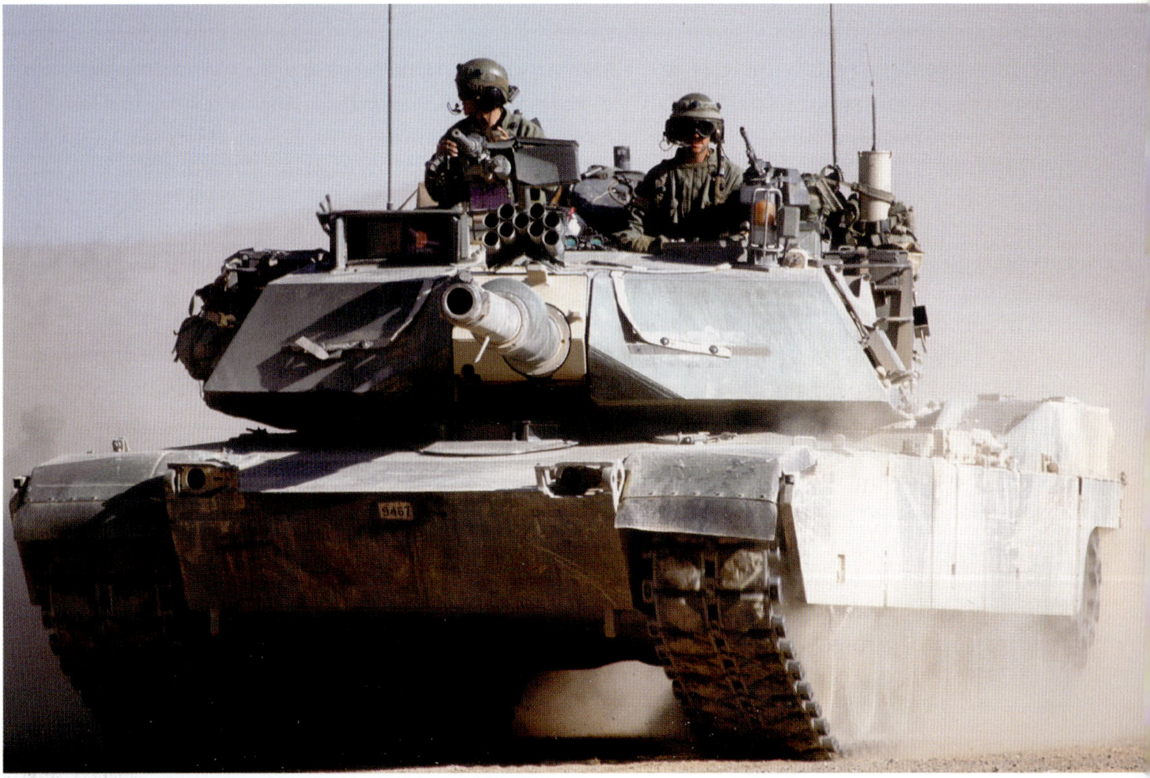

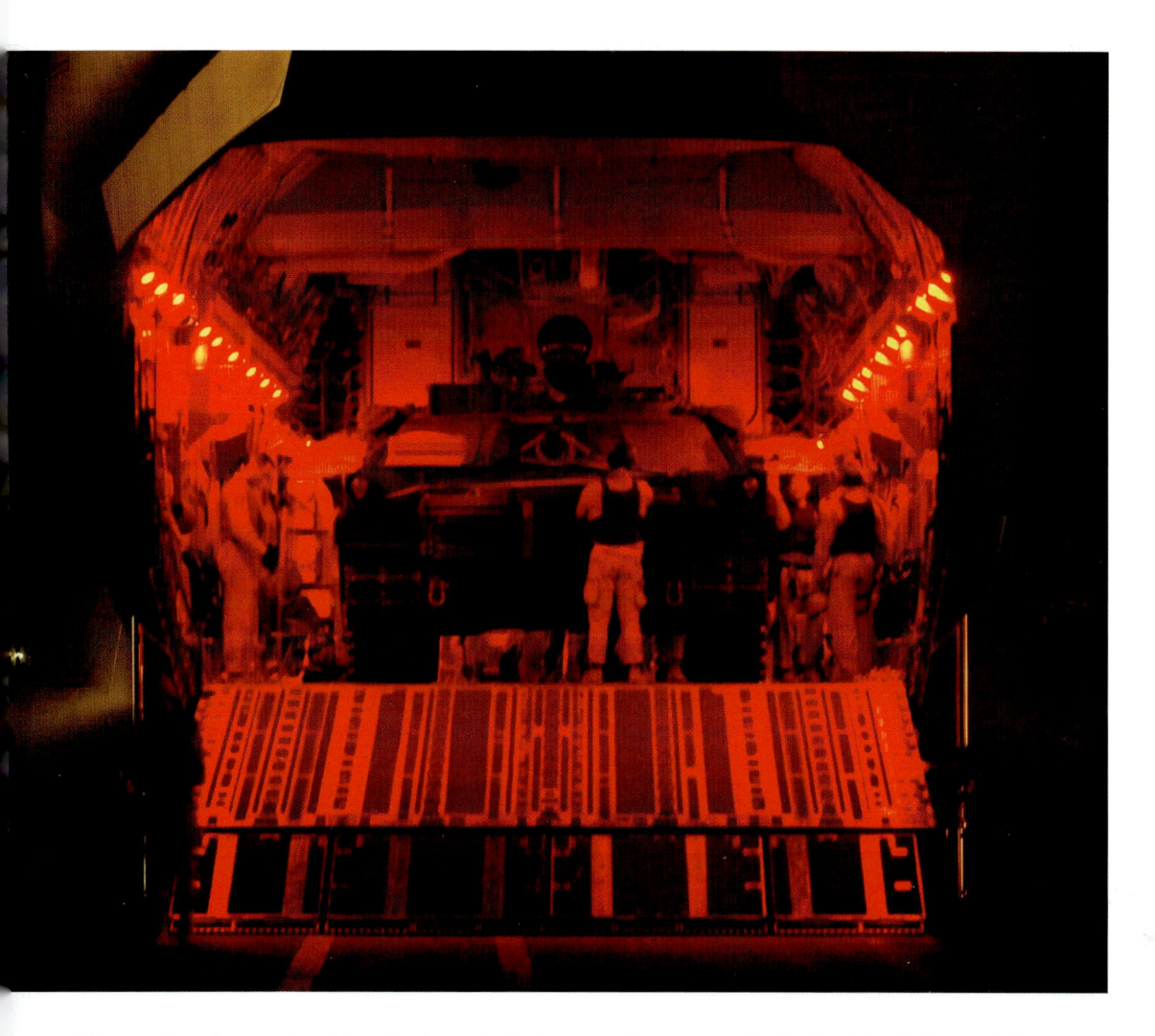

(**Opposite, above**) The British Army's 120mm main gun on both the Chieftain and the Challenger 1 used separately-loaded (two-piece) main gun rounds. This contrasts with the fixed (one-piece) semi-combustible cartridge cases used with the 120mm main gun on the Leopard 2. The projectile is loaded first, followed by the propellant. The tank's main gun was fully stabilized and came with a laser rangefinder (LRF). (*Dreamstime*)

(**Opposite, below**) A US Army M1A1 armed with a 120mm smoothbore main gun takes part in a exercise. The tank's exterior spotting feature is the larger and more pronounced bore evacuator than the previous 105mm main gun-armed version. Whereas the original M1 had stowage for fifty-five main gun rounds, the larger size of the 120mm rounds dropped stowage space on the M1A1 down to forty main gun rounds. Both the M1 and M1A1 had stowage for 900 rounds of .50 calibre machine-gun ammunition. (*Hans Halberstadt*)

(**Above**) Pictured here inside a US Air Force C-17 cargo plane is a single M1A1. The tank evolved from two separate efforts. First was the effort to integrate the West German-designed smoothbore 120mm main gun intended for their Leopard 2 tank into the M1 tank series. Second was a US Army product improvement programme (PIP) that included many features: improved armour and suspension system, a hybrid nuclear, biological and chemical (NBC) protection system, and upgraded transmission and final drives. (*DOD*)

(**Above**) The AGT-1500 air-cooled gas turbine engine of a US Marine Corps M1A1 tank is shown here being lowered into its rear hull. The M1A1 can go from zero to 20mph in about seven seconds on a level road. Top governed speed on a level road averages about 40mph for the M1A1. The original M1 had a maximum governed speed on a level road of 45mph. Cruising range on level roads was approximately 289 miles for the M1A1 and 275 miles for the original M1. (*DOD*)

(**Opposite, above**) Shown here in a training exercise is a US Army M1A1. One of the initial issues for the M1 and the M1A1 was the massive amount of air that had to be filtered efficiently for their gas turbine engines. When caught in sandstorms during Operation DESERT STORM in 1991, the engine filters of the M1A1s often became clogged with dust, as often as four times per hour of operation. The US Army introduced a pulse-jet filter cleaning system into the M1 tank series to solve the problem. (*Hans Halberstadt*)

(**Opposite, below**) A cutaway of a 120mm main gun High-Explosive Anti-Tank (HEAT) round. Because shaped-charge warheads must detonate away from a target at a certain distance to allow their jet stream to form correctly, the impact-switch assembly sits at the end of a stand-off spike. This is called PIBD: point-initiated base detonating. HEAT rounds see use against lightly-armoured vehicles and field fortifications, with a secondary role as a tank-killing round. (*DOD*)

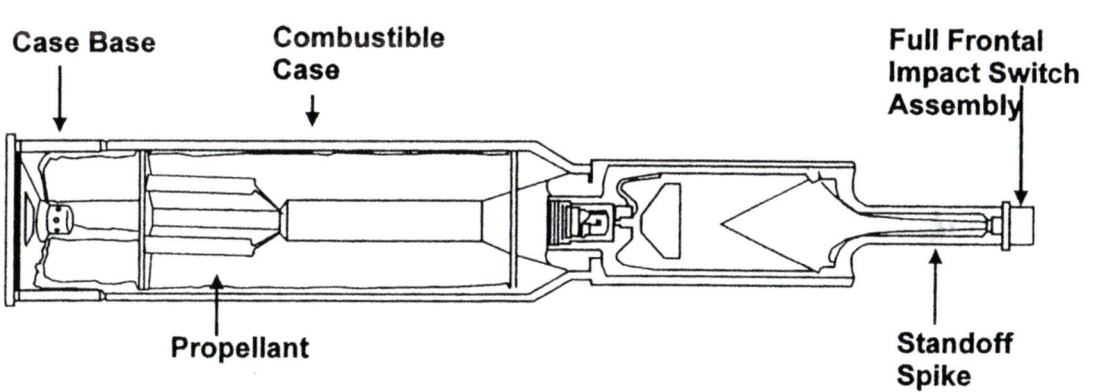

Case Base   **Combustible Case**   **Full Frontal Impact Switch Assembly**

Propellant   **Standoff Spike**

(**Above**) The main tank-killing round for the 120mm main gun on the M1A1 is an Armor-Piercing Fin-Stabilized Discarding Sabot (APFSDS) round shown here. APFSDS came into use because longer length-to-diameter (L/D) ratios were found to give even better areal density (energy per unit area of the hole they made). However, due to the lower axial mass moment of inertia inherent in the longer L/D projectiles, they could no longer be spin-stabilized. (*Richard and Barb Eshleman*)

(**Opposite**) US Marine Corps tankers are pictured here loading an M1A1 with 120mm Armor-Piercing Fin-Stabilized Discarding Sabot (APFSDS) training rounds, identified by a blue-coloured penetrator. When a live APFSDS round (with a depleted uranium (DU) penetrator) strikes armour, the impact heats the uranium to 7,000 degrees as it pushes its way through the armour. The longer the penetrator, the more armour it can defeat as it is consumed and shatters during penetration. (*Hans Halberstadt*)

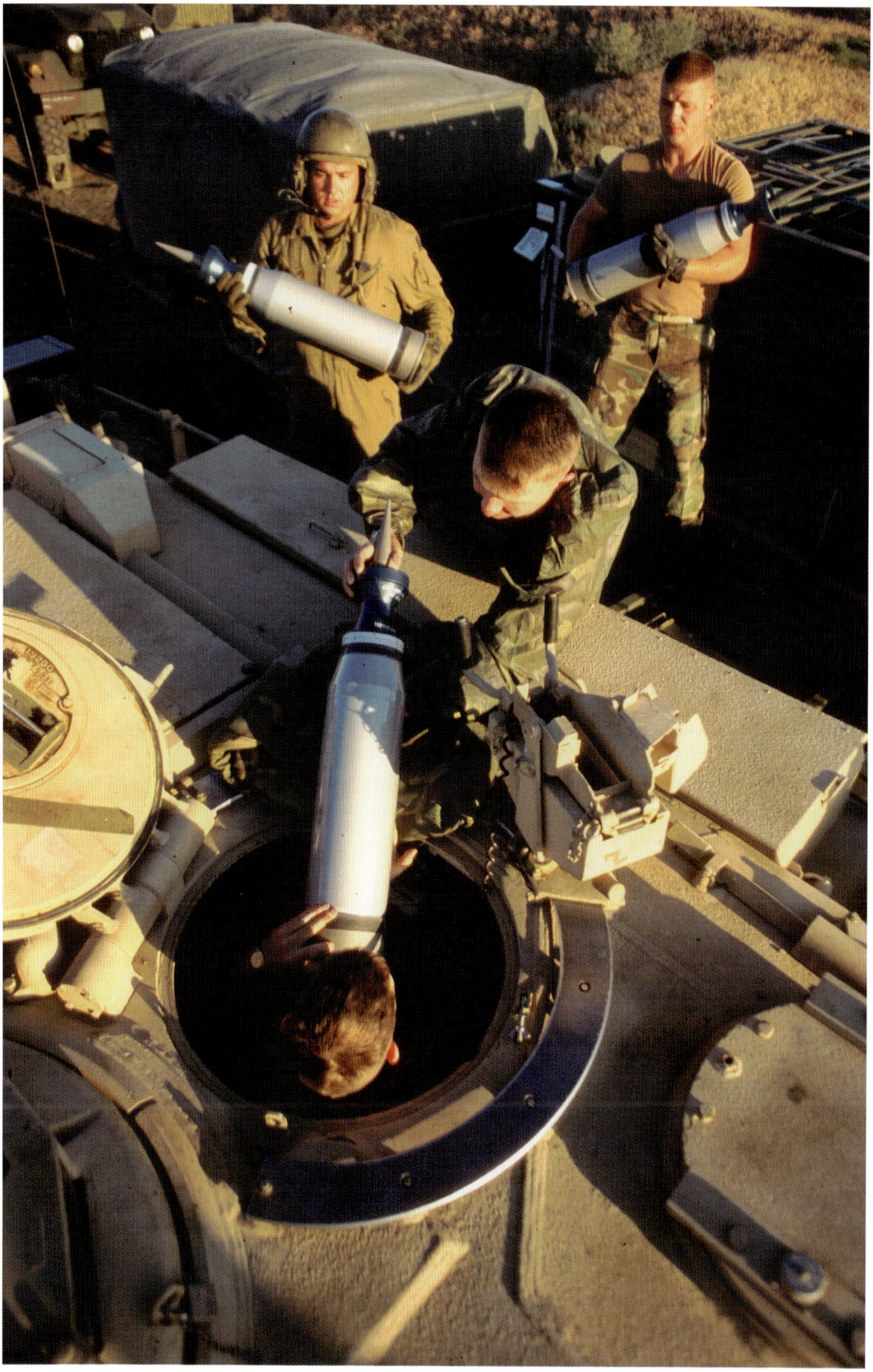

When the 120mm main gun on the M1A1 fires, an electrical current flows through a firing pin, setting off the cartridge's electrical primer in the firing chamber, just in front of the breechblock. An explosion (really a rapid burning of the propellant within the cartridge case) takes place. In less than 16.4ft and in less than a hundredth of a second, the projectile experiences more than 26,000 Gs as it accelerates past Mach 5 (3,580mph). The M829A4 120mm round does 1,670m/s or about 3,750mph. (*DOD*)